Opera
and
the Golden West

Opera
and
the Golden West
The Past, Present, and Future of Opera in the U.S.A.

Edited by
John L. DiGaetani and Josef P. Sirefman

Rutherford • Madison • Teaneck
Fairleigh Dickinson University Press
London and Toronto: Associated University Presses

Associated University Presses
440 Forsgate Drive
Cranbury, NJ 08512

Associated University Presses
25 Sicilian Avenue
London WC1A 2QH, England

Associated University Presses
P.O. Box 338, Port Credit
Mississauga, Ontario
Canada L5G 4L8

The paper used in this publication meets the requirements
of the American National Standard for Permanence of Paper
for Printed Library Materials Z33.48-1984.

Library of Congress Cataloging-in-Publication Data

Opera and the Golden West : the past, present, and future of opera in
    the U.S.A. / edited by John L. DiGaetani and Josef P. Sirefman.
        p.   cm.
    Based on a conference held at Hofstra University, sponsored by the
Hofstra Cultural Center.
    Includes bibliographical references and index.
    ISBN 0-8386-3519-9 (alk. paper)
    1. Opera—United States—Congresses.   I. DiGaetani, John Louis,
1943–   .   II. Sirefman, Josef P.
ML1711.064   1994
782.1'0973—dc20   92-55065
                                                                      CIP
                                                                      MN

PRINTED IN THE UNITED STATES OF AMERICA

for my parents, Romeo and Theresa DiGaetani

—J. L. D.

for my parents, William and Gussie Sirefman, and
for my wife Carol

—J. P. S.

Contents

Acknowledgments

This book grew out of a four-day conference at Hofstra University on the topic of Opera and the Golden West, or opera in America. The original focus of the conference was to celebrate the anniversary of Puccini's *La Fanciulla del West* at the Metropolitan Opera on 10 December 1910. From the desire to commemorate that premiere, the conference grew to the more general topic of opera in America.

We would like to thank the Hofstra Cultural Center for sponsoring this conference, in addition to Hofstra University for providing funding. We would particularly like to thank Natalie Datloff, Alexei Ugrinsky, and Athelene Collins of the Cultural Center for their help. In addition, we appreciate the support of Texaco, Inc. and W. M. Keenan, Manager of Corporate Advertising for Texaco. Regina Fiorito of the Metropolitan Opera Archive Dept. made a substantial contribution to the conference. The conference was enriched by the presentations of composers Bruce Adolphe, Leonard Lehrman, and Robert Starer of excepts from their operas and a musical lecture by Eve Queler. Finally, we acknowledge the contribution of Lucine Amara of the Metropolitan Opera to the success of this project.

Introduction

On 10 December 1910 the Metropolitan Opera presented the world premiere of Giacomo Puccini's *La Fanciulla del West*. Of course there were previous operas where some of the action occurs in the United States, ranging from Louisiana in Puccini's *Manon Lescaut* to a mythical Boston in Verdi's *Un Ballo in Maschera*. But *La fanciulla del West* was different. This was an opera set entirely within the United States—indeed, set in California, quintessence of the shining Golden West, a metaphor for the whole country and its noble ideals.

The ensuing century has witnessed the performance of the traditional repertory and a continuing fascination with foreign artists and conductors. Alongside these representatives of the Old World has been the development and outstanding success of homegrown singers and conductors. To a lesser but nonetheless significant degree, American composers have had their works based on American themes performed in major American opera houses as well as in regional and local theaters. The Metropolitan Opera's 1992–93 season included the world premiere of an opera to commemorate the five hundredth anniversary of the discovery of America: Philip Glass and David Henry Hwang's *The Voyage*. The season before, the Met premiered another highly successful American work, John Corigliano and William Hoffman's *The Ghosts Of Versailles*. Time will decide whether these works will become a part of the standard operatic repertory in America—as has, arguably, Douglas Moore's *The Ballad Of Baby Doe*. Business and economics will also prove their powers in the operatic field. We have experienced the expansion and contraction (and disappearance) of our opera houses with ever-changing phases of the business cycle and government arts funding.

This book is a celebration of opera's development in America. It focuses in part on early repertory and how European operatic masterpieces became part of American culture. This book also calls attention to the efforts of American composers as they continually tried to make original contributions to a foreign musical form. Throughout this anthology the authors, using a variety of approaches and styles, analyze the place of this art form imported from Europe.

In addition to where opera has been in this country, this anthology also has an eye on the future. Opera presentation in the coming century may be very different from the current experience. Economics, always a critical factor, may well dictate a different scale of production. Changing tastes in directorial and production values and the expansion of television and video into the home indicate evidence of a new era. As a result, this book is not only a celebration of the past and the present, it also anticipates what opera may be like in the years to come.

This anthology begins with a look at the earliest experiences of opera in America. Edith Borroff, in her "American Opera: An Early Suggestion of Context," argues that we have more of a tradition of opera than we may have thought. Thousands of American operas have been performed in the history of the art in this country, and that constitutes a tradition. Julian Mates's "Early Managers of the Repertoire" analyzes how impresarios governed opera at its beginning in America, often founding their own troupes. June Ottenberg's "New York and Philadelphia, 1825–1840: European Opera American Style" shows how these two cities soon dominated the presentation of opera in the nineteenth century, and how this tradition continued throughout the century and influenced opera all over America.

The second part of this anthology studies how opera gradually became a part of American culture, and how Europeans viewed this new country. Phillipa Burgess's "Popular Opera and Bands in the American Civil War" tries to prove that, ironically enough, the military bands in the Civil War did much to make Americans fans of opera. Mario Hamlet-Metz's "Old World Libretti for New World Settings," on the other hand, looks at how European composers first presented the new world on the operatic stage. Emanuel Rubin's "American Opera in the Gilded Age: America's First Professional Touring Opera Company" looks at a failure in American operatic history, the American Opera Company, and how that failure indicates much about how opera can succeed in this country.

Part 3 of this book focuses on the western United States, the Golden West as Puccini might have called it. Michael Dougan looks at the fascinating career of the tenor Pasquilino Brignoli, one of Walt Whitman's favorite tenors, and follows that career as Brignoli traveled throughout the United States, singing in both its major cities and its provinces. "Opera Activity in Texas before the Twentieth Century," by Gary Gibbs, examines Texas and its surprisingly early and yet significant operatic past.

In Part 4 this book looks at Puccini's *La Fanciulla del West*, which occasioned one of the most famous premieres in the history of American opera. Shelby Davis's "David Belasco and Giacomo Puccini: Their Collaboration" shows how these two geniuses worked together at the Metropolitan Opera Company, and how this joint effort resulted in one of the most successful premieres in the history of opera. Roxana Stuart's "Uncle Giacomo's Cabin: David Belasco's Direction of *La fanciulla del West*," on the other hand, studies the unique directorial methods of David Belasco and how he applied his method to this important premiere. Thomas Warburton, in his "Puccini's *Fanciulla* as Exemplar for American Composers" shows how Puccini's opera became a model for a series of American operas early in the twentieth century.

The influence of the European model on American opera, and America's continuing obsession with European opera, is the subject of Part 5 of this book. Michael Saffle analyzes America's early fascination with Wagner's final opera in "*Parsifal* Performances in America, 1886–1903: Changing Taste and the Popular Press." Zoltan Roman discusses the profound influence of Gustav Mahler, despite his short stay in this country, in "Gustav Mahler and Opera in America, 1907–1910." Nadine Sine's "Selling *Salome* in America" looks at the American public's shocked reaction to Strauss's opera, and how the press capitalized on the sensation. Jean-Francois Thibault's "Debussy's Unfinished American Opera: *La Chute de la maison Usher*" analyzes one of the most interesting fragments in operatic history, a product of Debussy's fascination with Edgar Allan Poe. Martin Chusid's "Verdi, America, and Adelina Patti" provides a historical context for a soprano who can be called the first American diva.

Part 6 looks at three modern American attempts at opera, attempts that succeeded to a degree. Alice Levine's "Kansas City Composer Meets Regency Dandy—Virgil Thomson's *Lord Byron*" analyzes the Virgil Thomson opera and its uses of its European subject matter. Marjorie Mackay Shapiro's "A Strange Case: Louis Gruenberg's Forgotten 'Great American' Opera—*The Emperor Jones*" looks at the very successful opening of a native American opera at the Metropolitan Opera. This essay also discusses why this successful premiere did not produce a standard repertory opera in America, though the opera was based on one of Eugene O'Neill's best plays. Giulio Gatti-Casazza staged many new American operas during his time as general manager of that theater. The Metropolitan Opera, for its move to its new home at Lincoln Center, again commissioned a new opera— discussed by Jon Solomon in "The Spectacle of Samuel Barber's *Antony and Cleopatra*."

Part 7 discusses how opera has, through a variety of means, become a part of contemporary American culture. Joann Krieg's "Adam in Wonderland: Krzystof Penderecki and the American Bicentennial" looks at the Lyric Opera of Chicago's attempt to commission a new opera on an American subject. Christopher Newton looks at one opera company's attempt to make opera a part of popular culture—in his "Modern Pop Currency in Contemporary American Opera: A Case Study of Elvis in Vancouver's Production of *Carmen*, 1986." Other attempts include Peter Sellar's controversial productions of Mozart's operas set in purely American settings like Trump Tower, a roadside diner, and Spanish Harlem. In the next essay, "Toward a Popular Opera," Sheila Sabrey-Saperstein argues for the increased use of the English language in operatic performances—through a variety of means—to meet audience demand in the United States.

Finally, Part 8 looks at the American Musical, especially the Broadway Musical, as America's unique contribution to the history of opera. In "More Singing! Less Talking!: The Operatic American Musical" Monica Albala looks at the increasingly operatic nature of the American musical. Joseph Swain's "Operatic Conventions and the American Musical" proves that the American musical often used techniques of European operatic composers, but adapted them for native purposes. Both essays suggest that the future of American operatic composition may lie with the Broadway musical. In the hands of people like Leonard Bernstein, Alan Jay Lerner, and Stephen Sondheim, the American Musical has certainly made significant contributions to the history of opera and musical theater in general.

Throughout *Opera and the Golden West* a variety of experts use a variety of styles to look at a peculiar combination, opera and America, trying to understand how these two seeming enemies became intimates. By the end of the twentieth century, all the major American cities and most of the minor ones as well boast of their own opera companies. In contemporary America, at last, opera is easily assimilated in what is certainly not the best of all possible worlds for the arts.

Opera
and
the Golden West

Part One
The Early Experience

American Opera:
An Early Suggestion of Context

EDITH BORROFF

We are seeing more and more studies of American operas, many of them excellent. Such studies, however, present a problem: they lack a context. Each opera is seen either totally *in ipso*, in a contained examination, or it is treated as alien. The underlying assumption, of course, is that such works are in fact exceptions, that American opera really does not exist as a tradition, as a separate art strong enough to have a genuine presence as a type.

I have known for a long time that American opera is in fact a strong musical reality, and it is difficult to say at what point my interest came into a sharper focus. Perhaps it was when, in 1976, I was commissioned to compose an opera by the Department of Theater at the State University of New York at Binghamton; the result of this commission was *The Sun and the Wind*, given four performances in April and May of 1977 and praised in a review in *Opera News*.

But the project on which I am now working—a bibliography of American opera—had its beginnings in 1984, when I was assigned to teach a graduate survey of Opera Literature. There is at SUNY-Binghamton an impressive opera program, an apprenticeship Masters Degree with the Tri-Cities Opera, and a well-considered professional company. So I had in the class a substantial number of students who were working deeply with six well-known Italian, German, and French operas during their two years in the program; I felt that they needed a genuine grasp of what is out there. Planning the outline was wonderful: I eliminated what they already knew—the operas of Verdi, Puccini, Wagner, and Strauss—and planned a real survey of everything else. I allotted three weeks to American opera because I believed (and still believe) that much of their professional future will devolve upon American opera; that was wonderful too. What was not so wonderful was trying to find the materials to present to the class during that three weeks. It was frustrating: I needed specific information on American operas; I needed scores and recordings.

I already knew it was useless to turn to Grout's *Short History of Opera*. That is essentially a history of Italian, German, and French schools with a few other titles sprinkled on the top like so much paprika on the stew. Twenty-five American works are mentioned over all, and no American work is discussed or given a musical example. The *New Grove* contains an extended article on Opera in general, but it has no section on American opera; two sentences sum up opera in the United States in the nineteenth century, beginning with the statement that there was "little important native-composed stage music in America"[1] and listing three works. A twentieth-century list comprises nine operas by seven New York men.

Thus the standard references give an impression of poverty. What is so terribly irritating to me is that European music gets all the adjectives and verbs, while American music is limited to nouns. In other words, European operas are dealt with in lively discussions, while American operas are given only as titles and composers' names on supplementary lists.

Knowing full well that a good deal of splendid music has long blessed American stages, I established a file of American operas, basically a card file of Americans who had composed operas, the titles of their works, dates of composition, and date and place of performance. I began with Julius Mattfeld's fine *Handbook of American Operatic Premieres: 1731–1962*[2] (a bibliography of operas produced in the United States), extrapolating works by American composers. Then I went through such works as the Hipscher study of *American Opera*.[3] I asked a lot of people how many composers they thought there were and got guesses of anything from twenty-five to a hundred, but none over a hundred. But by the time the course began, I had amassed data on 470 composers and 972 works.

The next frustration was that so few American works had been recorded. I checked Schwann and I checked the Louisville series (which is a good source, in fact), and I got enough to eke out the three weeks. Hearing that music, so much of it so good, led me to the determination to make a more penetrating study of American opera. At this point, I know a great deal more, yet in another sense I still know very little. All I am working towards at the moment is the publication of a bibliography of American opera. Until such an overall view is published, no study of individual works will be in the proper perspective.

I have continued to work with the file, and have managed a few sorties to libraries—notably a two-week study grant at the New-berry Library in Chicago. The project shows that American opera is a much greater field than any of us suspected: the file now stands at exactly 1,500 composers and 3,149 works, almost all of them produced. And I am only up to 1980—after that date, public interest expanded excitingly, and I am eager to get going into the eighties.

Probably the most important prerequisite for studying American opera is a willingness to study American opera. That may sound simple, but it is not. The simple thing is to study American opera as a subcategory of European opera, which it is not. It is, in fact, very different. European opera is basically and deeply suffused with Romanticism. But Americans were never Romantic die-hards in the European sense, and you will not find lush, harmony-driven stage works by Americans, except at the Met, which has produced only twenty-four American operas in over a century, in productions so basically European that they cast a pall over the whole perception of American opera. A case can be made that the production of operas by that house, in imitation of European models, has forced these operas into the European tradition rather than the American, and has not served the cause of American individuality or encouraged the development of a national consciousness. In any case, the first twenty-one of the Met composers, all of them men, of course, have in general been taken to represent the American contribution to the literature of the opera, specifically in style and generally in number and gender.

This is not a tract on women's studies, so I will add here parenthetically that of the 1,500 composers on my list, 173 are women—and that ratio, which is more than eleven percent, will probably shift upward slightly as I get into the eighties. The ratio was steadily ten percent until 1970, by the way, even in the nineteenth century. But in spite of this surprisingly high percentage of productions of operas by women, publication of those operas is less than one half of one percent of those by men; obviously some study is required so that we can understand that discrepency.

The twenty-second composer produced by the Met, that is, George Gershwin—whose *Porgy and Bess* finally made it into the fortress—is taken to represent a kind of slumming that "sophisticated" people enjoy so much, and that seems to me to be covered over with the Spanish moss of cultural snobbery which Boethius did us the disservice to endorse. In fact, I think we owe a tremendous negative debt to that worthy.[4] The Gershwin is, of course, an interesting work, but it was not his first essay in that form. In 1922 his one-act opera, *135th Street*, was produced in New Haven; and in 1925 *The Son of the Flame*, an opera he did with Herbert Stothart, was done in Wilmington and New York. *Porgy and Bess* is interesting too in having gone the same route as many distinguished works before it, not only Johann Strauss' *Die Fledermaus*, but also Mozart's *Abduction* and *Magic Flute*: from productions in houses that grand opera proponents considered less than respectable. This is a route being taken now by many works, from Stephen Sondheim's *Sweeney Todd* to Jerome Kern's *Showboat*, which was offered by five grand opera companies recently. So the question "What is an opera?" is never really answered, and I will have many impossible decisions to make in my study. The Gershwin, however, is not an issue: he composed his operas as operas, making informed decisions and making clear distinctions between his operas and his musical shows.

I was happy to have that two-week grant at the Newberry Library for two chief reasons. One is that this is a middle-western archive, and I am quite certain that wherever the secrets of American opera may lie, they do *not* lie at the Metropolitan Opera, or, for that matter, in New York or anywhere else on the East Coast. The second is that the notebooks of Eleanor Freer are there, and they comprise a tremendously valuable source.

Eleanor Freer was a Philadelphian, a singer, trained in France and married to a Chicago physician she had met in Europe. When they returned to the United States, they settled in Chicago and she became prominent in the musical life of that city. She studied composition as well as voice—with composer Benjamin Goddard. She arrived in Chicago ready, willing, and able to champion American opera.

Freer sponsored performances of American operas in Chicago during the twenties and thirties (she died in 1942), in a city much more centered in native musical experiment than the cities in the East.[5] And Freer composed at least nine operas herself, and what I have seen is perfectly good music, a good deal of it excellent.

But the most wonderful thing that Freer did for American opera was to establish (with the help of her friend Edith Rockefeller McCormick) the Opera in Our Language Foundation, which led to the support not only of foreign operas sung in English but to the greater sponsorship of American opera via the David Bispham Medal, an award given annually to American opera composers.

Production seems to have been a requirement for the award, but it also transpired that Freer herself saw to it that certain works were produced, thus making them eligible. I have found sixty Bispham medalists, but I am not sure that the list is complete. Most were awarded during Freer's lifetime, and most of the remaining were awarded in the five years after her death; I have found none after 1945.

The Bispham Medal was an inspired choice for a vehicle with which to promote American music. I presume that the initial expense, of having the matrix made, was the big item, and the reprinting of it relatively inexpensive; I know from the scrapbooks that each medalist received copious publicity, in the home town papers, in the towns where the operas had been produced, in music magazines, and in a variety of Chicago publications. And all that publicity, gained for individual composers, was publicity for American opera.

It is also a good list from which to begin a survey of American opera in general, for in many ways the list is representative and instructive. For it shows that operas were produced in many places, some of them expected, some of them very surprising.

The operas that I have found to date show productions in over 175 cities in forty-two states, plus Washington, D.C. and the provinces of Quebec, Ontario, and Alberta. New York City comes in far and above all the others, with 242 productions (but only twenty-four of them at the Met). The cities of Philadelphia and Chicago are the strongest after New York, with 46 and 42 productions. Boston comes in at half that, with 21, and San Francisco's 20 combines with Los Angeles's 18 to make California a strong state. The next highest is Seattle, with 16, but there are only 18 for the entire state; Cincinnati and Cleveland combine 16 and 12 to make Ohio a stronger state than Washington. Baltimore and Minneapolis each have nine.

New York State is strong also in the number of cities in which American operas have been produced: twenty-two in all. Rochester, of course, and Brooklyn (which likes to consider itself separate from those Manhattan opera houses), but Lindenhurst, on Long Island, producing in 1912, Carmel and Islip (also on Long Island), both in 1938—these are more surprising. Or Chichester, Clark Center, Glens Falls, Piermont, and Schroon Lake. One wonders at the strong motivation to pull these performances off. But if the study demonstrates anything, it is above all a strong affirmation of the unlikely and the musically heroic. I will not name 175 cities here, but I have the list for the perusal of anyone as fascinated as I am by wonder at the glories of productions in Springfield, Illinois, in 1882; Iowa City in 1939; South Bend, Indiana in 1925 (and a woman's work, at that); in Concord, Massachusetts in 1889; Brookline, Massachusetts in 1904 and 1917 (both of them women's works); Columbia, Missouri in 1887 (St. Louis in 1899 and 1903 seems less surprising somehow); Lincoln, Nebraska in 1912 and 1917; Yankton, South Dakota, in 1958; Denver in 1892—and the fact that operas have been produced in eight cities in Texas, the earliest in Fort Worth in 1926. That Philadelphia is strong is not surprising, since brotherly love extended to opera from 1767, when Barton's *The Disappointment* was anything but.

It is Chicago to which I return, however, for its forty-two productions represent an American splendor. Philadelphia had a long list of productions when Chicago was just a swampland; the first Chicago production of an American opera was in 1880. Four in the nineteenth century; one in 1909, then nine in the teens, ten in the twenties, eight in the thirties, and nine more before 1970. And seven of the forty-two were operas by women (only one of them by Freer)—that is one-seventh.

The statistics are fascinating. Freer's operas were produced in South Bend (Indiana), Lincoln (Nebraska), Houston (Texas), Milwaukee (Wisconsin), and Omaha (Nebraska), as well as Chicago. Alec Wilder's operas have been produced in seven cities; Claud Lapham's opera *Sakura* was sung in Japanese in Los Angeles (at the Hollywood Bowl) in 1933. And there were many American operas being produced in Europe: I have data on productions not only in London and Paris, but Graz, Frankfurt, Dresden, Venice, Florence, Bremen, Naples, Torino, Azziz (in what was then Bohemia), Freiburg, Munich, Hamburg, Wiesbaden, Berlin, Cassel, Braunschweig, Majorca, Posen, Lugano, Genoa, and Brussels. In other words, more American operas have been produced in Europe than at the Metropolitan Opera in New York.

We need a host of regional studies; everywhere I travel I find new examples for my file. And when the file is published it will be incomplete because I cannot go to every city in the United States. Every nook and cranny of this land can probably contribute something to a history of American opera.

We can no longer consider any American opera to be an exception: 3,149 works by 1,500 composers, produced in 175 cities in the United States and twenty-three in Europe add up to quite a bit more than a series of exceptions. And although I think my work represents a respectable percentage of them, I know very well that there are many yet to find.

I am eager to study more scores to see if I can begin to formulate opinions on the details of an American style. But I have already studied enough of them to be certain that before 1950 there was an American operatic literature with its own structural and stylistic signature, independent of European style, and that the characterization of that style will be a difficult and entirely worthy goal. I know that many of the musical works themselves are quite marvelous.

Scholars who have looked at one or two exemplars have consistently held them up to a European template and found them wanting. But it is equally true that European works, held to an American template, would be found wanting. *Salome*, the 1907 opera by Richard Strauss, for example, was used by one scholar in a comparison with Scott Joplin's *Treemonisha*. The Joplin does not have the huge sea of harmony, the magnificence of sound that the Strauss has—but we can reverse that and say that the Strauss does not have the instrumental clarity and delineation or the marvelous rhythmic vigor of the Joplin. I could even point out that the Strauss calls for an orchestra of over a hundred players, against which no singer in her right mind would choose to sing. But, from either side, such comparisons are, quite simply, a useless exercise. And yet, because we have, as it were, forged templates only for European music, the error is compounded again and again. American works are more sinned against than sinning.

American operas tend to be spare. The orchestra tends to be a small one (a pit orchestra, if you will), which, as a composer who called for exactly eleven instruments in *The Sun and the Wind*, I see not as being puny—far from it—but as allowing the voices and the instruments an extraordinary freedom and pungency, both American characteristics, I think. They are unpadded, and with the exceptions of the kinds of works that the Met has liked, quite free of pretension and melodrama.

Certainly a huge amount of work is waiting to be done. Work by composers, who will contribute further to the literature and perhaps lay the groundwork for international recognition of an American style. Work by producers, who are finding rewards (both artistic and financial) in American opera. Work by singers, of course, and the many other artists engaged in opera production. But work also by scholars, in finding our history and making it come alive. And other writers, perhaps in accounts of early opera in unlikely places, or in criticism (even newspaper reviews) that are based on solid respect for American opera. For there *is* a tradition of American opera, a tradition that I believe we shall all be hearing more about in the years to come.

Notes

1. *New Grove Encyclopedia* volume 5, p. 602.

2. Detroit Studies in Music Bibliography, #5. 1963. Published by Information Service, Detroit, Mich.

3. Edward Ellsworth Hipsher, *American Opera and Its Composers* (Philadelphia: Theodore Presser Co., 1927). This book has been reprinted by Da Capo Press.

4. Boethius's view of music was basically that of the superior master, who listened, and the inferior slave, who performed. This double standard had the positive effect of honoring the musical patron over the hired performer (we have, of course, Carnegie Hall, not Tchaikowsky Hall or even Philharmonic Hall); but it had the negative effect of demeaning the performer's art.

"For it is more meaningful and profound to know what someone else does, than to demonstrate oneself what one knows. For physical skill obeys like a servant, while reason commands like a mistress. . . . He indeed is a musician who, contemplating rationally, has been attracted to the science of singing, not by the servitude of performances, but by the command of speculation. . . . That man is a musician who, according to speculation or reason appropriate or adaptable to music, possesses the ability to pass judgment . . . "

There are many sources for these and other awfuls, but these are taken from the Ruth Halle Rowen *Music Through Sources And Documents* (Englewood Cliffs, N.J.: Prentice-Hall, 1979), p. 40f.

5. My mother was born and educated in Chicago. Her training in music was eclectic and advanced: when she went to Vienna to study at the Imperial Conservatory Master Class in 1913, Leopold Godowsky told her that she had the most perfect preparation of any student he had ever encountered. As a composer, she was more modern than women who had studied in the East. Chicago was also open to musical experiment: after World War I my mother was involved in experimental concerts of an instrument called the *choralcelo*, the first electronically motivated instrument; she gave recitals on that instrument (at the Potter Palmer mansion, on the near north side) for several years.

Early Managers and the Repertoire

JULIAN MATES

A distinction not often considered is the difference between the impresario or producer and the manager. An impresario or a producer may be responsible for bringing to an audience a special production or star or company; impresarios go back, in America, to the early days of the republic. A fine example of an early American impresario was Lorenzo da Ponte. He had an international reputation based on having written the libretti for Mozart's *Le Nozze di Figaro, Don Giovanni, Così fan tutte*. He became a Professor of Italian at Columbia University. And he owned a grocery store in the Bronx. Da Ponte may have helped bring the Garcia opera troupe here, though he claims in his *Memoirs* only that he was responsible for that company's presentation here of *Don Giovanni* in 1826.[1] Later, he negotiated for the Montresor opera company and was successful in bringing it to New York and Philadelphia in the 1832–1833 season. Manuel Garcia's company (including his daughter, later known as Madame Malibran) gave a series of seventy-nine opera performances in a year at the Park and Bowery theaters in New York. As with Da Ponte's various business ventures, his attempt at opera in America failed, but he had set up a tradition for the impresario leading directly to Sol Hurok and David Merrick.[2]

The manager's functions, however, often included those of the impresario—he needed to travel to Europe, for example, to seek out talent for his theater. John Bernard, one of three managers of a Boston theater in 1806, wrote of some of his responsibilities: " . . . to lease a theater was but a small part of the business; we needed actors and actresses, scenery, dresses, etc., such as could not be found on this side of the Atlantic, and it was, therefore, resolved that I should proceed to England to obtain all that was required. . . ."[3] The performers he sought included those who sang the popular comic operas of the day, works essential to all American theaters' repertoires. Theater managers have a long

tradition in America, and in many ways they are the most important figures to look at when attempting to find the roots of opera in
America.

I propose to discuss some early theater managers in America,
particularly those in America's theater centers, Philadelphia, New
York, Boston, New Orleans, and Charleston. And then I propose
to concentrate on one in particular, the New York theater at the
end of the eighteenth century, and William Dunlap, its manager.
By the late nineteenth century, the word "manager" had virtually
lost its meaning—or, rather, it had taken on too many meanings.
One scholar found five different men handling five different posi-
tions in connection with a single traveling company all referred to
as manager.[4] But the distinction among our early theater managers, those who flourished in the eighteenth and early nineteenth
centuries in America, was quite clear: the managers had three crucial functions. They selected the individual works to be presented
in their theaters, planned the overall repertoire, and hired the performers. (They had many other functions in connection with the
running of the company and the renting of theaters for their companies' tours, but these concerns are peripheral to the establishing
of an American repertoire.) In other words, whatever traditions
we have in the theater find their origins in the efforts of a very few
men. And if the response is, why, all they were doing was giving
the same pieces one might find in England, there are several re-
joinders that need to be made.

First, the English repertoire was extraordinarily diverse, thanks
in part to the need to evade various licensing acts. The result, since
musicals were not condemned, was a stress on music, so that ballad
operas, pasticcios, and comic opera, later English opera, were a
large part of the repertoire; and a rising middle class, insisting on
its own drama (that is, wanting itself and its problems represented
on the stage), found bourgeois prose tragedy introduced to the
repertory, and its concomitant, sentimental comedy, adding still
another segment to a repertory already heavy with revivals of
Shakespeare, Beaumont and Fletcher, and other great writers of
the English Renaissance.

Still another difference between England's repertoire and ours
resulted from an increasingly heterogeneous population here, so
that, for example, German drama flourished quite early in our history.

Finally, and the point may be the most important of all, even if
our repertoire were similar to that in England, we had no tradition
of drama, and so what was performed on our stages in the eigh-

teenth century became in time our *only* theatrical traditions. The first dramatic productions most Americans saw were in the repertory just described, and these formed America's idea of what constitutes theater.

The earliest managers, that is, those in eighteenth-century America, attempted to utilize the strengths of their companies—as Thomas Wignell and Alexander Reinagle did in Philadelphia, with a heavy stress on musical performances.[5] The earliest American troupes had been sharing companies similar to the makeup of such organizations in Shakespeare's day—each member owning one share, and the head of the company, by virtue of possessing costumes and props and scenery, plus making the traveling arrangements, owning two or more. Soon, however, still in the eighteenth century, authority shifted to one or two managers, men who had to do what the chief shareholder had done but who were now forced to pay salaries to performers (both in the pit and on the stage) and to the other employees of the theater. Managers in New York and Philadelphia and a very few elsewhere, in the early years, normally used one city as home base and toured, until gradually a set pattern of touring was established. Frequently, fit-up companies with a few actors and a musician or two would play the smaller communities it did not pay to send the full company to (here the old shareholding arrangement took over, despite the managerial system elsewhere). As more and more cities were established and grew, each became not just a stop on a tour but the home base for its own stock company.

Toward the end of the eighteenth century, then, the sharing system gave way (except over the summer when it was brought back for fit-up companies touring the American equivalent of the provinces) to the stock company, where the manager took the entire responsibility for the running of the company. One of the first things the larger stock companies did was to hire a star to fill houses, and the star system was launched—probably in the 1790s, some say with the hiring of James Fennell by William B. Wood.[6] Fennell illustrates one of the major difficulties in the hiring of stars: William Warren noted in his *Journal* in 1798 that Fennell "comes out of jail with a Sheriff's Officer behind the scenes every night he acts—."[7] Evidently, the thirty dollars per night for two weeks he received was not quite sufficient to release him from debtors' prison. In commenting both on the summer and on the star system, one of these early managers, William B. Wood, in his *Personal Recollections*,[8] spoke of another's management: "an excellent and prudent feature in Mr. Wignell's management, was his system of employing the company in the summer, during the regular recess. Besides the reasons formerly given, (to employ them at a distance from the cities during the season of fever,) it enabled him to avoid the annoyance and uncertainty of collecting so numerous a body together (frequently numbering seventy or eighty persons) for the autumn season at Baltimore, and also gave the junior portion of the performers the means of uninterrupted practice and study." During these times, he goes on, the management was on the sharing plan, "graduated by winter salaries; but the starring system ruined the old way."

All of the stock companies now were forced to hire stars, often for such exorbitant fees as to cause losses even with full houses. At the beginning, the star was a well-known performer—an actor, usually. Soon, the star might be a singer or a dancer. Later, a star might be an entire opera or dance company; in all cases the stock company was expected to support the star by acting, singing, and dancing. The point is worth stressing: aside from the stock company's repertoire, usually heavy with comic operas, in which all performers were expected to act but also to sing and to dance— aside from the standard repertoire, the stock company was expected to support the star, that is, to act in Shakespeare, to sing in opera, and to dance in ballet.

What had the manager to do with all this? It is worth noting some managers' activities in various cities. Alexandre Placide was the manager of Charleston's City Theatre in 1800—he was an actor and a dancer; for the opening performance of the new century, 1 January 1800, he selected a double bill: a play by Garrick, and *Rosina*, a comic opera. He offered music and pantomimes in summer gardens. Another Charleston theater manager, Charles Gilfert, a musician, composed for the theater. Regular opera companies came by in the early years of the new century—mostly named for their managers—the Madame Otto Opera Company, and the Seguins, for example, with such works as *La Sonnambula* and *Fra Diavolo*—and dancers such as Fanny Ellsler. Still another theater manager in Charleston was was W. H. Latham; formerly a singer, he emphasized the musical stage.[9]

Noah Ludlow, who managed theaters in many cities and, as a performer, sang and acted, notes that by the third decade of the nineteenth century, one could find permanent theaters in Pittsburgh, Cincinnati, Louisville, Nashville, St. Louis, Natchez, Mobile, and a choice of theaters in New Orleans. As he recounts the repertoire in each theater, comic opera led the way. Samuel Drake, a "very good musician," managed Kentucky theaters in

Lexington, Frankfort, and Louisville. When, in 1815, a season got under way in Pittsburgh, comic operas were performed the first two nights. The Louisville season of 1816 opened with a musical, and the year before Cincinnati had stressed English operas. Tuscaloosa, Alabama, in 1825, stressed both comic operas and, when the Seguins came by, such operas as *La sonnambula* and *La gazza ladra*.[10]

Sol. Smith, who managed for many years in partnership with Ludlow, wrote his memoirs, too, though he is considerably more anecdotal and, one suspects, more than willing to stretch the truth for a good story. Nonetheless, he tells of John Bernard in Albany, in 1814, giving whole comic operas, and he notes traveling to Cincinnati, the company in two skiffs; if one of them found the possibility of an audience, it flew a flag so the other would stop. A major part of their repertoire consisted of such comic operas as *The Poor Soldier*.[11] An interesting aside here—as one follows the careers of various managers, one notes that between seasons, especially along the frontier, they tended to act in some other manager's company. Away from the larger cities, the manager's functions increased. Sam Drake, who managed for a time the Columbia Theatre in Cincinnati, for example, frequently played two or three parts in one work, and after being killed in the last scene, had to fall far enough off stage in order to play slow music on an instrument as the curtain descended.[12] When gathering a company, the manager knew that *everyone* in the company was expected to sing in choruses, but some performers were especially hired to do the "singing business."

A major theatrical event, again the manager's responsibility, was the presentation in New Orleans of opera *in English*.[13] The work was *Cinderella*, and it was a hodgepodge of the works of Rossini, with *William Tell* heavily drawn upon. Philip Hone notes in his *Diary* the opera of *Rokeby* in the Park Theatre in New York with the same sort of approach. "The music," he says, "a considerable part of which is selected from various composers, is very fine, and the piece was well cast."[14] Besides grand opera in English, New Orleans, which had been hearing opera in the original tongue for many years, was now treated to comic opera: the *Barber of Seville* and the *Marriage of Figaro* (in English adaptations) plus *Love in a Village* and the *Devil's Bridge*. In the South, *William Tell* was a favorite comic opera afterpiece, containing many songs.

Smith writes of this bastard *Cinderella* when it was performed in Mobile, and his account gives some insight into the mind of a manager. "I had calculated greatly on this piece, it being the first opera ever presented with any completeness in Mobile. Music had always been my passion, and, if this opera succeeded, it was my intention to 'go in' largely for the production of that species of entertainment. I had personally attended and directed the rehearsals for two months, and, while I am free to admit that first-rate musical talent was not there to *insure* success, I do aver that every note of the opera was sung and played. . . ."[15] He then moved the successful production on to St. Louis. Smith lists some "horse pieces," or as they were later called, horse operas: *Timour the Tartar, Mazeppa, Forty Thieves, El hyder*, and *Cataract of the Ganges*. More about these later, when we look at circus managers as purveyors of opera. Meanwhile, Smith got up an opera burlesquing his own great success, called *Schinder Eller*, with music adopted from the opera.

Gradually two types of stock company began to emerge: one had a base in one or more cities and traveled a given route during the course of a year. The other had no particular base but went wherever there was the possibility of an audience.[16] What they had in common was their dependence upon comic operas at the heart of their repertoire. The patterns set by the early managers along the East Coast were replicated as other parts of the country were settled. J. S. Potter, for example, in Idaho, converted the Idaho saloon to the Idaho Theatre, presented songs and dances and comic operas, then hired as stars minstrels, variety troupes, circuses, and touring theatrical organizations.[17]

An excellent account of the managers' opening one part of California to theater is given by Douglas McDermott:

> The North-Central part of California was an economically and geographically unified region, and its theatrical unity was reflected in the touring circuits traveled by almost all performers. In this respect California's theatrical frontier was like the Eastern Seaboard when the Hallams monopolized it; like the Ohio Valley for Samuel Drake; like the Gulf Plains for Noah Ludlow, Sol Smith, and James Caldwell; like the Lake Plains for John Blake Rice, Dean and McKinney, McKenzie and Jefferson. Like their counterparts on previous frontiers, players in California toured because that was the only way they could reach an audience to support themselves for the entire year.[18]

This approach to California is important not only because the managers displayed the repertoire we have glimpsed but also because one sees "California's frontier theatre as a place where repertory stock companies, based in a large city, toured smaller settlements in a discrete geographic region, thereby maintaining the tradition on which the nation's theatre was founded."[19]

No matter where one looks in America, the beginnings of our theater followed this pattern. Mr. Harper managed a company that played in Providence and Newport in the summer and Charleston in the winter. John Bernard, who arrived here in the 1790s as an actor, spoke in his *Retrospections of America* of "three leading managements at this time in America, conducting three distinct circuits—in the North, South, and centre: that of Hodgkinson and Dunlap, who had succeeded Henry and Hallam . . . and whose principal cities were New York and Boston; that of Mons. Solee, whose headquarters was Charleston, but who migrated northward to Newberne and Richmond; and that of Wignell and Reinagle, whose home was Philadelphia, but who also paid visits to Baltimore and Annapolis."[20]

And always it is the manager who goes ahead to clear the way for his company. And frequently, it is the manager assembling a company, as Warren, for example, noted in his *Journals* how he and Reinagle rode about, finally ready to go to Annapolis in 1802, with eight actors, five actresses, one tailor, one property man, one painter, one call boy, and three musicians.

Still another good way to view the early manager is through his stewardship of the circus. Philip Astley in England made popular a form of circus featuring horsemanship, clowning, and musical theater, and this was the form our first circuses took. John Durang, one of the earliest managers to be born in America, notes in his *Memoir*[21] that John Bill Ricketts arrived in America in 1792, and opened a circus in Philadelphia, opposite the theater on Chestnut Street, and featured "dramatic burlettas, farces, operas, pantomimes, and ballet dancing on the stage, and all discription [sic] of horsemanship in the ring." He claims the operas were accompanied by a "full orchestra." Ricketts set up circuses in Philadelphia, New York, Norfolk, Charleston, Albany, Boston, and Hartford and generally alternated nights with the theater if indeed there was a theater or a performance in the cities in which he appeared.[22] In 1796, Ricketts changed his format from horsemanship and rope dancing to an evening that included stage performances as well. A ramp was constructed leading from the arena to a stage, thus allowing performances in the ring or on stage or a combination of the two. He began with horsemanship, rope dancing, and tumbling; he added more and more music, and fireworks, and a clown. Then shades and dancing and an exhibition of paintings. Next came harlequinades and pantomimes (in the eighteenth

century, pantomimes included singing), then Grand Pantomimes
with new music; then he advertised horse races, spectacles, interludes, concertos, songs. In Philadelphia he offered thirty-two different dramatic entertainments, mostly musical in nature, in his
circus.

Ricketts' chief competitor, Philip Lailson, opened his circus
with a French opera, Sedaine's *The Deserter*; Ricketts countered
with *La servante Maitresse*. Before the end of the century, Ricketts'
circus was featuring full-length operas.[23]

The circuses trained future theater managers in their companies
(witness Tony Pastor in the nineteenth century), but their major
effect was on the regular theaters which were hurt badly by musical
theaters' circus productions. For example, William Warren, in his
Journal of 1829, noted the circus in Baltimore competing against a
French opera company in the theater, managed by Blanchard; the
result was a circus featuring clowns, slack-wire dances, stars,
horses—and operas! The names of circus managers have come
down to us along with the section of the country to which they
brought entertainment—J. S. Potter, for example, in Idaho; Ed
and Jerry Mobie, whose circus troupe toured from Wisconsin to
Texas; Robertson in Boston; Joe Cowell, who took his circus
to New York, Boston, Philadelphia, Baltimore, Washington, and
Charleston. Cowell notes traveling south with a company of fifty-
five, including musicians. And he states the basic philosophy of
the circus manager: "In short, every novelty that money could
procure, *tact* invent, or unwearied industry produce, to excite
the creative appetite of curiosity, was served up in unceasing
variety."[24] When he left the circus, he joined with William Warren
and managed the Chestnut Street Theatre in Philadelphia. Victor
Pepin and John Breschard came to America for the 1807–1808 season and started a touring circus. By 1820 there were over thirty
rolling shows in New England and the Atlantic states, each featuring bands and most offering brief comic operas along with circus
acts. Through the 1830s one finds circuses with equestrian acts
combined with ballet and musical farces. By mid century, circuses
had reached the West Coast, and performances in Oregon and
Nevada are recorded along with those in California; rural Missouri
alone had sixty circuses before the Civil War.[25]

By the 1850s, circuses had begun to give up musicals, comic
operas, as part of their evening's entertainment. But for many
years the circus had brought the musical stage—comic and English
operas—to many parts of the United States where no other form
of entertainment had been given, where the circus was frequently

the first professional theater seen. The early circus managers produced what audiences wanted; what is interesting is not that people liked to see horsemanship but that they demanded operas in some form or another as well.

Managers of summer pleasure gardens were also responsible for heavily musical programs, often featuring comic operas. Ranelagh Gardens (managed by John Jones) and Vauxhall in the eighteenth century and Niblo's Garden in the nineteenth in New York were tremendously popular; and summer gardens in other cities were equally popular—for example, Charleston's Vauxhall Gardens flourished before 1800 with an excellent French orchestra under the management of the *theater manager* Alexandre Placide. Philadelphia and Baltimore also featured these summer pleasure gardens, sometimes in competition with each other. In 1798, New York had *three* of these—one managed by Joseph Corre, one by Joseph Delacroix, and one whose name is lost—but all featured musicians, singers, and dancers from the theater. By 1800, the Mount Vernon Garden gave theater performances three times a week and offered a full-length play or opera, and concerts followed the theatricals, and these too featured players from the Old American Company.[26]

By mid-nineteenth century, opera had achieved two separate audiences. Comic opera in all its guises remained in the popular theater. Its guises included melodrama (so much music was used that the melodrama's music was sold in the lobby of the theater), comic opera, ballad opera, and grand opera, especially when an opera company came by with a star. But the other audience for grand opera (even in its bastard form, that is, as a pastiche of popular operas) was now asserting itself. Anna Cora Mowatt's play *Fashion* of 1845 makes the point quite clear. Mrs. Tiffany: "Been to the opera, Mr. Fogg? I hear that the *bow monde* make their *debutt* there every evening."[27] But if Mrs. Mowatt laughed at the pretentiousness of the audience, Philip Hone, in his *Diary*, makes the point even clearer and without satire. In 1845 he wrote, "This opera of ours is a refined amusement, creditable to the taste of its proprietors [here the manager is at last coming into his own] and patrons; a beautiful parterre in which our young ladies, the flowers of New York society, are planted to expand in a congenial soil, under the sunshine of admiration; and here also our young men may be initiated into the habits and forms of elegant social intercourse, and learn to acquire a taste for a science of the most refined and elegant nature. . . ."[28] But long before this bifurcation was made into entertainment versus a social event, back when opera was a part of every company's repertoire, the audience's expectations were set and whatever traditions the American theater has were also created.

Up to now we have taken a sort of overview of the manager and his relation to the repertoire. Now, in order to see all this most clearly, it is necessary to focus on one period and one locale and one manager. William Dunlap was born in Perth Amboy, New Jersey, in 1766.[29] Despite the loss of an eye, his earliest inclinations were to be a painter. His father was a merchant, first in Perth Amboy and then in New York, and young William worked in the store, although he soon graduated to painting portraits—a growth industry in the Colonies. His first known portrait, at age seventeen, was of George Washington. His father, acknowledging some talent in his son, sent him to England to study with Benjamin West. He neglected his studies and became fascinated with the theater; his father brought him home, and he soon began to write for the stage. He married Elizabeth Woolsey (her brother-in-law was Timothy Dwight, later President of Yale).

Dunlap and a group of friends became literary critics, and shortly thereafter he was able to see one of his plays on the stage of the John Street Theatre—*The Father, or, American Shandyism*, produced in 1789. He later wrote of himself that "tragedies and comedies, operas and farces, occupied his [that is, Dunlap's] mind, his time, and his pen" (*History of the American Theatre*). The year 1796 was important in his life: his comic opera, *The Archers*, was produced, as was his *The Mysterious Monk* (later revised and performed in 1803 with the title *Ribbemont, or, the Feudal Baron*; and he became a manager—one-third interest in the American Company (his partners were Lewis Hallam and John Hodgkinson). By 1797 he had a one-half interest in the company and increased the number of his works produced in the theater, original plays and adaptations and translations. In 1798 he became sole manager of the company, and from here on, a study of the repertoire of the American Company (it was referred to as the Old American Company after competition in Philadelphia claimed to be an American company) is the study of how the manager shaped what Americans saw on the stage at the beginning of the young republic.

Dunlap remained as sole manager of the company as the John Street Theatre gave way to the Park Theatre. He was bankrupt in 1805 and went back to New Jersey. He returned to the theater as assistant manager in 1806 and retained a connection with the theater until 1811; although his formal connection to the theater was now over, he continued to contribute pieces, and his last translation and play for the theater were in 1828; four years later he published his Invaluable *History of the American Theatre*. He died in 1839.

Just to round out his career, one might note a total of over sixty plays, operas, translations, and adaptations for the stage, and his art—he created, in addition to portraits (mostly miniatures, as he traveled to an assortment of states, making scarcely enough to support his family) large, room-size paintings such as *Christ Rejected* in 1822 and *Death on a Pale Horse* in 1825. He published poetry, two biographies, a magazine, and a novel. He served for two years as assistant paymaster-general of the New York militia. He was Vice President of the National Academy (he was one of its founders). He published a children's history and one for adults of New York State. He died in 1839, but not before publishing two of the most important works on the arts in America—his *History of the American Theatre* in 1832, and his *History of the Rise and Progress of the Arts of Design in the United States* in 1834. Even this list of accomplishments fails to include other aspects of his life as revealed by his correspondence—his autograph collection, for example. It is safe to say that nearly everyone connected in any way with the arts in America in the late eighteenth and early nineteenth centuries was either a friend or a correspondent of William Dunlap.

All this serves as necessary background for William Dunlap's tenure as manager. Other managers also frequently created pieces for the stage, though it is possible that William Dunlap was the only manager who was not also a performer (he did play the flute, however). Certainly the *number* of his works for the stage exceeded that of any other manager: aside from his plays and libretti, his translations and adaptations during his tenure as manager made possible, sometimes within weeks, the best that was produced, not merely in England, but in France and Germany as well. He gained some knowledge of the theater as a reader and as a frequent playgoer in London and later in New York. Certainly, some knowledge of the basic repertoire came to him during those years. Also, he learned of the needs of a repertory company in terms of the frequency of productions and the use of stars. Basic to his learning, however, must have been his first year of partnership with Lewis Hallam and John Hodgkinson, then sharing the partnership with Hodgkinson alone, and finally managing the American Company all by himself. He learned, for example, that American managers sometimes rechristened their importations as if bringing in a new work or appealing to a specifically American audience.[30]

Two comparisons will help to make clear the continuity of his approach to the tradition he inherited as well as his similarity to other theater managers of his time. In 1796, the year William Dunlap joined the managers of the John Street Theatre in New York, the American Company put on ninety-one performances of forty-six different operas, pantomimes, and "other kindred works," specifically *musical* works.[31] This was out of a total of 117 different works for the stage (including both full- length works and the shorter afterpieces, sometimes two or three of these in an evening). So, opera and other musical-stage forms took up approximately 45 percent of the total repertoire when Dunlap joined the American Company in the middle of the year.

The first year in which he managed the theater by himself was 1799, and the figures I have been able to compile for that year show eighty performances of thirty-two operas and similar musical stage works.[32] These were included in a total repertoire for the year of eighty different productions. The ratio of musical productions to straight drama remains about the same as when William Dunlap first joined the company, presumably as a novice manager with little or no say about the repertoire. And if the total number is a bit lower in 1799, the answer may be that all sorts of exigencies prevented a full season, including the fact that the death of Washington necessitated the closing of the Park Theatre during a period of national mourning. Another way of looking at the theater, albeit somewhat outside our specific topic, is George C. D. Odell's note that the 1798–99 season featured eighty-eight performances, including forty-eight long works and forty-seven afterpieces—of which twenty-two long pieces and seven afterpieces were new to the repertoire; again, the musical stage works represented nearly 50 percent of the total. Dunlap as manager was able to make two of his own works part of the repertoire, considerably more than the one opera (*The Archers*) of the 1796 season.

The American Company's chief rival, and probably the best company in America in the last years of the eighteenth century, was that of Thomas Wignell and Alexander Reinagle in Philadelphia. A comparison with the figures of the New York company is revealing, even though the Philadelphia company was formed with the pecific idea that "operas" were to be their mainstay (in part because Reinagle, an intimate friend of Karl Philipp Emanuel Bach, was an accomplished musician and composer). Wignell and Reinagle built a new theater on Chestnut Street and by 1794 had built so powerful a company that the Old American Company gave over its Philadelphia territory to them.[33] Despite their heavy stress on musical theater, their figures are directly comparable to those at the John Street and Park theaters in New York.

In 1796, a year we have already examined for the Old American Company, Wignell and Reinagle featured eighty-six performances of sixty-four different musical stage pieces; in 1799, forty-six performances of thirty-three different operas and the like. In short, the number of musical stage performances, and their relationship to the rest of the repertoire, was similar in the two leading companies of eighteenth-century America.

Now it remains to examine the kinds of musical performance that William Dunlap produced, with some confidence that he is putting on the stage with few exceptions the same works one finds in Philadelphia—as well as in Boston and Charleston. Information is available for other cities (Hartford, Providence, and Baltimore, for example), but for the most part their seasons were offered by the three main companies (that is, Dunlap's, Wignell and Reinagle's, and Solee's) on tour. As Oscar Sonneck pointed out, "The history of opera in America during these [early] years is so clearly a part of the history of the Old American Company that a local treatment of the subject may conveniently be disregarded."[34]

Ballad opera was the earliest form of musical seen on the American stage, and ballad opera begins with *The Beggar's Opera*. Although *The Beggar's Opera* was not performed in 1796 or 1799, its descendants, other ballad operas, pasticcios, and comic operas, still trod the boards. Basically, ballad opera took songs everyone knew, that is, some folk songs and some songs from specific sources such as popular Italian operas, then set the songs to new words and stuffed them at frequent intervals into a comic plot. As popular songs began to be used up, pasticcios borrowed music from known composers, especially those who wrote popular serious operas. The final step into comic or English opera found one composer especially assigned to writing all the music for a given show. The composer was in a secondary role, and sheet music of the day nearly always mentions the author and infrequently the composer. The lines between the different forms are blurred since each contained elements of the others. While one of these three forms might be the main production on a given evening, each might also be cut down to serve as an afterpiece to another main work. An evening might feature a comic opera, a musical farce as afterpiece, and a pantomime as well (pantomimes often featured both songs and dances), making for a completely musical evening. In fact, it was rare in the eighteenth century in America to go to the theater and not find that the manager had provided an opera in same guise for the evening.

Even Shakespeare was frequently presented, if not as an opera, at least with many operatic appurtenances—songs, dances, duets, trios, and the like. England in mid-eighteenth century had put on, for example, a *Tempest* with thirty-two songs and duets and *A Midsummer Night's Dream* with thirty-three songs; much of the music was by Locke and Arne. And in this country, Charleston for example advertised an operatic *Tempest* with a "Dance of Demons" in Act II and Purcell's music in Act III, and a masque to follow. A performance of *Much Ado about Nothing* in May 1796, in New York, featured a masquerade and dance in Act II and a triple hornpipe at the end; this was shortly after a *Macbeth* that listed twelve vocal parts plus two principal characters in the witches' dance and extensive use of the music of Locke.[35]

As far as serious opera was concerned (that is, opera with recitatives as opposed to spoken dialogue), the form was available to Dunlap, but as manager he commented, "My taste was for simple melody, and I received more pleasure from the airs in *Rosina* than from all the bravuras of the Italian opera."[36] *Rosina* was a comic opera by Mrs. F. Brooke and William Shield (new orchestra accompaniments by Victor Pelissier), 1782, and Dunlap staged it three times in 1799, his first full season as manager. The music of serious opera was, however, frequently used with pantomimes and ballets and pasticcios.[37] J. Cobb and Stephen Storace, in England, attempted grand opera with *The Haunted Tower*, and despite his misgivings, Dunlap offered it twice in 1799.

Comic opera was probably the most important of the works for musical stage. There is no question that comic opera took up a large part of the repertoire and that its popularity never waned, or, better, led to the kinds of musicals popular all through the nineteenth century (thin on plot and thick with stage effects) and that, in turn, led to the musicals of today. A review in Philadelphia's *The Federal Gazette* (16 June 1790) of *The Duenna* (1775; book by Richard Brinsley Sheridan, music by Thomas Linley)[38] speaks of the opera as less perfect than *The School for Scandal* but more pleasing: "[The] author has rescued that species of the drama called opera, from the imputation of insipidity, to which, even in its native Italy, it has hitherto been subject. The combinations of wit, poetry and music . . . are the merits of the author. . . . The music of the *Duenna* (consisting principally in a fortunate adoption of the best Scotch airs). . . ."

Some comic operas were so popular on the stage that they were performed every year from their first appearance in New York through the end of the century—*The Agreeable Surprise*, for example (book by John O'Keeffe, music by Dr. Arnold); *No Song, No Supper* (book by Prince Hoare, music by Stephen Storace); *The*

Poor Soldier (book by O'Keeffe, music by Shield), *Rosina* (book by Mrs. Brooke, music by Shield). Most of these had "accompaniments" added by composers associated with the Old American Company.

Many of these comic operas were abridged and served as afterpieces. For example, *The Poor Soldier* was abridged to *Darby and Patrick*. Some comic operas were created originally as afterpieces and were called musical farce or operatic farce—*Edgar and Emmeline*, for example (with book by Hawkesworth and music by Michael Arne). One further subdivision was the musical interlude, merely an excuse for a song or two and a dance—sometimes an original work and sometimes a further abridgement of a comic opera. *Darby's Return* is an example of this form, not only presented by the manager William Dunlap but written by him as well.

American works were encouraged by Dunlap, such as *Edwin and Angelina* (book by Elihu Hubbard Smith, music by Victor Pelissier) and *Tammany* (book by Anne Julia Hatton, music by James Hewitt); Dunlap's own *Archers*, in 1796, with music by Benjamin Carr; and, in 1799, five performances of his *Sterne's Maria* with music by Victor Pelissier. Dunlap again appears as he presents an interlude, *Darby's Return*, a final shortening of *The Poor Soldier*. The manager was responsible with his partners for burlettas as well, those musicals with stories based on burlesques of classical incidents—Dibdin's *Poor Vulcan*, for example. Dunlap put on between five and ten original American operas and pantomimes in the 1799 season alone.

Robinson Crusoe, a pantomime, was also a Dunlap presentation. Pantomimes, unlike our current understanding of the term, in their eighteenth-century form included both spoken and unspoken action, songs and duets, dances, acrobatics, and special scenic effects. During his 1799 season as manager, Dunlap put six of these on the stage. A "pantomime ballet" stressed its dance over other aspects of the production; *Don Juan* was a 1799 example—one of the four or five different forms in which this ever-popular story was told on the stage. Masques, too, remained popular on the stage, with plots based on classic stories and featuring allegorical figures, and containing songs, dances, poetry, and spectacle; although English opera grew out of the masque, the two forms existed side by side for quite a while.

William Dunlap presented masques in 1798 (*Neptune and Amphitrite*) and 1800 (*King Arthur*). The only other relatively important musical-stage form of the eighteenth century was a kind of drama where everything was pushed to the background except scenic effects accompanied by music. Finally, same actors moved about the country performing a sort of olio of songs and recitations, but these are outside the purview of the manager.

William Dunlap, as manager of the Old American Company, was responsible for the repertoire, and many aspects of his influence have, perforce, been omitted, though they do bear peripheral reference to our topic. He was, for example, responsible for bringing to America the huge wave of popularity of August von Kotzebue (in fact, for a year or two, the Park Theatre was saved from bankruptcy by Kotzebue's plays). In 1799, fifty-four of ninety-four different performances at the Park belonged to Kotzebue.[39] But even here the operatic stage appears. An article in the *Monthly Magazine and American Review* of 1800 speaks of Dunlap's adaptation of Kotzebue's *Der Wildfang* as *The Wild Goose Chase*: "He [Dunlap] has divided the First Act into Two by the addition of song and made a comic opera of Four Acts. These songs are in the usual style of the English opera. . . . [W]e have no reason to be dissatisfied with the liberty he has taken."[40] The plays of Kotzebue, especially as presented by Dunlap, paved the way for melodrama, a dramatic form which would swamp the repertoires of theaters all over America—and melodrama, in its initial form, was a part of our musical stage heritage, helping to keep comic opera alive.

Soon, the Garcia troupe would arrive, and Madame Malibran, and grand opera in its original form and language would make its debut. And opera would go everywhere, though the manager was not always thrilled at the opportunity, as opera, said one manager, is "broken into fragments, scatters itself into the interior towns and cities, where, with scant orchestra and a chorus of eight or ten cracked voices, *Il trovatore, Il barbiere di Siviglia*, and all the other *Ils* of the Italian repertoire, are given to the worthy citizens of Peoria and Detroit. . . ."[41]

The eighteenth century, in America, found the managers shaping not only a repertoire to attract audiences, a repertoire largely made up of opera, but laying the groundwork for opera—indeed, for all forms of the musical stage—for years to come.

Notes

1. Lorenzo da Ponte, *Memoirs of Lorenzo da Ponte*, trans. Elizabeth Abbott, ed. Arthur Livingston (Philadelphia: J. B. Lippincott, 1929), pp. 448–449.

2. John Tasker Howard, *Our American Music* (New York: Thomas Y. Crowell Co., 1946), p. 239; David Ewen, *Music Comes to America* (New York: Allen, Towne and Heath, 1947), pp. 48–50.

3. John Bernard, *Retrospections of America, 1797–1811*, ed. Mrs. Bayle Bernard (New York: Harper's, 1887), p. 272.

4. Levi Damon Phillips, "Uses of the Term 'Manager' in 19th-Century U.S. Theatre", *Theatre Survey* 20, no. 2 (Nov. 1979): p. 63.

5. O. G.Sonneck, *Early Opera in America* (1943; reprint, New York: Benjamin Blum, 1963), p. 124.

6. William Winter, *Other Days* (New York: Moffat, Yard & Co., 1908), p. 24.

7. William Warren, *Journals* (1796–1831, original in Howard University, microfilm in Temple University).

8. William B. Wood, *Personal Recollections of the Stage* (Philadelphia: 1855), p. 58.

9. Stanley W. Hoole, *The Ante-Bellum Charleston Theatre* (Tuscaloosa: University of Alabama Press, 1946), p. 44.

10. Noah M. Ludlow, *Dramatic Life As I Found It* (1880; reprint, New York: Benjamin Blum, 1966), p. 267.

11. Sol. Smith, *Theatrical Management in the West and South for Thirty Years* (New York, 1868), p. 43.

12. Ibid., p. 23.

13. Ibid., p. 87.

14. Philip Hone, *The Diary of Philip Hone, 1828–1851*, ed. Allan Nevins (New York: Dodd, Mead and Company, 1936), p. 24.

15. Smith, *Theatrical Management*, p. 123.

16. Firman Hewitt Brown, Jr., *A History of the Theatre in Montana* (Ph.D. diss. Univ. of Wisconsin, 1963), p. 5.

17. Robert Franklin Eggers, *A History of Theatre in Boise, Idaho from 1863 to 1963* (M.A. thesis, University of Oregon, 1963), pp. 1, 10, 19.

18. Douglas McDermott, "Touring Patterns in California's Theatrical Frontier," *Theatre Survey* 15, no. 1 (May 1974): p. 19.

19. McDermott, "Touring Patterns," p. 19.

20. Bernard, *Retrospections*, p. 259.

21. John Durang, *The Memoir of John Durang*, ed. Alan S. Downer (Pittsburgh: University of Pittsburgh Press, 1966), p. 43.

22. Isaac J. Greenwood, *The Circus: Its Origin and Growth Prior to 1835* (Washington, D.C.: Hobby House Press, 1898), pp. 75, 69.

23. Thomas Clark Pollack, *The Philadelphia Theatre in the Eighteenth Century* (Philadelphia: University of Pennsylvania Press, 1933), Part II, Day Book, 1700–1800.

24. Joe Cowell, *Thirty Years Passed among the Players in England and America* (New York: Harper, 1844), p. 76.

25. Julian Mates, *America's Musical Stage: 200 Years of Musical Theatre* (Westport, Conn.: Greenwood, 1985), pp. 93–96.

26. Julian Mates, *The American Musical Stage Before 1800* (New Brunswick, N.J.: Rutgers University Press, 1962), pp. 29–31.

27. Anna Cora Mowatt, *Fashion*, Act I, in *The Longman Anthology of American Drama*, ed. Lee A. Jacobus (New York: Longman, 1982), p. 38.

28. Hone, *Diary*, p. 836.

29. Information on William Dunlap is drawn largely from four sources: his autobiographical essays in his *History of the Rise and Progress of the Arts of De-*

sign in the United States (1834; reprint. New York: Dover, 1969), I: 243–311; and his *History of the American Theatre* (1832; reprint, New York: Burt Franklin, 1963), vol. 13 and elsewhere. Also, two biographies: Oral Sumner Coad, *William Dunlap* (1917; reprint, New York: Russell and Russell, 1962); and Robert H. Canary, *William Dunlap* (New York: Twayne, 1970).

30. Sonneck, *Early Opera in America*, p. 79.

31. Summarized from Chart B, in Sonneck, *Early Opera in America*.

32. The statistics and information about authorship on this and the following pages were gleaned from the following: Sonneck, *Early Opera in America*; Oscar Sonneck, *A Bibliography of Early Secular American Music*, rev. by William Treat Upton (Washington, D.C.: Library of Congress, 1945); Oscar Sonneck, *Early Concert Life in America (1731–1800)* (Leipzig: Breitkopf and Hartel, 1907); Thomas Clark Pollack, *The Philadelphia Theatre in the Eighteenth Century*; Joseph N. Ireland, *Records of the New York Stage from 1750 to 1860*, vol. 1 (1866; reprint, New York: Burt Franklin, 1968); and George C. D. Odell, *Annals of the New York Stage* (New York: Columbia University Press, 1927), vols. 1 and 2.

33. Howard, *our American Music*, pp. 75, 78.

34. Sonneck, *Early Opera in America*, p. 76.

35. Julian Mates, "Shakespeare's Musical Comedies," *The Shakespeare Newslette* (Sept. 1961): p. 27.

36. William Dunlap, *History of the American Theatre*, p. 247.

37. Mates, *The American Musical Stage Before 1800*, p. 147.

38. Sonneck, *A Bibliography of Early Secular American Music*, p. 114; review cited in his *Early Opera in America*, pp. 82–83.

39. Sylvester Linus Kreilein, *August von Kotzebue's Critical Reception in New York City (1798–1805)* (Ph.D. diss., Univ. of Wisconsin, 1989) p. 41.

40. Cited in Ibid., p. 126.

41. Smith, *Theatrical Management*, p. 238.

New York and Philadelphia, 1825–40: European Opera American Style

JUNE C. OTTENBERG

Opera in New York and Philadelphia from 1825 to 1840 has usually been passed over by music historians and viewed as an unimportant subject for study. While other aspects of music in American have been scrutinized, this one, despite its colorful mix of opera styles and the availability of impressive annals gathered by scholars, has been ignored. Those annals reveal a thriving musical theater driven by the taste, customs, and economics of a time considerably different from our own. That taste emphasized English opera and musicians with only intermittent performances of Italian and French works. A fresh look at important individuals and the social/theatrical context in which they worked is merited and offers a productive approach to understanding the possible significance of this neglected area.

The fifteen years following Manuel Garcia's introductory "season" of Italian opera in 1825 reveal divergent images and an unstable equilibrium for opera. New York and Philadelphia were the largest cities in Jacksonian America, with the greatest variety of population, and, in the case of New York, the main place where opera was staged. Philadelphia was one of several cities to which companies went "on tour" when New York audiences began to diminish. New Orleans was the only other city with operatic activity comparable to that of New York and a special case because of its French population and culture.

Heterogeneous productions melded greater and lesser works that were staged with a few fine singers for a rather limited audience. The struggle to gain a firm financial basis for an operatic repertory revolved around the conflict of English, French, and Italian language works as companies vied for a restricted, fluctuating audience. English language opera, accessible to the broadest population and appealing by virtue of its strategically interwoven folk songs, was the accepted repertory which consistently dominated into the 1840s. French opera (hence language and culture) had the support of an excellent traveling company from New Orleans while the Italian repertory had advocates in Garcia, Da Ponte, and a few of the wealthier citizens. The scene was animated by a rising monied class seeking elitist symbols and institutions as well as by companies determined to survive in a competitive, mercantile environment. Although much of the repertory has been documented,[1] a large part of it is little known and undiscussed— likewise the collective impact of the major figures (the actors/ singers/managers/librettists/composers). Their endeavors and significance for this developing musical theater have been overlooked. The purpose of this essay is to review and examine the repertory, these individuals, and their ventures in context, thereby enhancing our knowledge and broadening our perspective on the period.

Background

New York, by 1820, had emerged as a city where business held the preeminent place while Philadelphia still treasured its label as the "Athens of America." In 1825 the Erie Canal was completed, connecting mercantile New York with the Great Lakes region, and for the next twelve years a relatively stable economy prevailed.[2] The populations of both cities, less than two hundred thousand, would increase with the large shift from rural to urban areas as jobs were created by developing industrialization and factory production. The resulting economic upheavals for the urban poor contrasted sharply to a stable, richer group that, by the 1820s, was wealthy even by European standards. This economic disparity disturbed the prevailing egalitarian ideal of Jacksonian America. That ideal had been articulated during the campaign of 1828 in a call (not unfamiliar) "against aristocracy, privilege, and government interference with a providential order . . . for the simple, the natural, the just."[3] This emphasis on man's equality, his individualism, and a natural order would linger for some time to come and permeate all attitudes and prejudices, including those towards theater and opera.

Those art forms were in general viewed with suspicion by religious groups and their leaders who saw the stage as a powerful vehicle that would sap moral fiber and inevitably seduce one into paths of evil. We should note that until well into the nineteenth century many American theaters, like the British, designated a particular section for prostitutes, thereby making them available and an accepted part of the audience. The clergy compared the "pit" of the orchestra to the "pit" of hell and attacked profanity on stage as well as stage references to God (positive or negative), costumes, and the actors themselves.[4] A churchgoer could hardly visit the theater. A persistent but opposing view held by non-religious critics saw the theater and opera as a possible vehicle of educational benefit and moral uplift. This attitude was reinforced in the 1830s by an upsurging spirit of reform and the general support for education and "improvement" that now became foremost among social concerns. Walt Whitman reflected a view held for many decades by certain commentators when he observed that "All—every age and every condition in life may with profit visit a well-regulated dramatic establishment, and go away better than when they came."[5]

The Repertory

Culturally this was British America supporting mainly English style musical theater. Even New York's most prestigious theater, The Park, was dubbed "Old Drury." The number and variety of productions called operas, comic operas, ballad operas, afterpieces, pasticcios and so on, all with a distinctive amount of music, are impressive and reflect a spectrum ranging from the naive to the sophisticated. Albrecht points this out in his coverage of the first thirty years of the century in Philadelphia, listing 258 works for that city alone. Close to 200 of these were in English (originally or in translation) while 155 were from the three major London theaters.[6] Since almost all theatrical endeavors entered through New York, a similar situation prevailed there. Strong British ties, covering all aspects of music and theater, would remain unbroken for some time.

A performance would consist of a longer work prefaced and followed by several shorter ones (a farce, afterpiece, etc.) to balance the evening's entertainment. The accessibility of the English language plots, the familiarity of the frequently used folk and folk-like tunes, staged by actors who could sing but were not primarily vocalists, characterized this opera. The actor/singers of these stock companies, however, as they were eclipsed by specialized performers who drew large audiences, would gave way to a "star" system.

English Works, Translations and Arrangements

A sampling of British works that migrated across the ocean, took root, and became perennial favorites would include *The Poor Soldier* (Shield), *The Beggar's Opera* (Gay), *The Castle of Andalusia* (Arnold), *The Haunted Tower* (Stephen Storace), *Love Laughs at Locksmiths* (Michael Kelly), and *The Devil's Bridge, or The Piedmontese Alps* (C. E. Horn and J. Braham). The first two are ballad operas, with music derived primarily from folk tunes. Arnold's piece, chosen to inaugurate the opening of the New Theater in Philadelphia in 1794, typified his "pasticcio" approach in its borrowing from other works of Handel, Arne, Giordani, and so forth. The Storace work, on the other hand, consisted mainly of the composer's own music and included a dramatically imaginative overture and several rather complex ensembles[7] (within or ending acts) all cast in the Viennese classical style. Michael Kelly reports in his "Memories" that he only wrote the melodies for his operas, which indicates that harmonization and instrumentation would have been done by others. The Horn/Braham collaboration (1812) established Horn's reputation in England as a first-class composer. Unquestionably he was a major figure in the production of English language opera and as such requires some explication.

Charles Edward Horn, influential as a singer, composer, manager, and finally publisher, arrived in New York in 1827. He opened at the Park Theater on July 20 as Seraskier in Storace's popular "rescue" opera *Siege of Belgrade*, followed several months later by his other most successful role, Caspar in Weber's *Freischütz*. Horn, a former student of the well-known singer Rauzzini, could encompass both tenor and baritone roles, had played double bass in the orchestra at Covent Garden, conducted the orchestras at Royal Gardens ("one of the finest orchestras in Europe"[8]), and, by the time he came to New York, had composed about twelve operas as well as songs, glees, two oratorios, etc. Clearly a versatile musician, he wrote five more operas in America, but was known primarily, until he lost his voice in 1833, as a singer/arranger. He adapted English versions of *Barber of Seville, La Cenerentola, Freischütz*, and *Zauberflöte* (among others), simplifying the orchestration to accommodate instrumentalists less able than their European counterparts. Horn's alterations of originals, no matter how disfiguring, did expand the vogue for Weber and continued the popularization of Rossini and Mozart. His version of *La Cenerentola* revived a recurrent hope expressed by the New York

Mirror (22 December 1832) that this would banish foreign language opera. Horn, also the teacher of Michael Balfe, the composer of numerous operas popular in America (*The Bohemian Girl* for example), actively promoted English ballad operas and works of Storace, Bishop, Arne, and his own.

Before Garcia's performance, audiences had seen major European operas only as translated, dim distortions of the originals.[9] Restructured plots and selected music (usually with changes) from a few Mozart and Rossini works were known mainly through the English translations and "arrangements" of Henry Bishop. In his version of *Don Giovanni*, called *Don Juan or The Libertine* (London, 1817; Philadelphia, 1827), most of the ensembles were omitted, most of the arias changed, and a duet from *Magic Flute* inserted along with dances by Mozart, Martini, and Bishop.[10] His *The Marriage of Figaro* (London, 1819, New York, Park Theater, 1823) underwent similar deletions and alterations as did his version of *The Barber of Seville* (London, 1818; New York, Park Theater, 1819). Bishop was not quite as artistically insensitive as one might conclude from this mangling of Mozart and Rossini. He was continuing the common and expedient British custom, encouraged and/or required by theatrical managers, of translating and adapting foreign language operas for London performances. Some of the resulting pieces with their distortions, euphemistically labelled "improvements," were then brought to this country by managers and performers. A notable example was Weber's *Freischütz* (Berlin, 1821), which had been so popular in London in 1824 that it ran in seven different English versions. One of these (probably Bishop's) was staged in both New York and Philadelphia in 1825. Also popular were Weber's *Oberon* (New York, September 1826), and *Abu Hassan* (New York and Philadelphia, November 1827).

Other Theater

Other current favorite theatrical productions were the dependable Shakespearean plays (often with some music), in particular *Hamlet, King Lear, and Richard III*. These always drew large audiences, but especially if illuminated by a star such as Edwin Forrest. Contemporary spoken plays (again with occasional music) would include Kotzebue's *Pizarro* or Sheridan's *School for Scandal*. The lighter fare melodramas of Pocock, *Rob Roy*, or Colman, *Mountaineers*, used inserted songs along with music as background to enhance action and atmospheric effects. Standard afterpieces such as Bickerstaffe's *Spoiled Child* (music by Arnold) or O'Keefe's *Poor Soldier* (music by Shield) could be depended on, in conjunction with some lengthier production, to fill a theater. Other types of entertainments[11] ran the gamut from the successful, if low-brow, spectacle, *The Cataract of the Ganges* described by Odell, to the sophistication of *Der Freischütz*. Often a viable play, then as now, appeared in several guises, as witness Scott's poem *Lady of the Lake*, first as spoken play, then as Rossini's opera, but in French (*La dame du lac*), and finally in Italian as *La donna del lago*.

Garcia's Season

Considering the prevalent English opera, Manuel Garcia's appearance with his Italian repertory and company in November 1825 at New York's most prestigious theater, the Park, was dramatic and challenging. His productions of Italian opera replete with its elaborate, highly sophisticated music performed by thoroughly professional singers and instrumentalists contrasted sharply with the less formal English operas' "play-with-music" style presented by actor/singers. In addition, a sense of elitism, exclusivity, and mystery was added to the musical magic of a Rossini or Mozart by the foreign language cloak that obscured the plot. The audience, instructed as to dress and deportment by the newspapers, comprised New York's rich and fashionable. Garcia followed his opening *Barber of Seville* (Rossini) by a season of Italian operas selected on the basis of their current popularity abroad. Audiences responded positively to the style and quality of performance in Rossini's *Tancredi, Otello, Il Turco in Italia, La Cenerentola* (already known in New York in an English version), and Mozart's *Don Giovanni*. These masterpieces added a new dimension[12] to the operatic scene, and although Garcia never went to Philadelphia, many Philadelphians came to hear him in New York.

In the opening performance, the orchestra of carefully selected instrumentalists performed with impressive skill.[13] The singing was superior, notably that of Garcia's seventeen-year-old daughter Maria who, rigorously trained by her father, had already made a successful debut in London and would soon achieve extraordinary fame in Europe as Maria Malibran. Garcia himself was a famous singer. He had created the role of Almaviva under Rossini in the 1816 Rome premiere of *Barber*, was active and highly regarded in

Naples, Paris, and London, and was one of the best-paid tenors of his time. By his late forties he was in London, declining vocally (a distinct throb had appeared and the volume had lessened),[14] in altercations with theater managers, and ready to seek new, less critical audiences. In the fall of 1825 Dominick Lynch, an emissary of the Park Theater's manager Stephen Price, had arrived in London looking for an opera troupe to import. Lynch, an amateur musician and enthusiastic patron of music active in the recently restructured Philharmonic Society, especially enjoyed opera.[15] Garcia responded favorably to the optimistic, rosy report of America's eagerness for Italian opera and agreed to bring his company (mainly his family) to New York.

Although initially popular because of its novelty and Maria Garcia's appeal, audiences for the Italian opera gradually decreased. Ten months and eighty performances later, having earned a gross of $56,685,[16] Garcia and most of his company left for Mexico. Initial interest in this foreign divertissement had waned. The significance of Garcia's single ten-month operatic season was twofold: first, the high quality (by American standards) of performances by experienced, professionally trained singers supported by a competent orchestra; and second, the staging of major works in a form close to the originals. The subtlety, informed sophistication, and technical demands of an aria such as "Una voce poco fa" stand at the other end of the spectrum from the stark simplicity, at times crudity, of songs from the widely popular ballad operas. Considering the usual English language repertory, surprisingly few criticisms were initially raised concerning the use of Italian. One suspects that the sophistication of the music and performance overcame any criticism regarding the use of a foreign language.

As "the magnet who attracted all eyes and won all hearts,"[17] Maria's charismatic quality became one of the main sources of the troupe's success. Her expressive quality and mastery of the difficult vocal technique required for the Rossini and Mozart repertory won dramatically positive responses from audiences. Now married to the forty-four-year-old merchant Eugene Malibran (March 1826), she remained in New York after the company's departure for Mexico to sing at the Grace Church and subsequently the newly built Bowery Theater managed by Charles Gilfert. There she appeared in some of the popular English works (Horn's *Devil's Bridge* and Arne's *Love in a Village*[18]), as well as *Don Giovanni* and, finally, a translation of Boieldieu's *Jean de Paris* introduced several months earlier by a French company in French. Then, having gained her professional experience in the provinces of America, she left for Paris, the opera capitol of the world, to achieve lasting fame as one of the greatest singers of the century.

French Opera Company

In July 1827 the French opera company (mentioned above) under the direction of John Davis opened its first six-month northern tour at the Park Theater in New York. A crucial aspect of this company was that it employed seasoned singers, musicians, and dancers imported from Paris. Equally important, their astute manager was experienced through his ten seasons of opera in New Orleans. In addition, the troupe had a strong, successful French repertory that included, besides the new "hit" Boieldieu's *La Dame Blanche*, works of Auber, Dalayrac, Isouard, Cherubini, and so on. The purpose of Davis's northern tour was to avoid the heat of the New Orleans summer, which discouraged theater attendance and often caused his performers to disband. The tour offered fresh audiences, continued employment, and hence a means of maintaining his company intact. The opening double bill of Isouard's *Cendrillon* and Dalayrac's *Maison à vendre* prefaced about forty operas that were staged over the next two months. The company then undertook three weeks at the Chestnut Street Theater in Philadelphia before returning to New York. Both cities saw sixty performances of thirty-two operas by fourteen composers.[19] The New York *American* noted, "This company is as good as those heard in the provinces of France and superior to those heard in the Capitals of Europe outside France."[20] New Orleans papers were similarly adulatory when the troupe returned home. Considering that city's lengthy operatic history and its variety of opera companies, the opinion carries some weight. During John Davis's six summer tours north (the last was in 1833), the most popular composers were Boieldieu with seven operas given fifty times (including performances in Boston and Baltimore) and Auber with seven works played forty-three times. The most frequent productions were *La Dame Blanche* (twenty-four times); *Der Freischütz*, translated as *Robin des bois* (sixteen times); and *Barber of Seville* (in French, of course, thirteen times). This exposure to such a consistently superior series of French performances enhanced the opera seasons of New York and Philadelphia. The variety, quantity, and fine quality expanded the audience's experience, raising the general level of taste and expectations.

The popular English opera repertory during this period of the late twenties and early thirties included two of Rophino Lacey's Rossini adaptions: *Cinderella* (with music from Rossini's *Cenerentola, Guillaume Tell, Maometto,* etc.) and *The Maid of Judah* (on Scott's *Ivanhoe* with music from *Mosè in Egitto*). The following consistently recurred on theater bills: Weber's *Abu Hassan*, Arne's English-language Italian-style opera *Artaxerxes*, Boieldieu's *The White Lady* (adapted by John Howard Payne), Auber's *Masaniello* (*La Muette di Portici*), Bishop's "Scott" opera *Guy Mannering, Magic Flute* in Horn's arrangement, and the shorter pieces *No Song No Supper* (Storace) and *The Quartette* (Horn). Among translations, *Cinderella, Barber of Seville, Freischütz, Marriage of Figaro,* and *Sonnambula* attained exceptional popularity, often due, in part, to a celebrity such as Malibran, Horn, or the Woods. Other singers whom critics noted as enhancing these performances included Mrs. Austin, greatly admired by the *Mirror*'s critic; Miss Hughes, noted for her "Cinderella" and role in the English *Freischütz*; and Mme. Feron and Mrs. Knight. Horn, until 1833, shone in his own works as well as *Freischütz*, while other popular male singers mentioned are John Sinclair, for whom Rossini had written the part of Idreno in *Semiramide*, and John Jones, composer/singer.

Da Ponte

In 1805 Lorenzo da Ponte, one of Mozart's librettists and a figure of some importance in opera's general development, had settled in New York after a period as a theater librettist in London. He reacted to the New Orleans company with the traditional Italian lack of enthusiasm for French music.[21] When he had gone to greet Garcia and identified himself as the librettist of *Don Giovanni*, Garcia was reputed to have responded by singing the opening of the opera's "Champagne" aria[22] to him. Da Ponte, now a teacher of Italian and a dealer in imported books, enthusiastically promoted Garcia's performances by attending them with his students, as well as printing and selling the libretto of *Don Giovanni* in English and Italian.[23] His relatively unsuccessful attempt to produce Italian opera in 1830 was followed by correspondence and eventually collabolation with Giovanni Montresor, a tenor/impresario then in Italy. In 1832 the two initiated, with Rossini's *La Cenerentola* (a dependable choice in any language), a season of Italian opera at the Richmond Hill Theater,[24] thus fulfilling in part the energetic da

Ponte's long-cheriched dream of personally bringing Italian culture to New York. What better medium than one in which he himself had achieved great success (albeit thirty-nine years before) and that the city had already briefly glimpsed? Richmond Hill's season ran from 6 October 1832 through 11 May 1833 with about fifty performances, excluding benefits, and including a tour to Philadelphia. Despite a fair company, good reviews, and weak competition from the current English opera, the enterprise lost money. Both da Ponte and Montresor were left with bad feelings and large debts. On the positive side, the company had premiered Rossini's *L'inganno felice* and *L'Italiana in Algeri*, Bellini's *Il pirata*, and Mercadante's *Elisa e Claudio*, all contemporary and successful in European theaters.

Undaunted by this financial failure, da Ponte now undertook to raise money for the construction of a theater specifically for opera. This separation of opera from the other types of stage entertainment with which it had previously been housed would give it (he hoped) a stronger, more permanent basis. He was, of course, replicating the European system. Support from wealthy citizens with strong cultural interests, such as Philip Hone, a former mayor of the city, and his friend Dominick Lynch, resulted in the construction of the Italian Opera House. It was thus:

> The auditorium was different in arrangement than any hitherto seen in America. The second tier was composed entirely of private boxes, hung with curtains of crimson silk; . . . The whole interior was pronounced magnificent, and the scenery and curtains were beautiful beyond all precedent. The ground of the front-boxes was white, with emblematical medallions and octagonal panels of crimson, blue, and gold. The dome was painted with representations of the Muses. The sofas and pitseats were covered with damask, and the floors were all carpeted.[25]

With da Ponte and his friend Rivafinoli, the managers for the first six months, the financial basis for the seasons proved totally impractical and doomed to failure.

Philip Hone noted in his diary,[26] November 1835, two elements fused in opposition to the acceptance of Italian opera: one was the use of a foreign language and the other the aristocratic atmosphere that the boxes induced. Although undoubtedly true at the time, these were the very elements that eventually gained opera support from those socially elite elements, of which Hone was one, seeking class symbols. Hone then added, "[T]he immense houses which Mr. and Mrs. Wood bring nightly to the Park, prove that the New

Yorkers are not devoid of musical taste, notwithstanding that the Italian opera does not succeed. . . . " In a word, there was no reason for Italian opera to exist, especially in the face of a successful English opera that flourished unconcerned with attempts to establish a foreign language opera (Italian or French).

The Mr. and Mrs. Woods that Hone mentions had arrived in New York from London in 1832 and were about to introduce one of their most successful works in English, Bellini's *La sonnambula*. One of their other big attractions was the ever-popular *La Cenerentola* in English. In the fall of 1833 they had staged twenty works of ballad and grand operas in Philadelphia at the Chestnut St. Theater, where they had opened with *Love in a Village*. Armstrong describes Mrs. Woods as an authoritative performer with a "rich and powerful voice . . . of great facility."[27] He also observes that she taught Mr. Woods most of what he knew about music.

In 1836 the Italian Opera House, following a second disastrous attempt at Italian opera, became the National Theater with a repertory expanded beyond opera. Two years later a trio of singers, Arthur Seguin, John Wilson, and Jane Shirreff, successfully inaugurated Rooke's *Amilie, or the Love Test* there. Despite the financial panic and a severe depression from 1837 to 1841, most established theaters survived and a few new ones appeared. In 1839, one year after da Ponte's death, the National Theater burned down, and in 1840 Stephen Price, the enterprising manager of the Park Theater who had originally commissioned Dominick Lynch to seek an opera company in London, died. An era had ended. Da Ponte had labored long and determinedly to bring Italian opera to America, and despite the many obstacles, problems, and failures he was crucial in its beginnings and future. He was aided by a number of others, including Maria Malibran, our first superstar prima donna who transfixed audiences, and the essential background figures such as Price, Hone, and Lynch who respectively offered practical and financial support.

Conclusion

Opera was attended by a small audience drawn from a limited but expanding population still close culturally to Britain and still using (in its wealthy class) only limited, rather private symbols of class distinctions.[28] English style opera, dominated the period of 1825–40, with French and Italian works appearing only sporadically. Performances may have varied, but English language or translations were considered as essential as the combination of opera with other miscellaneous entertainments to round out the evening. The afterpiece or farce now functioned in the manner similar to that of the "lieto fine" (happy ending) of the eighteenth century *opera seria*. Before the segregation of opera, drama, comedy, etc. into special, separate theaters, opera coexisted, democratically, with all other entertainments on one stage. There were no purists' objections to following a translated *Don Giovanni* with an afterpiece. No one was excluded intellectually or financially since the audience supported opera it could understand and went where the price was uniform.

Garcia's staging of Rossini and Mozart masterpieces with their florid arias and sung recitatives was a revelation not only of artistic refinement, but the genre's potential excitement. John Davis's New Orleans company mounted first-class performances of a fine contemporary French repertory typified by spoken dialogue and shorter solo airs. Maria Garcia, under the tutelage of her truly gifted father, enamored her audiences and became the standard by which all female singers were evaluated for several decades. Thus the Garcias paved the way for da Ponte's efforts to establish a permanent Italian opera.

The wealthy patronage essential from opera's birth had been exposed to the enchantment of the Italian and French styles as well as its aristocratic associations. In the next decade Italian opera in particular would attract the attention of the socially elite as they realized that its symbolic significance of exclusivity and prestige could be used to establish their own social hierarchy. As Philip Hone had noted, there was now no reason for Italian opera to exist in America. The mellifluous marriage of Italian poetry and music had little meaning for or impact on an English-speaking audience, especially since the same lovely melodies with words one could understand were accessible at a theater where prices better reflected egalitarian principles.

Notes

1. Julius Mattfeld, *A Hundred Years of Grand Opera in New York: 1825–1925* (New York: New York Public Library, 1927). W. G. Armstrong, *A Record of the Opera in Philadelphia* (Philadelphia, 1884). George C. D. Odell, *Annals of the New York Stage* (New York: Columbia University Press, 1928), vols. 3 and 4. Henry A. Kmen, *Music in New Orleans: The Formative Years, 1791–1841* (Baton Rouge: Louisiona State University Press, 1966).

2. Edward Pessen, *Riches, Class, and Power before the Civil War* (Lexington, Mass.: D. C. Heath and Co.), chapter 7.

3. Michael A. Lebowitz, "The Jacksonians: Paradox Lost?" in *Towards a New Past: Dissenting Essays in American History*, ed. Barton J. Bernstein (New York: Random House, 1968) p. 69.

4. David Grimsted, *Melodrama Unveiled: American Theater and Culture 1800–1850* (Chicago: Univ. of Chicago Press, 1968). Chapter 2 has a detailed discussion of these attitudes. Grimsted notes a certain subtle rivalry for the individual's time and money existing between church and theater.

5. Quoted in ibid., p. 35.

6. Otto E. Albrecht, "Opera in Philadelphia, 1800–1830," *Journal of the American Musicological Society* 32, no. 39 (Fall 1979): p. 498.

7. J. Ottenberg, "Popularity of Two Operas in Philadelphia in the 1790s," in *International Review of the Aesthetics and Sociology of Music* 18, no. 2. The work had only two folk tunes and some borrowing from Paisiello, Marini, etc.

8. Quoted in Richard Montague, *Charles Edward Horn: His Life and Work (1786–1849)* (Ph.D. diss., Florida State Univ., 1959), p. 11.

9. Opera, however, had been offered in New Orleans in French since 1796 when Gretry's *Sylvain* is listed. See Kmen, p. 58.

10. Frederick Corder, "The Works of Sir Henry Bishop," *Musical Quarterly* 4 (1918): 78–97.

11. Extensive listings appear in Joseph N. Ireland, *Records of the New York Stage from 1750 to 1860* (New York: Benjamin Bloom, 1966), 2. See also Odell.

12. Mattfeld, *Hundred Years*, p. 21, gives a full listing of the repertory.

13. Ibid., p. 19. Mattfeld also gives some details of the Garcia company.

14. Howard Bushnell, *Maria Malibran: A Biography of the Singer* (University Park: Pennsylvania State Univ. Press, 1979), p. 3.

15. Vera Brodsky Lawrence, *Strong on Music: The New York Music Scene in the Days of George Templeton Strong, 1836–1875*, vol. 1 of *Resonances 1836–1850*. (New York: Oxford Univ. Press, 1988), p. xl.

16. Mattfeld, *Hundred Years*, p. 20.

17. Bushnell, *Maria Malibran*, pp. 63–64 from *Albion*, cited by M. Sterling Mackinley, *Garcia: The Centenarian and His Time* (London, 1908).

18. Mattfeld, *Hundred Years*, p. 22.

19. Kmen, *Music in New Orleans*, p. 112.

20. Ibid, p. 113.

21. This controversy is well-known and long-lived.

22. Mattfeld, *Hundred Years*, p. 19.

23. Sheila Hodges, *Lorenzo da Ponte: The Life and Times of Mozart's Librettist* (London: Granada Publishing, 1985). This offers a needed reassessment of da Ponte through a wealth of clear, well-researched information.

24. Soon to be renamed the Italian Opera House.

25. Ritter, quoted in Mattfeld, *Hundred Years*, p. 32.

26. Ibid., pp. 32–34.

27. Armstrong, *Record*, p. 39.

28. Pessen, *Riches*, chap. 11.

Part Two
Opera: Becoming Part of American Culture

Popular Opera and Bands in the American Civil War

PHILLIPA BURGESS

Opera excerpts were used for the purposes of popular entertainment extensively during the American Civil War. Arrangements of opera made for performance by the military brass band was, to a large extent, responsible for the broadening of the public perception of opera in the military camps or at the home front. This was achieved through their recognized military association and pageantry at a time of heightened patriotic fervor.

The bands were an informal ensemble that removed opera from the confines of exclusive indoor performance areas and presented the catchy tunes of an opera without the encumbrance of the not-so-catchy recitatives. To the Civil War soldier, the bands provided a daily acquaintance with opera melodies, since the soldier had very little other forms of entertainment; and the nomadic nature of the soldier and the bands provided an opportunity to come into contact with bands from different parts and cultures of the continent. This encouraged the dissemination of opera from band to band as its popularity was quickly recognized.

Most of the military functions of the soldiers of the American Civil War were accompanied by music, either the more simple field music of fifes and drums or bugles, or the more complex arrangements provided by the regimental or brigade brass bands. However, very little time of the military was spent performing military functions, and time spent behind picket lines or in the evenings in camp was often occupied by music performed by the brass band. Early in the war, many of the existing militia bands and city bands enlisted as a group, thus providing for the entertainment of the members of their regiment with repertoire already established and rehearsed. Patrick Gilmore's Band from Boston joined the Twenty-Fourth Massachusetts Volunteer Regiment, much to the appreciation of other volunteers. This was recorded by John Partridge, who wrote to his sister on, 19 April 1862 the following letter:

> I don't know what we should have done without our band. . . . Every night about sundown Gilmore gives us a splendid concert, playing selections from operas and some very pretty marches, quicksteps, waltzes and the like, most of which were composed by himself or by Zohler, a member of his band[1]. . . . Thus you see we get a good deal of new music, notwithstanding we are off here in the woods. Gilmore used to give some of the most fashionable concerts we had at home and we lack nothing but strings now. In their place however we have five reed instruments, of which no other band can boast.[2]

Patrick Gilmore had become leader of the Boston Brigade Band in 1859, following his successful work with his previous band in Salem, Massachusetts. This was noted by Dwight in his *Journal of Music* when it performed in Boston as part of the Promenade Concerts given in 1857.

These Promenade Concerts were given by the better brass bands in the Boston area (such as the Germania, Hall's Boston Brass, Gilmore's Salem Brass, and Bond's and Flagg's Cornet Bands[3]) and were organized by the City of Boston in recognition of the popularity of these bands. As brass bands were an outgrowth of the pageantry associated with the national enthusiasm for militia, they originally performed music that was appropriate for military functions—such as recruitments and parades. Band arrangements of operatic literature were very popular for these purposes, and with some of these bands branching out from their military beginnings in the late 1850s as their musicianship exceeded the limited requirements of a militia brass band, these popular operatic arrangements became an established part of their repertoire. The selection of the program for the Promenade Concerts of 1857 reflects the popularity of these arrangements, especially as this provided an opportunity for the better bands to showcase their ensembles in the more formal setting of the Music Hall.

Initially, Dwight's reception of the concept of these concerts was less than enthusiastic, although he accepted them in preference to performances by less well-rehearsed bands and encouraged them only in that they provided some music for the public at an inexpensive cost.

> Better the most hacknied ditties, better negro melodies, "anvil choruses," and clap-trap polkas, quick-steps, patriotic airs, or any music, we would say, than none at all. . . . What is humdrum to our ears may

be the preparation of thousands for the appreciation, some day, of something a little nearer to the character and dignity of Art.

We rejoice therefore in everything that is done to furnish the people, the masses, freely or at small cost, with frequent feasts of music such as they have most delight in, provided it have some true pretensions to excellence both in composition and performance. . . . We rejoice to believe, too, that our popular street music, especially the music of our bands, which always feels its way by consultation of the public pulse, is better than it was, and on the whole improving.[4]

Despite his well-stated antipathy towards brass bands and his strong distaste for works arranged for them from orchestral and operatic literature, Dwight had to admit to the immense popularity of these concerts, which had to be repeated three times a week for over a month in August and September of that year. By the close of the season the popularity of the concerts had increased until there was no longer any room for promenading.[5]

Through his criticism of the band arrangements it is possible to identify some of the concert pieces as well as the instrumentation of the performing ensembles. It seems from his review from August 1857 that a Rossini overture was played, as well as an arrangement of his *Stabat Mater*. Other arrangements seemed to have included the trio from *Lucrezia Borgia* and the "Miserere" from *Il trovatore*.

Dwight's final analysis on the Promenade Concerts was that until bands include other instruments besides brass in their complement of members, then brass bands must suffice for the purposes of providing entertainment and education for the public.

For ourselves, we would rather listen only to marches and the waltzes [in brass band music]; but these give hardly sphere enough to the musicians, and would keep the public out of the fashions of the day in music, which might cause some murmuring; they know the *Trovatore* is now fashionable, and they must have a taste of it, even from a cornet band.[6]

As a result of the recognition gained by Gilmore through the performance of the Salem Band in this Boston concert, as well as Gilmore's own ability as an organized manager and showman, Gilmore was appointed leader of the Boston Brigade Band in 1859. Gilmore was able to reorganize both the instrumentation and the repertoire of the band to include reeds, orchestral and operatic literature well-arranged for the ensemble, and a reintroduction of some older band literature that had been abandoned with the advancing instrumental technology that produced the saxhorns and the string-linkage rotary valve. At Gilmore's first concert with his new band in Boston, *Dwight's Journal of Music* quotes from the *Courier* as it praises the addition of reed instruments on a permanent basis to the band.

> The Courier of Monday gives the following account of Mr. GIL-MORE'S CONCERT.—The first appearance of Mr. Gilmore's new band last Saturday evening gave assurance of much success in its future operations. The audience was immense and the applause abundant, compelling many encores not anticipated. . . . His military band consists of some thirty-five members, among whom are the proper proportion of players upon reed instruments—flutes, clarinet, hautboys, bassoons.[7]

The success that the *Courier* critic felt to be assured for the Gilmore Band was shown to be justified in the programs and repertoire that the band performed. Later that year, the Gilmore Band had the honor of being the final band to appear in the third season of Promenade Concerts given in Boston, and the program for that date indicates the importance of opera as the staple not only for the Gilmore Band but for the entire promenade season. (As the concert advertisement suggests, Gilmore had taken over management of the Promenade Concerts, and, as a businessman, ensured its adherence to popular taste.) Out of the twelve pieces performed on this concert, four were from opera, with another being a selection from the Rossini *Stabat Mater*. All four of the opera excerpts were from the Italian repertoire. They were the finale from Donizetti's *Lucrezia Borgia*; a selection from Verdi's *Lombardi* (first time performed); the overture from Rossini's *Italian in Algiers*, and the cavatina from Verdi's *Nabucco*.[8]

The most "fashionable" of all of Gilmore's concerts from this period was probably the last one that the band gave before leaving with the Twenty-Fourth Massachusetts. This concert lists five operatic excerpts out of a possible twelve, despite the patriotic nature of the concert. The operatic excerpts used here were mainly Italian, although a selection from the German opera *Martha* was also included. The Italian works were a grand aria from Verdi's *Nabucco*; a selection from Verdi's *Ernani*; the "March Militaire" from Verdi's *Sicilian Vespers*, and the overture from Rossini's *Barber of Seville*.

It was with this repertoire that Gilmore marched off to war, and it was with this repertoire that Gilmore and his band entertained the troops while they served with the Union army. Gilmore's Band remained with the Twenty-Fourth as they served in North Carolina, until his band was mustered out in 1862 when the war department reduced the number of bands by attaching them to the brigade level only.[9]

Gilmore and his repertoire continued to be influential in the Massachusetts area as he attempted to continue the subscription concerts of the Gilmore Brass Band as well as to participate in recruitment drives in Boston, although many of his band members volunteered for service and were used either as infantrymen or bandsmen. At this time, Gilmore also become responsible for the organization and rehearsal of bands about to became active with newly formed regiments, one of which accompanied General Banks on his campaign in Louisiana.

In 1864, Gilmore was invited by General Banks to organize the music for the celebration of the inauguration of General Hahn as governor of Louisiana. Gilmore's extravaganza involved over 500 bandsmen, a 5000-strong chorus of adults and children, church bells, thirty-six artillery pieces, and fifty anvils. Besides such required patriotic airs as "Hail Columbia", the program included a performance of the Anvil chorus from Verdi's *Il trovatore*.

> Patriotic songs were sung by the little folks; five hundred musicians filled the air with sweet sounds, and in the "Anvil Chorus," which was sung, fifty sons of Vulcan kept time on as many veritable anvils. . . .[10]

Another established band that enlisted for the war included the young men from the Moravian band of Winston-Salem, North Carolina. This band joined with the Twenty-Sixth North Carolina Regiment, Confederate States of America, and its military service is recorded in the diaries of Julius Leinbach with the band books preserved by the Moravian Music Foundation. From these sources it can be seen that the band began with seven members and never exceeded a complement of ten brass players plus two drummers.

This band accompanied their regiment through the entire conflict, and were even heard to play polkas and waltzes at the battle of Gettysburg where their services as bandsmen were more highly valued than their services as stretcher bearers. The function of this band as a battle band playing for the troops on the front line explains the smaller size of the band and the relative simplicity of their repertoire, which allowed for playing and movement on the field with minimal interruption to the flow of the music. Despite this required simplicity, the band books of the Twenty-Sixth North Carolina Regimental Band have opera arrangements in approximately fifteen percent of their selections, demonstrating that opera was used regardless of the standard of the band.

Although the band was of German origin, the band books show that almost all the opera performed was of Italian origin, with the only two German operas being Flotow's *Martha* and Weber's *Der Freischütz*. The incidence of opera in their band books occurs mainly after their first book, suggesting that these were collected following the beginning of their enlistment. Once in the field, the band frequently heard other bands and copied arrangements from these bands. One band that impressed them more for their arrangements than for their playing was the band of the Sixth Mississippi. Eleven pieces from the repertoire of the Twenty-Sixth North Carolina Band come from Hartwell, the director of the Mississippi band, and were probably copied into the band books while they were in camp or at a concert together.

Below is a list of the books and their operatic content, demonstrating the effect that contact with other bands had upon the repertoire of the band. (The band even managed to obtain some arrangements by Claudio Grafulla, a Yankee band master.)

BOOK ONE
Grand March in *Norma*, Bellini.
From *Bohemian Girl*, Balfe.

BOOK TWO
Excerpt from *Lucia di Lammermoor*, Donizetti.
Chorus from *The Child of the Regiment*, Donizetti.

BOOK THREE
Excerpt from *Lucia di Lammermoor*, Donizetti.
Quickstep from *Martha*, Flotow.
The Prophete March, Meyerbeer.
Quartette from *Der Freischütz*, Weber.
Ballade from *Zampa*, Herold.
Aria from *Child of the Regiment*, Donizetti.

BOOK FOUR
March from *Belisario*.
Romance from *Lucreia Borgia*, arr. Grafulla
"Then You'll Remember Me" from *The Bohemian Girl*, from
    Balfe.
Quickstep from *Trovatore*, Verdi.

BOOK FIVE
Air from *Falstaff*, Balfe.
Scene and Prayer from *Der Freischütz*, Weber.
Quickstep from *Sicilian Vespers*, Verdi.

Very little reference in given in the diaries about which numbers
were played for which occasions, although they do mention performing "some of [their] best"[11] for General Lee when he personally thanked them for their musical efforts. Some of these best
arrangements may well have been included on the program for the
concert given following their return home. They had hoped to raise
enough money to replace the instruments they had lost at the close
of the war, and for this purpose the repertoire chosen was likely to
reflect the quality of the performers upon popular numbers. One
of the numbers selected for this concert was the quickstep from
Trovatore, testifying to its prominent place in the repertoire of the
band.

The books of the Twenty-Sixth North Carolina Band contain
several numbers arranged by Grafulla. Grafulla had established his
reputation as both band leader and band arranger prior to the war
when he directed the Seventh Regimental Bank of New York. This
band enlisted with the Seventh New York Regiment in 1861. The
band lasted three months in the war before they were mustered
out, but like Gilmore's Band they continued to support the war
effort through benefit concerts, and Grafulla continued to write
band arrangements that appear in many of the surviving band
books, such as the Twenty-Sixth North Carolina (already mentioned) and the Port Royal Band.

Many of his operatic arrangements were "potpourris"—medleys
of the most popular tunes form an opera. One such was the potpourri from William Fry's opera *Leonora*. This work was whistled
to Grafulla some time after he became hand master of the Seventh
Regimental Band in 1860. By the end of that evening, Grafulla had
arranged a potpourri using the tunes, and it was performed that
night. This arrangement "became very popular with the bands
shortly afterwards."[12]

During the war, the practice of compositing tunes from half-
remembered snatches seems to have become more common as
band masters, searching for new literature and remembering a tune
form an earlier visit to an opera or a concert, wrote arrangements
for their bands based upon these tunes. The Port Royal Band
Books contain one such number, which is referred to by the title

"Prisoner's Song from *Il trovatore*." While this arrangement contains some of the features of the Verdi work, such as triple time and guitar-like accompaniment, the melody has enough differences between the two versions that it could be mistaken for an original composition by the band master.

The military bands provided an important service through the entertainment that they provided for the people at home or on the front. Their informal performances provided settings for the popular consumption of music of which opera excerpts arranged for the band were among the favorites. The orchestrations tended to be primitive since the band musicians generally moved in blocks of chords, often playing at the unison. However, the movement of bands through the various battlefields and encampments of the Civil War disseminated popular operatic music throughout the war zones as soldiers were daily serenaded by the strains of opera literature.

Notes

1. It is possible that by crediting Gilmore and Zohler as composers of the music performed by the band, John Partridge is referring to arrangements of music by these men.

2. John Partridge to Fannie L. Partridge, 19 April 1862, manuscript in the Chicago Historical Society.

3. John S. Dwight, "Musical Chit-Chat," *Dwight's Journal of Music*, 25 July 1857, p. 135.

4. John S. Dwight, "Promenade Concerts," *Dwight's Journal of Music*, 1 August 1857, p. 141.

5. John S. Dwight, "Musical Chit-Chat," *Dwight's Journal of Music*, 12 September 1857, p. 191

6. John S. Dwight, "Musical Chit-Chat," *Dwight's Journal of Music*, 8 August 1857, p.151.

7. John S. Dwight, "A New Band," *Dwight's Journal of Music* 16 April 1859, p. 21.

8. Boston Music Hall, "Gilmore's Promenade Concerts," Concert Program, 24 September 1859.

9. Despite the ordinance that disbanded the regimental band, some officers maintained their regimental bands at their own expense, and many bands that survived the cut-backs maintained their original, regimental titles.

10. "The Inauguration," *New Orleans Times*, 5 March 1864, p. 1.

11. Julius Leinbach in a speech before the Wachovia Historical Society in Winston-Salem, North Carolina, in Donald M. McCorkle, "Regiment Band of the Twenty-Sixth North Carolina," *Civil War History* (Sept. 1958): 224.

12. William Bayley in Kenneth E. Olson, *Music and Muskets* (Westport, Conn.: Greenwood, 1981), p. 228.

Old World Libretti for New World Settings

MARIO HAMLET-METZ

With the exception of occasional travel accounts, and epic poems such as Ercilla's *La Araucana* in the sixteenth century, the New World was practically unknown in European literature until the end of the eighteenth century; what was said about it constituted mere idealizations serving the authors' purposes (moralistic, political, or philosophical) and gave a totally distorted description of both the lands and their inhabitants. This was indeed the case with the Abbé Prévost and Voltaire, the first two major writers who used the New World as an original setting in their writings; in 1731, Prévost published his semi-autobiographical, moralistic novel *Manon Lescaut* in which he denounces the corruption reigning in France after the death of Louis XIV. The last part of his novel takes place in a Louisiana described as a barren, inhospitable territory where only outlaws and criminals could survive. Manon could not, that is the author's point. The purely fictional description has nothing to do with the articles published in *Le Mercure* in 1717 and 1719 that had originally inspired Prévost and that gave an almost idyllic tableau of the region. Voltaire's tragedy *Alzire ou les Américains* (1736), set in colonial Peru, is also pure fiction; in it, the author defends the value of civilization and of Christianity against the most primitive and brutal forces of nature as represented by the Incas. In Voltaire's *Candide* (1759), South America is also used as an ideal background for the hero's apprenticeship into the absurdities of life. (Interestingly, these three works were used for opera librettos long after the authors' lives.)

Subsequent literary works, especially those written for the stage at the end of the eighteenth and early nineteenth centuries, were profoundly influenced by the French Revolution. The desire to change the old order suddenly became a necessity and, in their eagerness to develop new forms (the birth of popular melodrama, for one, dates from this time) and find original subjects, the young generation of playwrights, including librettists, looked for sources

71

of inspiration in foreign literatures as well as in distant real-life places and characters. On the lyric stage, a most successful production of this period, and one that must be regarded as, if not the first, one of the first large-scale spectacular works, a true forerunner of Grand Opera, was the Spontini/Jouy *Fernand Cortez*, which premiered at the Paris Opera in 1809 and was an enormous success. In the interesting foreword, Jouy argues that his libretto follows history closer than most literary works and that he has chosen it because it suits the lyric stage ideally, with a brave yet compassionate hero and a story full of striking events; as for the use of horses on stage (a novelty on any stage), Jouy says that rather than impress the spectators' eye (which he certainly did), his true intention was to recreate the surprise and the terror that the sight of these animals must have caused among the natives. Although structurally still reminiscent of *opera seria*, especially in the happy finale, the love story of Cortez and the native Amazili, and the villainous behavior of Amazili's brother the High Priest, are definitely melodramatic in spirit and seem to foreshadow the Romantic drama of the years to come. While Cortez's heroism and generosity (he offers a peaceful settlement to Montezuma) can be easily explained in political terms during the Napoleonic era, the nobility of Montezuma (he recognizes Cortez's heroism from the beginning and in the end renounces his intentions of burning the city and welcomes the Spaniards) must be viewed as a wise reaction on the part of a defeated leader who acknowledges the superiority of a victorious conqueror. (The French always were fascinated by the conquest of Mexico and loved to compare the humane Cortez with the ruthless Pizarro, the conqueror of the Incas.)

Because of the thematic and stylistic merits that made the Abbé Prévost's *Manon Lescaut* so attractive to Romanticists and Realists a century after it was published, this novel never did lose its popularity. Not only was it frequently mentioned in important literary works by the main authors of the nineteenth century, but it was adapted on at least three occasions to the lyric stage, by Auber/Scribe, Massenet/Meilhac and Puccini/Civinini-Zangarini. While the Massenet heroine dies before leaving for the New World, the last act of the other two *Manons* does take place in Louisiana, a Louisiana that in the Auber/Scribe opera offers the audience some local color scenically and linguistically. The third act shows first a rich apartment on a plantation on the Mississippi, with plenty of seemingly happy slaves singing about the joys of working for a fair master, in a picturesque Indian-sounding dialect. Then, in the final scene, the weakened Manon, reunited with Des

Grieux, flees with him to the desert and dies at the entrance of a forest (!), in the presence of a group of black slaves who have arrived too late to rescue the two lovers and who lament the heroine's death with words said no longer in the previous jargon but in a most French romantic manner. The Christian thought on the part of the slaves finds the prolific Scribe at his creative worst.

In Puccini's *Manon Lescaut*, the New World is mentioned in the third act, during which it becomes obvious that it is a most undesirable place where only the enamored Des Grieux seems anxious to go. As in Auber, the last act of *Manon Lescaut* takes place in America, on a vast desert plain on the borders of New Orleans. The geographically unrealistic landscape is purposely desolate to imply internal desolation and death and is really not important, except that the dying Manon is fully aware that her fatal beauty is once again responsible for her downfall, this time in a land she mistakenly believed to be peaceful.

One of the opera librettos with a South American setting inspired by a tragedy by Voltaire was *Alzira*, an opera with a prologue and two acts by Verdi, composed in 1845 to a libretto by the well-known Salvatore Cammarano. It was a hasty product of the so-called "Galley years," and its book seems to have been a poor choice—a Cammarano choice—for a time when Verdi was working mainly with plots that would invariably touch at some point, directly or surreptitiously, the patriotic fiber of his fellow Italians. Here, one expects in vain an outburst by the tenor or a chorus singing words filled with the deeply felt patriotic message to which Verdi had already accustomed his audiences, even in operas that were not necessarily patriotic, such as *Ernani*. On the contrary, towards the end of the opera, when the Peruvian Alzira is to marry Gusmano, the Spanish tyrant, rather than lament this forced wedding, her maidens actually rejoice. Perhaps Verdi did realize that the original text, with its typical eighteenth century Voltairian message, was far removed from his own political and philosophical views as well as from his clearly Romantic aesthetic preferences. In fact, it is hard to believe that the aesthetically Schiller-Hugo-minded Verdi was too keen to work on a book that portrayed the oppressed natives as the truly cruel ones and the tyrannical invaders as the virtuous ones, such as appears from the very first scene in the Prologue, where the Indians drag the enchained old Alvaro and sing ferociously with Otumbo, their leader:"Die, die covered with insults. . . . O brothers, who died of your wounds, / Rise howling from your graves . . . / Intone together the hymn of triumph, / While he breathes his last breath." It is also unlikely that Verdi genuinely cared for either Zamoro (nicknamed Ernani's South American cousin), the sincere but unwisely generous hero who in the end finds happiness after stabbing his rival, nor for Gusmano, the unsympathetic tyrant whose last-minute act of nobility (he forgives Zamoro) totally contradicts his previous behavior. At this point of his career, Verdi did not seem to care too much about" local color" either: the sets, on the Rima river and in the city of Lima, do not have any importance, nor are they described musically, as the composer would do later on so creatively in his *Aïda*. But determined as he was to establish his reputation as an opera composer, Verdi took on his task, accepting the Cammarano libretto, where politics and philosophy became secondary to the love triangle.

Offenbach's *La Périchole* (1868), an *opéra bouffe* with libretto by the prestigious Meilhac-Halevy team (*Carmen*), offers a colorful South American setting as well. The opera is based on a Mérimée book, which in turn was based on the real story of the eighteenth century Micaela Villegas, a half-Indian Peruvian actress who became the Viceroy's mistress and finished her days in a Carmelite convent in Lima. She owes her nickname to the Viceroy himself, who, tired of her, called her "Perra Chola" (Mulatto Dog). The opera tells us how La Périchole caught the eye of the Viceroy, how this ruler arranged for her to get married so she could officially enter the Palace and become his mistress, and how La Périchole tricked the Viceroy twice, first by marrying the man she really loved (Piquillo), who was drunk at the time of the wedding and did not realize until later that his wife was the Viceroy's mistress, and at the end, by freeing Piquillo from prison and escaping with him. There is a moment of seriousness in the opera when, at the end of Act II, the furious husband insults everyone at court, giving away to the Viceroy the most seductive and false-hearted woman ("la femme la plus séduisante et la plus fausse en même temps"), in a scene taken from Donizetti's *La Favorite* and that had also been seen in *El gitano*, a very popular French play of the 1830s. But everything ends happily, as La Périchole is allowed to leave with her beloved Piquillo and keep the jewels given her during her affair. In spite of the setting, we learn very little about Peru in this opera. The libretto says that we are in Lima, in the eighteenth century, to be precise on a square, facing the Cabaret of the Three Cousins. Then, in Act II, we move on to the Palace of the Viceroy in Lima, from where we see a vast bay and a general view of the city. Act III takes place in the prison. It could be anywhere, but it really is Paris. The characters and the innuendos of the plots are no more

South American than the setting. The fashionable Spanish accents and the hypocrisy at the Court of Napoléon III and Empress Eugénie, the escapades of the Emperor, the cruelty and selfishness of the courtiers, and the overall gay Parisian atmosphere of the times are all there. It could not be otherwise *chez* Offenbach. La Périchole's final address to the world ("Peup' d'Amérique, de l'Espagne et du Pérou") in which she tells her story may be a proforma reminder to the audience that it is all a Peruvian tale, but this reminder does not make the entire piece any less French in spirit and in word.

One should also mention in passing Verdi's *La forza del destino*, based on a drama by the Duque de Rivas. One would assume that the Spaniards would present to readers or audiences—to the rest of the world—a positive image of the peoples or the lands that used to be part of their Empire. Not at all. The literary works produced in Spain show nothing but contempt for the colonies. In the name of pride, of purity of blood, the Spanish authors seem eager to stress the racial and social inferiority of the inhabitants of their territories, with total disregard for their human values or feelings. The case of Don Alvaro (which is pertinent to us here) is typical: a son of a patriot and the last Inca Princess, he was born in prison, grew up in a desert, and is alive only because his royal lineage is unknown. When Melitone describes him to Don Carlo, he refers to him as a skinny, swarthy person with devilish eyes. And Don Carlo, once he confronts him, does not hesitate to provoke him with the ultimate insult: "You come from an ignoble stock. . . . Your blood has a mulatto tinge to it."

At least two different (and how different!) teams of European composers/librettists of renown have used the United States as setting for their operas. Chronologically, Puccini and his collaborators Guelfo Civinini and Carlo Zangarini came first, with their adaptation of Belasco's *The Girl of the Golden West*, which premiered at the Metropolitan Opera in 1910. Granted, the literary source for this opera is a play by a well-versed American who had given a melodramatic but, he thought, highly believable account of the Gold Rush period. Puccini did not have to start from scratch in creating either the physical setting, the overall reigning mood, or the psychology of the individual characters. Yet Puccini's Wild West is impregnated with unmistakable touches of sentimentality; Wallace ("What will my old folks do way back home") and Larkens ("I want the plough and I want my mother") are genuinely two Italian immigrants suffering from a severe case of homesickness. Rance himself is nothing but an embittered, love-hungry sentimental. And the much-exploited western clichés, such as the trigger-ready attitude of most white regulars in Minnie's Saloon, and especially the Indians, Jackrabbit and Wowkle, seem to lose their original authenticity and acquire a new, more human albeit unrealistic dimension. But undoubtedly the least authentic and most Puccinian character of all is Minnie herself; her exquisite fragility and sensuality are easily detectable behind her apparent masculine strength and determination. That she is a sensuous girl becomes evident even before she meets Johnson, when she refuses Rance's advances. Her subsequent discovery of love and sex is not too far removed from the Straussian Salome. From the theatrical standpoint, we have in *Fanciulla* an interesting case of intelligent adaptation: Puccini kept the original crust (setting and most of the characters) but handled it with a smoother hand, giving it a very distinctive Italian (Tuscan) flavor, which ultimately explains much of the enduring success of the piece throughout the world. We are hardly in the presence of a realistic description of the New World here either, but the sensitive characters who populate this Puccinian Wild West are more simpatico than the insensitive "Good or Bad ones only" found in Westerns, of which *La fanciulla del West* is certainly a direct ancestor.

On the opposite extreme of Puccini's *La fanciulla del West*, lies the utterly unattractive and decadent city of Mahagonny, a creation of Weill and Brecht, and a pretext for the Marxist Brecht to display his anti-capitalistic ideas. Although *The Rise and Fall of the City of Mahagonny* contains indeed a visionary warning to the German people about the imminent downfall of the Weimar Republic, it is set in a mythical American South populated by a terribly disgusting, greedy bunch whose materialistic philosophy of life, eloquently expressed in the third act, is totally immoral. In spite of this opera's undeniable musical merits and the power of its message, this is art for ideological sakes at its purest and it too, myth or not, contributes to the perpetuation of a prejudicial, negative image of the New World.

For a native, the absurdities of the American plots are very easy to detect, and can indeed provide for good inside ethnic jokes. But when these absurdities pass for truths (as they often do) they can be harmful. Ever since the early nineteenth century, the three Americas have been used as setting (mostly picturesque and exotic) and its inhabitants as characters (mostly stereotyped) in plots (mostly prejudicial) that range from the humorous to the tragic to the mythical. Rarely do the works inspired by European authors give a realistic let alone sympathetic account of this region, of its cultural richness, of the human values of its people. In studying the Art of the Old World—literature and music, in this case—it is interesting to observe that many of the early prejudices of the Europeans against the peoples of the New World that are somewhat subdued yet very much alive nowadays stem from such damaging statements as the one found in the opening lines of Voltaire's *Alzire*, a play to be used for an opera libretto, and chronologically the first one using the American setting. In it Voltaire seems to justify the cruel treatment of the ferocious and monstrous natives in the name of civilization: "L'Américain farouche est un monstre sauvage."

Sources

BOOKS

Abbé Prévost. *Manon Lescaut*. Paris: Garnier, 1965.
Osborne, Charles. *The Complete Operas of Verdi*. New York: Knopf, 1970.
———. *The Complete Operas of Puccini*. New York: DaCapo Press, 1981.
Voltaire. *Alzire ou les Américains*. In *Oeuvres completes*. Paris: Garnier, 1883–1885.

LIBRETTI

Brecht, Bertolt. *The Rise and Fall of the City of Mahagonny*, music by Kurt Weill, 1929.
Cammarano, Salvatore. *Alzira*, music by Giuseppe Verdi, 1845. (Cited English translation by David Johnson, in booklet included in the complete recording of the opera, Orfeo Records, 1983.)
Civinini, Guelfo, and Carlo Zangarini. *La fanciulla del West*, music by Giacomo Puccini, 1910.
Jouy, Etienne. *Fernand Cortez*, music by Gaspare Spontini, 1817.
Meilhac, Henri, and Ludovic Halévy. *La Périchole*, music by Jacques Offenbach, 1868. (Cited English translation by Béatrice Vierne in booklet included in the complete recording of the opera, EMI Records, 1982.)
Oliva, Domenico, Marco Praga, Giuseppe Giacosa, Luigi Illica, and Giulio Ricordi. *Manon Lescaut*, music by Giacomo Puccini, 1893.
Piave, Francesco Maria. *Ernani*, music by Giuseppe Verdi, 1844.
———. *La forza del destino*, music by Giuseppe Verdi, 1862. (Cited English translation [no credit given] in booklet included in the complete recording of the opera, RCA Records, 1977.)
Scribe, Eugene. *Manon Lescaut*, music by Francois Auber, 1856.

American Opera in the Gilded Age: America's First Professional Touring Opera Company

EMANUAL RUBIN

History, they say, is the record left by the victors. This is the story of a glorious loser in American music. Both the meteoric success of the American Opera Company and its subsequent humiliating failure are indications of the position of music in America's "Gilded Age," and to some extent, of the role of the popular press in defining that place.

In 1885 the American Opera Company was founded in New York City to provide a professional outlet for young American artists and with the avowedly democratic intent of bringing world-class opera to a broad spectrum of the American public. Performing the best of the standard repertoire and featuring some of the finest artists from Europe and America in brilliantly staged productions, it won the admiration and patronage of New York music lovers and garnered sufficient support to undertake a national tour in 1886. It was greeted with popular enthusiasm and widespread critical acclaim in major cities across the country as well as in New York, and appeared to be well on its way to achieving both of the principal goals of its founder and mentor, Jeannette M. (Mrs. Francis B.) Thurber.

By 1887, though, the company was in dire financial straits. Stranded in the Midwest, where funds ran dry on the last leg of its second national tour, members of the cast had to be bailed out by a wealthy patron. By the end of that same season the company was bankrupt, its sponsors resorted to chicanery to extricate themselves from its financial burden, and members of the company were forced to sue for their wages. Much to the delight of New York's newspaper readers, who followed the story avidly, real and imaginary scandals among the wealthy backers of the company made daily headlines as the American Opera Company, renamed the

78

National Opera company in an attempt to hide assets from its creditors, succumbed in a flurry of charges and countercharges to the success of the high society orientation of the Metropolitan Opera. All this came about due to the efforts of two idealists: Jeannette M. Thurber and Theodore Thomas.

Theodore Thomas is well known to students of American music, but his patron, Jeannette M. Thurber (1850–1946) is a more obscure figure. Although most of her work was done behind the scenes, she was an important influence on the course of music in America. More than simply a donor of funds, she brought to the music scene in New York the dreams of a visionary, the management skills of a labor negotiator, and a dedication to music education that mark her, even today, as one of the most intelligent and effective patrons ever to take a stand for American music. She spent her life and a good portion of her appreciable wealth in the service of her musical ideals. Imagination, high artistic standards, and indomitable energy established the National Conservatory of Music as one of the finest institutions of post-secondary music education ever to rise in America, and it was her dream to duplicate that success with the American Opera Company.

In 1883 she had underwritten Theodore Thomas's notable concerts for young people in New York City, and in 1884 she provided the city with its first Wagner festival[1] It was an artistic success, but lost money on a heroic scale, leaving its guarantor with bills reported at $1.5 million. Typically, rather than discouraging Mrs. Thurber, this project only spurred her to greater efforts on behalf of American music. Noting the lack of opportunity for young American singers, she began to gather a group of wealthy patrons together as early as 1878 to remedy that situation by providing vehicles for American singers to appear onstage in New York. She carried that idea to its logical conclusion by organizing the American Opera Company and its companion, the National Conservatory of Music in 1885,[2] then went on to sponsor the debut of the Boston Symphony in New York in 1888–89 and bring Anton Dvořák to New York as head of her conservatory in 1891.

The two institutions were conceived as an interlocking pair. The aim of the conservatory, modeled after the *Conservatoire de Paris* where Mrs. Thurber had been a student herself, was to provide a locus for training young American musicians to take a place in the opera company. As a matter of fact, the first account books of the conservatory show the name of the school as "The American School of Opera."[3] On 15 April 1886, only four months after incorporation, the name was changed at Mrs. Thurber's petition, probably to make clear the financial distinction between the two entities.

The American Opera Company maintained several firm policies that displayed Mrs. Thurber's touch. It eschewed the "star system," championed native singers, and translated all operas into English. Its prospectus boasted that it had, among other features, "[t]he largest regularly trained chorus ever employed in grand opera in America. . . . The largest ballet corps ever presented in grand opera in America and as far as possible, American in its composition. . . . Four thousand new and correct costumes for which no expense has been spared . . . scenery . . . painted by the most eminent scenic artists. . . The musical guidance of Theodore Thomas . . . [and] the unrivaled Thomas Orchestra."[4] It was Mrs. Thurber's avowed aim to transplant opera onto American soil by creating reasonably priced performances of the highest quality. The first production was the American premiere of Goetz's *Taming of the Shrew* on 4 January 1886 at the Academy of Music.[5]

An additional motivation for forming the company was social. The Academy of Music on East Fourteenth Street had been the socially correct venue for opera at least since 1878 under the financing of August Belmont, and the Academy undertook to offer four operas a season under the management of Colonel George Henry Mapleson after 1880. The Academy could not accommodate all the wealthy who hoped to take boxes, though, and the "old money" —the Bayards, Cuttings, Lorillards, Van Rensselaers and their ilk—were not amenable to the influx of the *nouveaux riches*— the Astors, Vanderbilts, and their crowd. William K. Vanderbilt is rumored to have offered $30,000 for a box, but was politely turned away.

It became necessary, then, to build a new opera house to accommodate the needs of the new wealthy. So in 1880 a corporation was formed and the Metropolitan Opera opened its doors with the performance of Gounod's *Faust* on 22 October 1883. Boxes, which sold for $12,000 to $15,000 a season, could not be had. With a capacity of 3,045 one might think that there should be other seats in the hall from which to hear the performance, but one's box at the opera was a statement of wealth and social position, not merely a listener's chair. "From an artistic and musical point of view," wrote Henry Theophilus Finck the morning after the opening, "the large number of boxes in the Metropolitan is a decided mistake. But as the house was avowedly built for social purposes rather than artistic, it is useless to complain about this."[6] Irving Kolodin, recounting the tyranny of Caroline Astor over New York society at that time, notes:

> In those relatively innocent times there were fewer ways in which the possession of large sums of money could be demonstrated than there are now. . . . One of the few ways by which such a tangible superiority could be made visible was the possession of an opera box. To be sure, the cost was trivial . . . but the value of the boxes was really proportionate to the number of persons who wanted, but could not have them.[7]

Mrs. Thurber, on the other hand, had a further end in view. She wanted to create a company that would feature American performers and educate America nationwide to the social and musical joys of opera. Her aspiration was to create a *national* opera company coupled to a *national* conservatory, housed, for convenience, in New York, but traveling to branches in major cities all over the country to present, as the *Prospectus* put it, "Artists . . . of the front rank of American singers . . . supported by an *ensemble* which has never been equaled in this country." Her plan was initiated as announced: twenty-nine lead singers were employed for the opera, twenty of whom were American.[8]

At the beginning, the celebrated Belgian Baritone, Jacques Bouhy, who had created the role of Don Escamillo in *Carmen*, was employed as Director of the conservatory at the lavish salary of $9,000 per year—about $100,000 in 1988 dollars. By comparison, the average annual salary for urban workers in 1880 was about $588.[9]

Both the American Opera and its companion school were endorsed by enthusiastic incorporators who, among themselves, "owned or represented about one half of the wealth of the nation," in the only slight exaggeration of one commentator.[10] These included Andrew Carnegie as President, with fellow New York multimillonaires August Belmont, Levi P. Morton, Henry Seligman, Brayton Ives, H. J. Jewett, and Deacon White. The board also included many from the West, such as N. K. Fairbank of Chicago packing house wealth, George M. Pullman (Chicago, sleeping cars), W. D. Washburn (Minneapolis, flour), Charles Crocker (San Francisco, railroads), and John W. Mackay (mining).[11] With the backing of that formidable list of incorporators, Mrs. Thurber approached the one man who was in a position to lend national, if not international, prestige to the post of director, America's best-known conductor: Theodore Thomas. One of Thomas's biographers lamented:

> [T]hey approached him with this proposal and he accepted it. Despite the warnings of clearer-sighted friends, despite the lesson he had received at Cincinnati, he accepted [their offer]. He believed with all his heart in the fable about the millionaire and art. God knows why he should have believed it, except for the reason that he wished it to be true.[12]

Thomas threw himself into the company wholeheartedly, hiring singers, editing scores, even making his own English translations for the performances. He too was not in favor of the "star system" on which the Metropolitan Opera was run, but preferred ensemble opera, an approach in which "all the concomitant parts . . . [were] equally balanced and excellent."[13] The repertoire put into rehearsal in that first season included an astonishing number of operas, eclectically chosen from both classic and modern operas by French, German, and Italian composers:

Orpheus and Eurydice (Gluck)
The Merry Wives of Windsor (Nicolai)
The Flying Dutchman (Wagner)
Faust (Gound)
The Taming of the Shrew (Goetz)
Lakmé (Delibes)
The Magic Flute (Mozart)
The Huguenots (Meyerbeer)
Martha (von Flotow)
Aïda (Verdi)
Nero (Rubenstein)
Lohengrin (Wagner)
The Marriage of Jeannette (Massé)

The opening night was 4 January 1886 at the Academy of Music. "It went without a hitch," wrote Russell, "a fact that caused universal comment and amazement. "

> The scenery, all specially painted by famous artists, was wonderfully good and beautiful, all the accessories were adequate, the chorus covered itself with glory, the soloists sang adorably. Critics, commentators, sceptics, joined the public in one swelling hymn of laudation. Operas had not been so produced in the memory of living man. What

struck everyone was the flawless perfection of the details and their relation to the harmony of the whole.[14]

In view of the Metropolitan's single-minded emphasis on stars
and its reputation for poor, if not downright shoddy, staging, little
wonder that there was such enthusiastic response to the results of
Thomas's meticulous work. The National Opera Company not
only had excellent lead singers, but also "an incomparable orchestra, a fresh young chorus, always correct, sure and in tune."[15] Of
course it helped that chorus members were full-time employees
with regular rehearsals conducted by their own chorus master. The
young company embarked almost immediately on tour. In February they moved to Washington, returned to New York for performances in March, then to Philadelphia, and in November went
to St. Louis, accompanied by praise at every stop.

Only one flaw marked that first, brilliant season, but it was a
most serious one: an enormous deficit that caused many of Mrs.
Thurber's co-sponsors to back away from the project. Not the least
of those defectors was Andrew Carnegie, who was replaced as
president by Theodore Thomas. To avoid outstanding bills and
frustrate lawsuits, the American Opera Company was dissolved
and reorganized for 1886–87 as "The National Opera Company of
New Jersey," a plan that allowed the new company to assume the
assets of its predecessor but walk away scot-free of its debts.
Thomas, deeply committed to the project, stayed on to conduct
the National Opera in New York and on its transcontinental tour.

The second season the renamed company opened with great success in New York, and quickly became the most talked-about
musical topic of the year. As the most obvious of the policy revisions, Emma Fursch-Madi was brought in as prima donna. She had
been at the Paris Opera and was known to New Yorkers from having sung the role of Ortrud in *Lohengrin* at the Metropolitan
Opera's first season. The season was crowned with the National
Opera's American premiere of Rubinstein's *Nero* at the Metropolitan Opera House. The production was acclaimed as having been
"placed upon the stage on a scale of splendor never before given to
opera in this country . . . sung with enthusiasm, intelligence, and
artistic devotion."[16] As far away as Chicago critics proclaimed,
"The National Opera Co. is making a decided success at the Metropolitan Opera House, and notably with Rubenstien's *Nero*."[17]
In spite of rumors of fiscal problems caused by poor management, Charles Locke, the company's manager, announced that the

National Opera Company, like its predecessor, would undertake a
transcontinental tour.

With the unanimous acclaim of the New York and Boston critics
in their ears, the National Opera Company sped off across the
country. The tour ran into increasing financial problems on its
westward leg, culminating in a comic opera fiasco in Omaha where
they ran out of money to pay for the transportation of performers
and baggage and had to be bailed out from New York before they
were permitted to leave. The train was only a few miles out of
Omaha, though, when they were informed a mistake had been
made and they would have to pay $7,000 more if they wished to
continue. "They are now back in Omaha," reported the papers,
"with board bills eating up Mr. Washington Connor's contributions, and waiting pensively for some fortunate breeze to blow a
monied man their way."

The story is told with some relish in the New York *Times* of 14
April 1886:

Manager Locke's Success
The National Opera Company Gets Out of Omaha

Omaha, Neb., April 13—The National Opera Co. met with another
batch of trouble today. They should have left this place at one o'clock
last night for San Francisco, but the Union Pacific Railroad refused to
move a wheel until manager Locke paid $8,400 in transportation. Su-
perintendent Hayes of the Wagner Sleeping Car Co. also appeared on
the scene and held both trains and baggage until he was paid $2,000.
After considerable telegraphing today, Washington Connor, the Wall
Street broker, wired funds sufficient to help Mr. Locke out. About
eight o'clock tonight they proceeded in the direction of San Francisco.
The receipts of the three performances here only reached $7,000, of
which amount the opera company received $5,000. The male members
of the company amused themselves during the day by playing football
on the platform of the Union Pacific Station, while the ladies spent
their time in the sleeping cars playing cards and reading novels.

Arriving in San Francisco on 17 April, they performed brilliantly. The enthusiastic public demanded that they stay on for an additional, uncontracted performance. One paper exclaimed on 23
April that "*Lohengrin* by the National Opera Company, was the
finest operatic performance ever presented to a San Francisco audience." That last evening marked another memorable fiasco.
Steam lines constructed under the stage to provide "smoke" for the

final scene of Rubinstein's *Nero*—the burning of Rome—burst:

> Fragments of the main pipe shot into the air, and out poured a great cloud of steam, not from many places, as ordered, but from one. The chorus shrieked and started to run, the orchestra stopped, the players sprang from their seats. . . . "Go on!" [Thomas] hissed, and continued to beat as if nothing had happened. "Go on! Go on!" The orchestra pulled itself together, the chorus caught up a note, the voices quickly rose and the scene ended, illumined with fire effects the stage manager had not dreamed of. . . . People said it was the best fire scene ever put upon any stage and the newspapers praised Thomas for arranging it."[18]

Leaving San Francisco a day late but showered with popular accolades, the company chartered three trains for a race to make their scheduled performance of *Lohengrin* at Kansas City. That trip contributed still more stories to the mythology of the company, breathless tales of hotbox fires and railroad cars careening around turns on two wheels at seventy miles an hour to the accompaniment of prayers from the musicians. One member of the orchestra reported of the Kansas City performance, "I have never known it to go better. We were too excited to be tired. Sometimes a performance on bare nerves is the best in the world."[19]

Back in New York, the shell game that had buried the debts of the old American Opera Company and reclaimed its assets to flourish anew as the National Opera Company did not go unchallenged. Thomas had gamely swallowed a loss and continued as director because of his faith in the ideal. Emma Fursch-Madi, however, was not of such a benevolent disposition. An article titled "A Prima Donna Sues for Her Salary" (5 February 1887) affirmed that Mme. Fursch-Madi, prima donna of the National Opera Company, sued Charles E. Locke for $679 in back salary owed her up to 8 April 1886.

The tour was an artistic triumph conducted against a backdrop of fiscal chaos and internal bickering. In Chicago, after one blow-up, Herr Heinrichs, the choral director, discharged a number of singers for incompetence; however, all those discharged were Americans, leaving a chorus of 84, 66 of whom were Germans. When one of the fired American singers protested and threatened to sue, he was rehired as an assistant stage director, although he had no experience in stagecraft. At the same time that notices were appearing in Syracuse papers heralding upcoming performances of *Martha*, and other cities were looking forward eagerly to tour performances of *Lakmé* and Rubinstein's *Nero*, other, more foreboding notices appeared in the same papers. The St. Louis *Tribune*, for example, reported on 24 March, that "The American Opera Co., Limited, of New York, which started out with such grand prospects and was merged into the National Opera Company of New Jersey, has, in its legal evolutions toward dissolution, fallen into the hands of a receiver."

The company quickly countered with a story that appeared in the *New York Herald* two days later (25 March 1887):

The Opera is Prospering
No Receiver for the National Company
False Report Denied

"There is not a particle of truth in the report that the National Opera Company has gone into the hands of a receiver," said Mr. Jaffre, the cashier of the company, to a *Herald* reporter who sought an interview with Mr. Locke at the Brooklyn Academy of Music last night.

As a matter of fact, newspapers played a key role in keeping the story of the National Opera Company in front of the public. There were eighty-four articles about the National Opera Company in the 1887 New York *Times* alone, even more remarkable when one considers that they were away on tour that year more than they were in the city. Articles such as "Mrs. Thurber's Triumph" (21 February 1887) supported the endeavor to the city's philanthropists:

Notwithstanding all, one cannot but admire the pluck of Mrs. Thurber, who has now raised for her scheme and spent about a quarter of a million dollars. Everyone hopes that the coming season will be the turning point in the company's career, and that New York capitalists will be found so impressed with the excellence of its performances as to put their hands in their pockets and establish the organization upon a firm footing.

Lawsuits, though, made better press than Mrs. Thurber's protestations or the critical acclaim the company was gathering across the country, and the broader public was more fascinated by the spectacle of the high and mighty scuffling among themselves than the prospect for native opera. On the same dates the National Opera Company scored so brilliantly in San Francisco and Kansas City, New York papers were full of articles about the company fighting off suits from creditors. The tone was almost salacious, as in the delicious headline "Six Poor Deceived Girls" atop a story of 28 April 1887. One of the members of the chorus, Alice Richards, sued the California millionaire Charles Crocker for back salary she was sure she would never get from the defunct American Opera Company or its successor:

The American Opera Co. was a defendant in seven separate cases before Judge Ehrlich in the city court yesterday. Six of the defendants were described by their lawyer, W. W. Badger, as "poor deceived girls." The other was a poor deceived man, William Parry, the stage manager.

The poor deceived girls sat in two rows in the back part of the room, jauntily dressed and trying to look sad. One of them, Alice Richards, a ballet girl, who was engaged for $20 a week, now enjoys the distinction of having sued more millionaires in a given time than any girl in New York.

She first sued the American Opera Company for $380 or 19 weeks salary, and then, anticipating a failure to collect in that quarter, brought separate suits against C. P. Huntington, Charles Crocker, J. Pierpont Morgan, Andrew Carnegie, and Henry Seligman, stockholders, each for $146 for damages.

Mr. Parry and Miss Richards won their suits, but the hounding of the reporters did not let up. Neither did the problems of the National Opera Company. By 10 June the company had worked its way back to Toledo, Ohio. Most members of the company had stopped receiving paychecks and Thomas, who had received none himself, "paid the living expenses of the penniless and brought them back to New York."[20] He managed to fulfill performance contracts as far as Buffalo, but finally had to throw in the towel there on 15 June."[21] About 20 June they returned to New York, where Thomas immediately withdrew from the company, and on 9 July, he severed all connections with it in a distressed letter, writing, "We have had in ourselves all the elements for good work and prosperity if only the first and vital condition of success in any undertaking had been observed . . . namely, prompt payment of all employees."[22] Mrs. Thurber, left holding the bag, claimed that the financial difficulties were due to the fact that subscriptions, amounting to a quarter-million dollars promised in several cities, had not been paid.

By the middle of July almost one hundred members of the National Opera Company, including Theodore Thomas himself, were suing for back pay. Other members of the company formed a committee to meet with Mrs. Thurber, deciding that they might catch more flies with honey than vinegar. According to a story in the *New York Herald* of 25 July 1887, the property of the company had been stealthily removed to New Jersey, where it was stored in an abandoned skating rink in Jersey City Heights. Mrs. Thurber sued the corporation herself, engaging District Attorney Winfield to represent her in the Hudson County Civil Court in an attempt to recover at least the amount she had loaned the company. The assets of the company, originally valued at $150,000, were sold for $26,101.

What had happened? Why, in the space of less than two years' time, had the experiment in "American" opera gone from a brilliant beginning to such ignominious failure? There is no question about the quality of the company, the artistry of its performers, or the readiness of late nineteenth-century American audiences to welcome opera enthusiastically. Nor is there any doubt that Mrs. Thurber's American Opera Company was well received and widely supported at the time of its inception. The combination of lavish productions and low price, though, left the company with a deficit at the end of its first season, a disability from which it never recovered. Theodore Thomas's biographer, perhaps, put it most succinctly:

> The notion that any enterprise taking money from the public must be self-sustaining to justify its existence is bred in the Anglo-Saxon bone.
> . . . [T]he eminent gentlemen that Mrs. Thurber's eloquence and the popularity of her husband had induced to join in the American Opera Company believed they were starting a business enterprise like any other, and when they heard that it had not paid its way in one whole season of experiment, they called it a failure and scrambled ashore.[23]

The assumption, not confined to Anglo-Saxons, was that only those enterprises that survived in the marketplace could be called successes, and failures should be cut loose as quickly as possible.

At a later date Theodore Thomas was asked about the cause of the American Opera disaster. He attributed it to "inexperienced and misdirected enthusiasm in business management, and to misapplication of money."[24] But that widely quoted remark only reflects the story as seen through Thomas's eyes. Charles Locke, manager of the company, seems to have been caught between Thomas on one side, demanding more rehearsal time, a larger chorus, and fuller instrumentation, and Mrs. Thurber on the other, calling for better stage effects and richer costumes. They complemented one another in their naive neglect of fiscal reality. Liberal with her own money where artistic standards were concerned, Mrs. Thurber expected others to follow suit. Rather than a check on Thomas's fertile imagination and perfectionism, she was a goad.

The press, too, played its part. This was, after all, the era of "yellow journalism," and New York's "opera war" was good copy. When it appeared to be fading, a well-placed article on one side or the other could be counted on to stir things up again. Proponents of any point of view could, and often did, make their points in the daily papers. One unsigned article of 6 January 1887 from the *New York Evening Post*[25] bravely charged editorial bias against Mrs. Thurber's undertaking:

A New York Press Raid
How a Meritorious Enterprise Is Methodically Dragged Down

The newspaper campaign, which has been in progress for some time against the National Opera Company . . . has been such a remarkable development of modern journalism that a complete history of its rise, powers, and career should be put upon record for future reference.

The article goes on to laud Mrs. Thurber and her supporters for their faith in American opera against the opposition of the press then plunges into the meat of the charges:

Scarcely a newspaper held out an encouraging hand. They did not content themselves with hostile and malicious criticisms of the performances, but they gave the widest publicity to all kinds of rumors which were started in the byways and gutters of the musical world for the injury of the enterprise . . . Its first season ended, not only without collapse, but with honor. Yet nearly the whole press of New York had done its best to ruin it.

The author continues, citing several of the rumors that had been reported with malicious delight by the press. One resulted from the company dismissing, as he put it, "a few incompetent ballet girls and a few other unnecessary employees."

Here was a noble "find." The "Cyrus W. Field" started the story that the girls were sent to New York in a "box car," and the other papers held up their hands in horror and started an army of reporters to the freight station to await the girls' arrival and interview every one of them. When they came in decently, in a comfortable car, the "box car" report was not contradicted, but the interviews were published and the girls kept the sensation alive for several days.

The writer attributes the opposition to people with commercial interests in the arts. As the "opera war" of the 1880s wound down, it became clear that the fashionable *haut monde* of New York would take their opera in the boxes at the Metropolitan, and for the astute newspaper publisher, that was where the profit lay. He concludes by citing an unnamed newspaper manager, who is quoted as having said (apparently to Mrs. Thurber), "You will get just as much help from the newspapers as you are willing to pay for. You say you are working for art, but you are really working for money and must share your profits with the newspaper that helps you."

There were still other issues. Lack of any brilliant "stars" militated against the larger box office returns generated by their presence, and though the principal singers were fine musicians they did not attract the awe, adulation, and wonder of such personalities as the brothers De Reszke or a Marcella Sembrich. Then, too, resentment of Thomas's success was not unheard of among New York's professionals, and with the failure of the National Opera Company many musicians as well as patrons turned against him. His biographer, at least, felt that not so mysterious:

> [H]e had committed the unpardonable sin; he had wrought impiously toward the great American deity, which is Success. How had he? Why, if he had not failed himself he had been connected with something that failed, and failed notoriously. He had better have committed forgery or burglary. . . . It was a colossal wreck, Thomas was on board; enough, he goes down with the rest.[26]

In fact, Thomas was financially and professionally ruined by the company's collapse and, to add insult to injury, was even named as defendant in suits brought by the same people whom he had supported out of his own pocket.

Other supporters identified the culprit as the Eurocentrism of the arts establishment. The bitterest of those articles was one by Blakely Hall that appeared in a number of papers across the country on 10 and 11 March 1887.[27]

> Society as such does not smile upon the national opera. It is a pity and it is unfair to the last degree, for there can be no question of the critical excellence of the performances now being given at the Metropolitan Opera House. But society will not have it, so the great auditorium, which was ablaze with diamonds and showy toilets during the German opera season, is dimmed by the sober costumes of the poor relations and out-of-town cousins of the millionaire box-owners. It would

be difficult to describe in detail the change that has come over the entire opera house, but the effect is palpable. When a small section of society does venture out to one of the performances of the National Opera, it comes late, talks as though bored to death by the performance, and retires early. It is a pity that nothing that is American can become fashionable in New York. . . .

Quaintance Eaton may have written the American Opera Company's most poignant obituary: "Founded in innocent good faith by Jeannette Thurber . . . [it] had bickered and broken on the road after only two seasons. Theodore Thomas' yearnings for an opera of his own went with it, as did the fortunes of many well-known singers."[28] The failure of the American—or National—Opera Company left only a faint ripple in the pool of America's musical history, one that is already forgotten by all but a few scholars. It represented a far-reaching scheme that was ahead of its time, or at least not in harmony with the time in which the principals lived. It was an unsuccessful attempt to mold the distinctly "American way" of producing opera as business, with private, not public, support. A more successful route was exemplified by the towering success of the Metropolitan Opera, where one segment of our society found a niche for opera in their lives and built a house to nurture it.

Mrs. Thurber's concept was entirely too idealistic for that entrepreneurial age. Opera succeeded in New York when it was subsidized by the wealthy for the wealthy; but it retained the associations of that social setting as a stigma for many years, making it a subject for coarse, demotic parody as populism swept the country. One need only think of the running joke about the boredom of opera for "real Americans" that was a central feature of MacManus's comic strip, *Bringing Up Father*, for some thirty years. The success of the Metropolitan Opera House in becoming one of the most brilliant opera venues in the world was gained at the expense of opera's entering the mainstream of American culture. Perhaps—just perhaps—if Mrs. Thurber's concept had worked, the history of opera in American might have taken an entirely different turn.

Notes

1. Although preceded by sporadic attempts to present Wagner's operas under less than fully professional conditions, this constituted the first full-scale production of Wagner's major works as a series in the United States. In 1859 Carl Bergmann had given the American premiere of Wagner's *Tannhäuser* at the old Stadt

Theatre in the Bowery with the assistance of the Arion chorus. A second Wagner production did not take place until 1870, when A. Neuendorf put on *Lohengrin* at the same hall. While extracts had been presented in concert form, these were the only complete productions of Wagner operas preceding Mrs. Thurber's 1884 festival.

2. A more detailed appreciation of Mrs. Thurber and her National Conservatory of Music can be found in an article by the present writer in *American Music* (Winter 1990–91).

3. This account book, which runs from 1 Dec. 1885 through 1898, can be found among the papers of Richard Irvin in the New York Historical Society. The book is headed on page 1 "The American School of Opera," but after that the heading changes to "The National Conservatory of Music."

4. Selected from the prospectus published in full in Rose Fay Thomas's *Memoirs of Theodore Thomas* (New York: Moffat, Yard, Co. 1911), pp. 283–85, hereafter *Memoirs*.

5. This view is substantiated by Nicolas Slonimsky in *The Plush Era in American Concert Life* (New York, 1961). Emile Serposs is mistaken in the *New Grove Dictionary of Music and Musicians* (IV: 36), where he says that the first season was 1886–87. There may have been some confusion over the troupe's renaming as the National Opera Company (see below).

6. *New York Evening Post*, 23 October 1883. Many of these citations from newspapers are taken from scrapbooks kept by Mrs. Thurber, who apparently subscribed to a national clipping service. Not all of those clippings are fully identified, while some of them, identified or not, are in such a state of deterioration as to make them partially illegible. Mrs. Thurber's scrapbooks are now in the New York Public Library, Performing Arts Division, where they are filed under "National Conservatory of Music." They will be referred to in this paper as "Thurber Scrapbooks."

7. In *The Metropolitan Opera 1883–1935*, p. 2.

8. A complete list of the principal singers engaged for the first two seasons, taken from Theodore Thomas's *Musical Autobiography* (1905; reprint, New York: Da Capo, 1964), p. 188, follows:

Sopranos: Kate Bensberg, Minnie Dilthey, Christine Dossert, May Fielding, Helen Hastreiter (of Louisville), Emma Juch, Pauline L'Allemand (of Syracuse), Annis Montague, Charlotte Walker.

Mezzos and Contraltos: Sara Barton, Helen Dudley Campbell, Jessie Bartlett Davis, Mathilde Muellenbach, Mathilde Phillipps.

Tenors: George Appleby, William Candidus, William H. Fessenden, Whitney Mockridge, Albert Paulet, Charles Turner.

Baritones: George Fox, William H. Lee, William Ludwig, Homer A. Moore, Eugene E. Oudin, Alonzo E. Stoddard.

Basses: William H. Hamilton, John Howson, Edward J. O'Mahoney, Myron W. Whitney.

9. Based on figures in *Historical Statistics of the United States from Colonial Times to 1970* (Washington, D.C.: Bureau of Census, 1975).

10. Charles Edward Russell, *The American Orchestra and Theodore Thomas* (New York, 1927), p. 162.

11. A complete list of incorporators is given, along with the Prospectus for the corporation, in *Memoirs*, p. 285.

12. Russell, *American Orchestra*, p. 163.

13. *Memoirs*, p. 278.

14. Russell, *American Orchestra*, p. 165.

15. *Century Magazine*, May 1886. Quoted by Rose Fay Thomas in *Memoirs*, p. 286.

16. *New York World*, other information lacking in the Thurber Scrapbooks.

17. *The Inter-Ocean Journal*, 26 March, 1886 (Thurber Scrapbooks).

18. Russell, *American Orchestra*, p. 176.

19. Ibid., p. 177.

20. Ibid., p. 178.

21. George Upton, alone among those who have written about the National Opera Company, says that there was one last, convulsive performance, without Thomas, at Toronto following the Buffalo engagement. (Cf. Thomas's *Musical Autobiography*, p. 191.)

22. *Musical Autobiography* p. 192.

23. Russell, *American Orchestra*, pp. 168–69.

24 Quoted by George Upton in his editing of Thomas's *Musical Autobiography*, p. 193.

25. *Boston Transcript*. The Thurber scrapbooks contain a number of copies of this same article from other, unidentified papers.

26. Russell, *American Orchestra*, p. 179.

27. The Omaha *Herald* is clearly marked, as is the Kansas City *Times*, but it is difficult to make out the others from the state of the scrapbook.

28. *The Miracle of the Met* (New York, 1968), p. 85.

Part Three
Opera in the Western United States

Pasquilino Brignoli:
Tenor of the Golden West

MICHAEL B. DOUGAN

In 1851, when opera in New York was only some twenty-five years old, Donald G. Mitchell, a cultivated music lover who wrote under the pseudonym of "The Lorgnette," defined opera singers and managers as

> . . . missionaries, who have, with a disinterestedness and love of souls, most commendable, left the attractions and luxuries of European Society, to come to this land of almost Pagan socialism; and they are here putting forth their best efforts in a variety of ways, to raise us from our lost condition, and to bring us nearer to the elevelated plane of fashion, morals, liberality, and taste, which they have left behind them. They find too, fortunately, not a few, who are willing to take them by the hand, and cheer them in this undertaking—nay, to give them the aid of the little piquant paragraphs of praise, which go forth like so many gospels of mercy, to redeem us from our social barbarism, and to gather us into the sheepfold of—opera-goers.[1]

Given the state of American culture, the task was enormous. Although opera in New York properly began with the arrival of the Manuel Garcia troupe in 1825, the public was perverse. Lacking state support and rich benefactors ready to underwrite deficits, impresarios came and went. Only slowly did the public's taste improve. "I was too classical for them," Belgian violinist Henri Vieuxtemps recalled, for audiences responded best to variations on "Yankee Doodle." [2] The greatest promotion of the age, the American tour of Jenny Lind, took place under the auspices of P. T. Barnum, a master of hokum. Maria Piccolomini in 1858 was advertised as a lineal descendant of Charlemagne and the great-granddaughter of Max Piccolomini.[3]

Properly promoted, there was money to be made in educating the public. Although fifty cents was probably the prevailing rate and the public gaped at prices above a dollar, tickets to Lind's concerts sold as high as $6.50. Georgia Congressman Howell Cobb, who wrote his wife that the Swedish Nightingale "can't turn a tune to save her life" and that he was "lost in the most discordant rhapsodies of melodious incongruities," nevertheless attended three consecutive concerts in Philadelphia at a cost of $6.00 a ticket.[4]

What Americans sought out in music was the sensational. In the 1840s, it was the rivalry between the "Belgian Paganini," violinist Henri Vieuxtemps, and the "Norwegian Paganini," Ole Bull, in a struggle that took on most of the elements of a tractor-pulling contest. Opera, which labored under the Protestant prejudice against the theater, was probably more sung at home through the circulation of sheet music than heard in the flesh. Support for opera performances rested on an uneasy alliance between a growing core of music lovers and the rich in quest of outlets for conspicuous consumption.[5]

By the 1850s, Americans had been exposed to a succession of good performers. In 1854, for example, dramatic soprano Giulia Grisi and Giuseppe Mario, the world's undisputed greatest tenor, arrived for a series of performances in New York. Beginning at Castle Garden, they moved uptown and inaugurated opera at the Academy of Music, a building that served as the musical mecca of New York for the next forty years. Despite their eminence, the venture lost the promoters $2,000 a night, and the couple soon removed to Philadelphia and Boston before returning to Europe. They left behind a standard that critics continued to apply for the next several decades.[6]

Into the void left by their departure leapt Ole Bull, whose skill on the violin contrasted sharply with his inaptitude both as a social reformer and a musical missionary. In the former capacity, he announced a competition with a thousand dollar prize for the best opera by an American on an American subject and promoted the creation of an American musical conservatory. More daringly, in the spring of 1855 he organized an opera company built around soprano Clotilde Patti, an older sister of the future diva Adelina, and mezzo-soprano Madame Vestvali, whom long-time critic Robert Grant White called "the tallest woman that I ever saw upon the stage; I believe the tallest woman I ever encountered." [7] On the male side, Bull had arranged to have a new tenor, Brignoli, and a new baritone, Amodio, brought over from France. Before they arrived, however, Bull had run to ruin and his creditors seized upon their contracts.[8]

Determined that the show must go on, a committee continued the season, and both men made their debuts on 15 March 1855 in a performance of Donizetti's *Lucia di Lammermoor*. Although Brignoli had to stand comparison with the incomparable Mario, Amodio had no such competition. Amodio, White recalled, "had one of the most beautiful baritone voices ever heard. It was of almost unexampled richness and sweetness,—a large, free-flowing voice, and seeming almost as flexible as that of a tenore di grazia." Unfortunately, he looked like "Falstaff singing in Italian. When he appeared in a close and antique costume, with a little round hat upon his little head, he looked like a plum pudding set upon sausages." [9]

Brignoli, the *Times* reported, "does not depend upon the roar for his principal effects" and possessed a voice of "sympathetic sentimental sweetness." Although calling him a poorer Mario, he was, nevertheless, "the most agreeable tenor we have had for years." [10] And so he remained for over twenty-five years.

His full name was Pasquilino Brignoli. As this first name was too much for the American public, he invariably signed his name with a "P." Some thought that stood for Pasquale, but it was a matter of little relevance since most mid-nineteenth-century male singers went by their last names alone (e.g., Mario, Rubini, Tamberlick, etc.). In time, he became "Dear Old Brig."

He was born in 1824 in Naples, where his father was a glove manufacturer. Of his early life, there was much conjecture, for Brignoli was noticeably reticent. American diva Clara Louise Kellogg, noting that he had pierced ears, thought that he might have been a sailor, but "he would never let anyone mention the subject." He also refused to wear earrings on stage. Curiously, among his compositions was a song entitled "The Sailor's Dream." [11]

His musical career began when his singing at a party attracted the attention of Madame Alboni. American pianist Louis Moreau Gottschalk, who met him in Paris in 1849, claimed he was "under the amorous aegis of the beautiful Madame R."[12] At any rate, he made his debut in Paris in Rossini's *Moise en Egypte* but left the stage for further study at the Paris Conservatoire. A second debut took place at the Theatre des Italiens as Nemorino in Donizetti's *L'Elisir d'amore*. In 1854, he is recorded as having sung at the Paris Opera.[13] Except for a few seasons at Covent Garden late in his life, he never returned to Europe.

Brignoli arrived in America in company, musically speaking, with the great middle Verdi operas. A few weeks after his debut in *Lucia*, the company presented the first American performance of *Il trovatore*. Although it became customary to claim that Manrico is a role for the heroic tenor, Brignoli made it his own, singing it perhaps a thousand times. What that first-generation audience heard differed from later performance standards. As originally written, there was no high C at end of "Di Quella Pira" until Tamberlink inserted one, and Brignoli would sing only up to a B-flat.[14] Other Verdi operas featuring Brignoli included the American premieres of *La traviata* (3 December 1856, New York Academy of Music), *I vespri siciliani* (7 November 1859, New York Academy of Music), and *Un ballo in maschera* (11 February 1861, New York Academy of Music). The *Ballo* performances were conducted by Emanuele Muzio, Verdi's personal friend and student. President Abraham Lincoln attended one performance but did not stay to the end.[15]

Brignoli also appeared in the American premieres of Donizetti's *Betly* (25 October 1861, Philadelphia Academy of Music) and Luigi Arditi's *La spia* (24 March 1855, Philadelphia Academy of Music). The last-named opera came about as the fruit of the Ole Bull American opera competition. Arditi, best known in musical history for his song, "Il bacio," won the prize with an opera based on James Fenimore Cooper's novel *The Spy*. This work soon vanished, but the tenor aria "Colli nativi" was frequently performed separately.[16]

Almost immediately, Brignoli became the indispensable tenor, participating in every New York season for the next two decades. In Philadelphia, he sang 174 times in opera alone, beginning with the opening of the Academy of Music on 25 February 1857. The opera on this occasion was *Il trovatore*, and "society was out in force" to cheer on the Leonora, Marietta Gazzaniga, and Brignoli.[17] There was less cheering two nights later at a performance of Lucia when a certain Mme. De Paez was so bad that impresario Max Maretzek was warned that she would be "hissed off the stage should she appear again before the audience."[18] The Philadelphia performances with Gazzaniga and Brignoli in *La traviata* precipitated a major morality debate over the obscenity of the subject matter. Verdi's music helped undermine the power of the clergy in their struggle against the theater.[19]

Brignoli was also present for a musical event of the greatest importance. On 24 November 1859, Adelina Patti, the daughter and sister and sister-in-law of opera singers, made her adult debut in *Lucia di Lammermoor* at age sixteen. Despite the recent hanging of John Brown and the threatening war clouds, the public sensed her greatness. Within a few years, she demanded and received $5,000 for each performance delivered to her by two o'clock in the afternoon.[20]

Meanwhile, Brignoli went on piling up success after success. The "youth of rather an elegant and distinguished presence" appeared on stage, a hostile critic wrote, "as awkward as the man that a child makes by sticking two skewers into a long potato." [21] By 1862, he had what Gottschalk called an *embonpoint*, as the thin young man of the 1840s became a stout tenor who ate huge quantities of raw oysters before every performance. Henry E. Krehbiel recalled that "he probably ate as no tenor ate before or since—ravenously as a Prussian dragoon after a fast." [22] Billed as the Primo Tenore Assoluto, he became a matinee idol, attracting the idolatrous attentions of thousands of young girls who bombarded him with love notes. An observer noted in 1858 that this "Adonis of the Opera, Brignoli, drew upon himself two thousand black lenses, for the ladies stare boldly and sigh sentimentally, whenever he goes on." [23] At first he tried to answer the notes, but finally gave up and added them to his collection, while humming Leporello's Catalogue aria from *Don Giovanni*.[24]

Although sopranos came and went, Brignoli remained remarkably consistent. Unlike the tenors of popular legend, he was a good musician. As a pianist, he occasionally played on stage with Gottschalk and had committed the Hummel A-minor concerto to memory. He composed a number of songs and dedicated to band conductor Patrick Gilmore "The Crossing of the Danube," which, like Tchaikovsky's *1812 Overture*, had booming cannon, charging infantry, buglecalls, and other effects.[25]

Vocally, his longevity was achieved by refusing to force his voice or sing high Cs. "Screaming is not singing," he told Chicago critic George P. Upton. "Let those fellows wear their throats out if they will; Brignoli keeps his." [26] Doubtless another contributing factor was his lack of acting.

Critics early on commented on his behavior on stage but were unacquainted with the cause: Brignoli suffered from extreme stage fright. Nervous to the extreme, he carried around a stuffed deer's head. When things went well, he patted it approvingly, but if something was wrong, he swore and pounded on it. In his contracts, which he would never sign on a Friday, he always wanted matched black horses to carry him to the theater.[27]

In 1864, the bored public turned to a tenor named Mazzolini, of hard and forced voice and uncertain pitch, but who, Gottschalk observed, "screams loud and for a long time, which always pleases the bulk of the public." Brignoli had been out west performing, and on his return, the tenors became rivals. Mazzolini appeared at Brignoli's first performance sporting enormous glasses and causing the tenor to think the evil eye was after him. Brignoli canceled a second performance, but returned after a trip to Boston to renewed acclaim.[28] Not until Italo Campanini arrived in the 1870s did Brignoli have a serious rival.

On stage in *I Puritani*, he stood in one spot "and thrust one arm out, and then the other, at right angles from his body, twenty-three consecutive times." [29] In London, where he appeared for the first time in 1865, the *Times* noted "his extreme nervousness" and found him "a very gentlemanly lover, if not an energetic one."[30] A New York critic suggested "he should be made to wear trousers full of thistles to keep him awake." [31] Another idiosyncrasy was that he would not touch another singer during a performance, which doubtless detracted from his love scenes. "His repose on the stage is death-like," the New York *Sunday Atlas* reported on a performance of Pacini's *Sappho*, "and enough to throw a cold chill over the impassioned Gazzaniga."[32] Furthermore, singers tried to stay far away, for his method of vocal production spewed forth copious quantities of saliva. Luigi Arditi recalled that in a production of *Don Giovanni*, the Donna Anna was wearing a very handsome and expensive dress: "During the famous trio, Madame Lablache watched Brignoli very anxiously, and finally, unable to contain her fears any longer, she whispered to him in a voice full of appeal: 'Voyon, mon cher ami, ne pourriez vous pas, une foi par hasard, cracher sur la robe de Donna Elvira?'"[33]

As time went on, the criticisms increased. Robert Grant White, who liked his tenors "red with warm blood," quibbled with Mario and blasted Brignoli: "There never was a tenor of any note in New York whose singing was so utterly without character or significance, and who was deficient in histrionic ability. His high and long-continued favor is one of those puzzling popular freaks not uncommon in dramatic annals."[34]

Henry Edward Krehbiel in reply observed, "Let us hope, in a spirit of Christian charity and something more selfish, that Brignoli never read these severely critical words. His vanity was that of a child, and they would have grieved him inordinately."[35] Another of his defenders wrote: "The fact is, his voice alone is worth more than others acting and singing combined. He is, besides, the most elegant gentleman upon the lyric stage. His fine person, his almost beautiful face, his incomparable voice, added to his manliness and gentleness off and on the stage, will always render him a favorite par excellence in spite of the most ingenious critical industry."[36]

Perhaps because of his fears, Brignoli did not follow the paths trod by Adelina Patti and Maria Malibran, who made their professional debuts in America and their careers internationally. By the late 1850s he was receiving $1,500 a month, which a *Dwight's* correspondent considered more than he would have gotten in Europe.[37] Instead, Brignoli turned to the provinces of America. As a result, his name is nowhere to be found even in the *New Grove's Dictionary of Music and Musicians*, but instead belongs to the history of the civilizing of America.

Nineteenth-century opera generally resulted from the efforts of individual impresarios. Max Maretzek, Moritz and Max Strakosch, and Colonel James H. Mapleson were the men most active in Brignoli's time. In general, an impresario recruited the leading singers. The Strakosches drew on the Barili-Patti family, building companies around their talents. Besides the leading singers, it was necessary to secure an orchestra and perhaps a chorus. Four Germans constituted the chorus at the Philadelphia Academy of Music. Stage scenery was limited, but backdrops were in use. Those painted by Russell Smith for the Philadelphia Academy of Music attracted much critical acclaim.[38] Singers were responsible for their own costumes. Mme. Pauline Colson from the New Orleans Opera was probably unique in sewing her own clothes and in attempting stylistic authenticity. Critic Frederic Louis Ritter recalled that operas were "sometimes put on the stage with a good deal of scenic splendor and brilliancy, and represented with acceptable dramatic ensemble. Chorus and orchestra were, at the same time, rather effective, and well balanced in number and proportion."[39] Touring companies often numbered fewer than sixty persons and used very limited orchestras.

Repertoire depended on the available artists and public interest. In general, companies opened a run with some old bel canto favorites—*Lucia di Lammermoor* or *Lucrezia Borgia*—and then moved to the current favorites—*Il trovatore* and *La traviata*—(*Rigoletto* was less popular during Brignoli's time). After these came the novelties, which might include new works or revivals of old works. Mozart's *Don Giovanni* was sometimes attempted, but less was seen of his other operas. The end of the season often consisted of portions of operas. On tour with Brignoli one could invariably count on seeing the "Tower Scene" from *Il trovatore*, sometimes paired with an act or two from *The Barber of Seville*, *Don Pasquale*, or the "Garden Scene" from *Faust*.

Protestant prejudices remained a factor. Some, like the young George Templeton Strong, refused to attend the opera at all despite being familiar with much of the music.[40] Many more objected to Sunday performances. After the Civil War, a wave of Sunday "blue laws" hit the nation, and Brignoli was one intended victim. In Memphis in 1870, the ministers tried to prevent the presentation of a Sunday afternoon sacred concert but could find no relevant city ordinance. They proceeded to wait on the mayor, urging him to ban the concert, and then published a card in the papers warning the public of the dangers involved. The concert took place as planned, with parts of Rossini's *Stabat Mater* and "celebrated new mass," a Grand Sacred March, and solos by Cicconi, "the celebrated clarionet soloist." Laboring under the fear of arrest, Brignoli did not sing his best.[41]

In the formative period of American opera, twenty years before Brignoli, it had been necessary to "gild the lily" by inserting English songs, Scotch ballads, and other popular music into the operas. Although this practice had died out in the major cities, it was still alive and well in the provinces. *The Barber of Seville*, with its Lesson Scene, provided an obvious opportunity for sopranos, but Brignoli utilized the same device, singing what became his signature tune, "Good-bye, Sweetheart," composed for him by John L. Hatton, the noted composer of "Simon the Cellarer" and "The Arab's Farewell to his Favorite Steed." "Shall we," asked Henry E. Krehbiel a quarter of a century after Brignoli's death, "be ashamed for having thrilled a little when we heard his 'Coot boy, sweetheart, c-o-o-o-t boy!' thirty years ago? I trust not."[42]

Singers performed often as much as five times a week. In the bigger cities with a larger repertoire, there was some rest. Brignoli avoided the roles of Ernani and Pollione in *Norma*, thus giving a chance for others to sing. Adding to a singer's work were encores. On one occasion in Boston, Brignoli did not want to repeat the Miserere and was hissed from the stage. "He took his revenge," *Dwight's Journal of Music* reported, "by singing more exquisitely than ever . . . extracting applause from the unwilling hands of those who only just before had hissed him."[43] Artists tried to make things easier by making cuts in the score. One Boston performance of *Un ballo in maschera* with Colson and Brignoli was advertised as complete. However, the soprano omitted her aria, "Ma dell'arido stelo divulsa," the Act III scene between baritone and soprano was cut, and Brignoli left out his aria, "Ma se m'e forza perderti." They made up for it with long intermissions.[44]

A season consisted of how many performances profitably could be given. Most impresarios worked only a few months or weeks ahead. In Philadelphia, the Maretzek company, which opened the Academy of Music, left to fulfill other engagements but returned a few months later. Since Philadelphians were determined to reclaim the nation's cultural lead from New York; the project was so well patronized that the company promised sixteen performances but gave twenty-five. On the strength of this success, Maretzek was encouraged to organize the Philadelphia Opera Company for the 1858 season. However, the recession of that year undermined community support. Although Gazzaniga, Brignoli, and Amodio were the best America could assemble, in the second week the bass Joseph Tagliafico demanded the $500 due him or he refused to sing. The company soon disbanded, and the next opera season was brought by the Strakosch forces.[45]

In working the provinces, less flexibility existed. Promoters tried to gauge what the demand would be, what competition existed from English or German troupes, and what halls were available. Since the same theaters served both legitimate drama, minstrel shows, and opera, the problems were complex. In Savannah in 1870, the theater cost $250 per week. A $50 deposit was needed to get the gas turned on. Extra police cost $4 per night; the state charged $25 for a license; the county demanded $1.50 per day; the federal tax was 2 percent; billboards cost $40; and the hotel charged $2.50 per day. These fixed charges could bankrupt a company. The Grau Associated German Artists, which toured extensively after the Civil War, were beset upon by a Georgia sheriff with no less than six writs and lost their properties and wardrobes.[46] In commenting on the scarcity of performances in smaller places, the Savannah paper praised Brignoli, noting, "It is not often that a manager can be found who is willing to incur the risk." [47]

Some places were best avoided altogether. Gottschalk remembered an 1862 concert at Wilmington, Delaware, which netted the pianist, Brignoli, and three others the sum of $25. Three years later Gottschalk returned but found that only eight tickets had been sold. New Jersey towns were considered particularly hopeless.[48]

During his first seven or eight years, Brignoli was the indispensible tenor for every major opera company, but during the 1860s he undertook the role of impresario. The Civil War initially curtailed opera, and one traveling concern, the Holman National Opera troupe, was accused by a Northern critic of expressing sympathy for the South when in the South and for the North when on the other side of the Ohio River. At the start of the war, a number of major singers left for Europe, so Brignoli concertized a great deal. With Gottschalk he visited St. Louis, Cincinnati, Milwaukee, and

Cleveland in 1863. In Chicago, where Brignoli and Colson virtually began that city's rich operatic history on 22 February 1859, the war so cut into attendance that the singers eliminated chorus and orchestra to compensate. Critics charged that such "operatic concerts" consisting of detached scenes were too "tame," and the practice was abandoned after the war.[49]

By the late 1860s, Brignoli was past his prime. As the Cleveland *Leader* noted after an 1869 concert, he "dawdled through his part with the same listless indifference with which he has sung 'Good-bye, Sweet Heart, Good-bye' and the 'M'appari tut Amore,' for us during the last dozen winters."[50] Similar comments could be heard in Boston or New York. Thus, Brignoli tried to stir up new interest by embarking on a farewell tour. This device, common to theater artists and used so extensively by Adelina Patti that it became a joke, failed miserably for Brignoli. In reviewing his Cleveland offering, the *Leader* called him the "eminent but somewhat faded tenor" and concluded, "this quackery should receive the snubbing it deserves." [51] Apparently, Brignoli abandoned the series and instead turned to the South, where new operatic vistas opened.

"No better medicine to reconstruct the South in the matter of music could be selected," editorialized the New York *Herald*, and in the spring of 1869 at least three different opera troupes invaded Dixie.[52] Brignoli's consisted of forty-five persons. "The Prince of Tenors" was supported by Marie Louise Durand, a Charleston native, and the company hit Washington, Richmond, Norfolk, Raleigh, and Charleston before arriving in April in Savannah. In contrast to the blasé audiences of the North, Southerners found so much enjoyment that in Savannah the troupe scheduled an extra concert. Brignoli sang the familiar "Good-bye Sweetheart" and with Steffanoni played his "popular and romantic symphony," "The Sailor's Dream," on two pianos. From there, the troupe headed west to Atlanta.[53]

Atlanta, destined to be the capital of the New South, was a tough nut to crack. Audiences, the *Daily New Examiner* noted, were "an abomination and a nuisance. " Applause consisted of "whooping, shouting, shrieking, groaning, whistling, stomping, grunting, coughing, sneezing, rapping, wheezing, shouting, and bellowing." [54] Known as a "one night town," "Atlanta," the *Daily New Era* ruefully admitted, "has not the taste to appreciate anything good unless it be fashionable, unless it is a circus, a negro minstrel troupe or a variety show." [55] Grau's German Opera company went to pieces there, and two other companies, including one led by Max Strakosch in 1866, preceded Brignoli's arrival with indifferent results.[56]

Despite the omens, Brignoli was again successful. "As a whole," one paper noted, "no better company ever traveled through the South, and we have never heard one as good." Brignoli was "mellow" and Durand had "few equals." [57] Cautiously, he only scheduled two performances there. The troupe then headed westward, passing through New Orleans and eventually reaching San Francisco by November.

During the next ten years, Brignoli was almost continually on the road. In 1870, he secured the services of Isabella McCulloch, a Southern songstress from Columbia, South Carolina. Known as Sallie while at school, her publicity created the image of a Southern belle forced upon the stage after the Civil War had destroyed the family fortune. As such, she immediately enjoyed the support of all the white Democratic papers in the South.

McCulloch, who became the second Mrs. Brignoli after the first, Madame Morensi (in reality an English singer named Kate Duckworth) died, had a voice of "great compass and surpassing sweetness." She had already appeared in New York and with the Parlor Opera troupe in the South. The Memphis *Daily Appeal*, disappointed with the reception tendered her, observed that "had Miss McCulloch appeared as Signorina McCulina, or some other outlandish name, she would have been greeted with crowded houses." [58]

In acquiring McCulloch, Brignoli seems to have merged his forces with the Parlor Opera and launched a new campaign. This one took opera to Little Rock, Arkansas, a town that in its fifty-year history had never received any cultural enlightenment. The troupe left Memphis, with the Sunday concert controversy raging, and steamed down the Mississippi before ascending the Arkansas River. Besides McCulloch and Brignoli, the forces included Antonia Henne, an American mezzo-soprano very active in oratorios; baritone Signor Petrelli; and bass Signor Borbagelato, "remarkable for one gesture—a sawing and beating on the air with his right arm, that was awkwardness itself." [59] The conductor was Paolo Giorza, an active ballet composer and later the founding musical father of Seattle. It took five days to make the trip.

For some entirely unknown reason, Little Rock received no less than six performances. *Martha*, *Lucia di Lammermoor*, and *Il trovatore* were given in full; on Sunday came the inevitable sacred concert. On Monday the company presented one act each from Gounod's *Faust* and Donizetti's *Lucrezia Borgia*. Henne's small part was enlarged by stopping the action and allowing her to render "Do you think of me?" During *The Barber of Seville* on Tuesday, Brignoli managed to get in "Good-bye, Sweetheart, Goodbye" and the evening concluded with the Tower Scene from *Il trovatore*. During the engagement the local press got involved in a political proprietary battle over opera. The *Republican*,speaking for the carpetbag element, lauded culture and early promoted the performances. The *Arkansas Gazette*, Democratic, was early indifferent until it discovered the Dixie connection with Miss McCulloch. Then she became all the rage since the *Gazette* barely mentioned anyone else. The *Republican* and apparently the public took Miss Henne to heart, and for good (or perhaps bad) measure, the German-language newspaper, the *Staats Zeitung*, called Brignoli "much sung out." Brignoli resented that, and also some *Gazette* comments about his graying hair. In reply, the *Staats Zeitung* claimed its comments had been misinterpreted and the *Gazette* retracted the comment about the hair.[60]

The return trip to Memphis demonstrated some of the risks involved in touring. The troupe lost a day when just below Helena their boat came upon the burning wreckage of the *Maggie Hayes*, which had burst a boiler, killing the captain and seriously scalding several of the passengers and crew. The passengers of the *Commercial*, led by Colonel Robert Crockett, nephew of the deceased Davy, took up a collection to which the theater troupe generously donated. Other stops on this far-ranging jaunt included Galveston, Texas, and Mobile, Alabama.[61]

If Brignoli hoped to make himself a permanent Southern favorite by relying on McCulloch, he was disappointed. Her light soprano, "of good quality, but delicate in its texture and quickly exhausted," noted the New York *Times*, was put to the most astonishing uses.[62] With roles ranging from the coloratura Oscar in *Un Ballo in maschera* to Bellini's *Norma*, Mozart's Donna Elvira, *Lucia di Lammermoor*, and both Leonora and Azucena in *Il trovatore*, it was small wonder that her career was short.

By the mid-1870s, Brignoli had switched his attentions elsewhere. He became the leading tenor for Christine Nilsson, the new Swedish nightingale. George Bernard Shaw recalled seeing Nilsson, "after listening with a critical air to 'Ah si, ben mio' sung by a tenor who must have been a veteran when she was in her cradle, slap the patriarch on the back with a hearty bravo at the end."[63] It was in Madame Nilsson's behalf in Chicago where he was laughed off the stage after telling the audience in English that the soprano was "a leetle 'orse."[64] The American diva, Clara Louise Kellogg, who wrote affectionately of him in her autobiography, came next. Last was Emma Abbott, who began her career in English opera and switched to Italian. Critics in the 1870s began to note faults. In Philadelphia, inveterate operagoer William G. Armstrong noted considerable loss of quality, although an individual performance might still measure up.[65] On 26 February 1877, the Academy of Music staged a twentieth anniversary of its opening night. The house was "very large and brilliant," but time had marched on. Amodio was dead, and Gazzaniga, "a huge melancholy wreck," sang Azucena rather than Leonora. McCulloch essayed that role, but was "wretched, flat and weak." As for Brignoli, Armstrong adjudged him "tolerable."[66]

Since Brignoli had always lived beyond his means, which at one time amounted to $3000 a week, retirement was impossible. His voice weakened on top, and to compensate he ran forward to the footlights to sing his high notes, once getting caught on the wrong side when the curtain fell. In order to stay employed, he took on new roles like Pollione in *Norma* that were wrong for his voice and of secondary importance.[67] His final New York performances were with English opera troupes, a great comedown for the faded tenor. George Upton met him in Chicago in fall of 1884 when Adelina Patti was singing Lucia at McVicker's Theatre and recalled:

I asked him if he was going to the opera. He mournfully shook his head and exclaimed: "No! I cannot afford it, and I will not ask them for a pass. I sang in Lucia when she made her debut. To-night she must transpose her part. Old Brignoli can still sing his where it is written. Adelina gets $5000 a night; old Brignoli gets fifty cents" . . . We shook hands and parted. Some friends helped him get to New York, where he died a few weeks later. In his death one of the purest and most perfect exponents of beautiful melody passed away.[68]

Ironically, had he lived a little longer, Mapleson reportedly had plans to reunite the two for a celebration of Patti's twenty-fifth anniversary.[69]

Richard Grant White might have been unable to understand the enthusiasm that Brignoli inspired, but a greater critic had the last words. Wrote Walt Whitman of Brignoli:

As down the stage again,
With Spanish hat and plumes, and gait inimitable,
Back from the fading lessons of the past, I'd call, I'd tell, and own,
How much from thee! the revelation of the singing voice from thee!
So firm—so liquid-soft—again that tremulous, manly timbre!

The perfect singing voice—deepest of all to me the lesson—trial and test
of all:
How through those strains distill'd—how the rapt ears, the soul of me
absorbing
Fernando's heart, Manrico's passionate call, Ernani's, sweet Gennaro's,
I fold thenceforth, or seek to fold, within my chants transmuting,
Freedom's and Love's and Faith's unloos'd cantabile, (As perfume's,
color's, sunlight's correlation:) From these, for these, with these, a
hurried line, dead tenor,
A wafted autumn leaf, dropt in the closing grave, the shovel'd earth,
To memory of thee.[70]

Notes

1. Donald G. Mitchell, *The Lorgnette or Studies of the Town by an Opera
Goer* (New York: Stringer & Townsend, 1851), p. 149.

2. Henri Vieuxtemps's autobiography, *Dwight's Journal of Music* 41 (5 Sept.
1881): 119. Hereafter cited as *DJM*.

3. Henry S. Holland and W. S. Rockstro, *Madame Jenny Lind-Goldschmidt:
Her Early Art-Life and Dramatic Career*, 2 vols. (London: John Murray, 1891),
2: 369. Daniel G. Mason, ed., *The Art of Music* (New York: National Society of
Music, 1915), p. 133.

4. Horace Montgomery, "Howell Cobb, Daniel Webster, and Jenny Lind,"
Georgia Historical Quarterly 45 (March 1961): 37– 41.

5. Vera B. Lawrence, *Strong on Music: The New York Music Scene in the
Days of George Templeton Strong, 1836–1875* (New York: Oxford Univ. Press,
1988), 1:192–290.

6. Robert G. White, "Opera in New York," *Century Magazine* 24 (June
1882): 193– 95.

7. Ibid., p. 197.

8. Frederic L. Ritter, *Music in America* (New York and London: Johnson Reprint Corporation, 1970) 316–17; Max Maretzek, *Sharps and Flats* (New York:
American Musician, 1890), 1:17.

9. White, "Opera," p. 199.

10. *New York Times*, 31 October 1884.

11. Clara Louise Kellogg, *Memoirs of an American Prima Donna* (New York:
Putnam, 1913), p. 24.

12. Louis M. Gottshalk, "Notes of a Pianist," *Atlantic Monthly* 15 (April
1865): 575.

13. Jean Gourret, *Dictionnaire des chanteurs de opera de Paris* (Paris: Editions
Albutros, 1982), p.70.

14. Julian Budden, *The Operas of Verdi* (New York: Oxford Univ. Press,
1979), 2: 98. Budden called the role of Manrico "the essence of the heroic tenor."

15. George C. D. Odell, *Annals of the New York Stage* (New York: Columbia
Univ. Press, 1931), 7: 347. Budden 2: 421.

16. Odell, *Annals*, 6: 478. Luigi Arditi, *My Reminiscences* (New York: Dodd,
Mead & Co., 1896), p. 29.

17. John Curtis, "One Hundred Years of Grand Opera in Philadelphia" (typescript, Historical Society of Pennsylvania, 1920), p. 543.

18. Nicholas B. Wainwright, ed., *A Philadelphia Perspective: The Diary of Sidney George Fisher. Covering the Years 1834–1871* (Philadelphia: Historical Society of Pennsylvania, 1963), p. 268.

19. Curtis, *100 Years*, p. 551.

20. White, "Opera in New York," p. 205–6.

21. Henry C. Lahee, *Grand Opera in America* (Boston: L. C. Page & Co., 1902), p. 157; White, p. 199.

22. Jeamme Behrend, ed., *Notes of a Pianist—Louis Moreau Gottshalk* (New York: Knopf, 1964), p. 52; Henry E. Krehbiel, *Chapters of Opera . . .* (New York: Henry Holt and Company, 1909), p. 84.

23. *DJM* 13 (1 May 1858): 39.

24. *DJM* 15 (5 March 1859): 389.

25. Behrend, Notes, p. 52; Lahee, *Grand Opera*, p. 162; George P. Upton, *Musical Memories—My Recollections of Celebrities of the Half Century, 1850–1900* (Chicago: A. C. McClung & Co., 1908), p. 124.

26. Upton, *Musical Memorices*, p. 122.

27. Kellogg, *Memoirs*, p. 22–29.

28. Behrend, *Notes*, pp. 160– 61.

29. Kellogg, *Memoirs*, p. 29.

30. London *Sunday Times*, 28 May 1865.

31. *DJM* 13 (3 July 1858): 109.

32. Ibid.

33. Arditi, *Reminiscences*, p. 197.

34. White,"Opera in New York," p. 199.

35. Krehbiel, *Chapters of Opera . . .* , p. 83.

36. *DJM* 18 (13 October 1860): 232.

37. *DJM* 15 (5 March 1859): 389.

38. Fisher Diary, p. 269.

39. Ritter, *Music in American*, pp. 350–51.

40. Lawrence, *Strong on Music*, p. 22.

41. Memphis *Appeal* 26, 30 January, 1 February 1870.

42. Krehbiel, *Chapters of Opera . . .* , p. 83.

43. *DJM* 18 (30 March 1861): 423.

44. *DJM* 18 (16 March 1861): 422.

45. Curtis, *100 Years*, p. 579.

46. Peg Gough, "On Stage in Atlanta, 1860–1870," *Atlanta Historical Bulletin* 21 (Summer 1977): 37–38; Savannah *Morning News*, 2 April 1870.

47. Savannah *Morning News*, 9 April 1869.

48. Behrend, *Notes*, p. 257.

49. Upton, *Musical Memories*, p. 232.

50. Cleveland *Leader*, 18 October 1869.

51. Ibid.

52. Quoted in Savannah *Morning News*, 30 March 1869.

53. Savannah *Morning News*, 3–18 April 1869.

54. Atlanta Daily *New Examiner*, May 1870.

55. Grigsby H. Wotton, "New City of the South: Atlanta, 1843–1873" (Ph.D. diss., Johns Hopkins, University, 1973), pp. 265–266.

56. Gough, "On Stage in Atlanta," pp. 38–43.

57. Atlanta *Daily New Era*, 24 April 1869.

58. Little Rock *Arkansas Gazette*, 5 February 1870; Atlanta *Daily New Era*, 23 May 1868; Memphis *Daily Appeal*, 11 June 1868.

59. Odell, *Annals*, 9: 73; Memphis *Daily Appeal*, 1 February 1870.

60. Michael B. Dougan, "Bravo Brignoli! The First Opera Season in Arkansas," *Pulaski County Historical Review* 30 (Winter 1982): 74–80.

61. Ibid.

62. New York *Times*, 23 April 1866.

63. Bernard Shaw, *Music in London* . . . (New York: Vienna House, 1973), 1: 202.

64. Upton, *Musical Memories*, p. 124.

65. W. G. Armstrong, *A Record of the Opera in Philadelphia* (Philadelphla: Porter & Coats, 1884), p. 143.

66. Curtis, *100 Years*, p. 328.

67. Odel, *Annals*, 11: 96.

68. Upton, *Musical Memories*, p. 125.

69. Krehbiel, *Chapters of Opera* . . . , p. 124.

70. Walt Whitman, *The Complete Writings of Walt Whitman* (New York: G. P. Putnam's Sons, 1902), 2: 308.

Opera Activity in Texas before the Twentieth Century

GARY D. GIBBS

When one thinks of Texas, the first thing to come to mind is probably not opera. It is somewhat difficult to imagine the cowboys and farmers sitting down for an evening's entertainment of *La sonnambula* at the local theater in nineteenth-century Texas. Since its earliest days, however, there was an element of the population in the state who appreciated and enjoyed the genre of opera. This essay will provide a broad overview of opera activity in Texas before the twentieth century.

In 1836, Texas won its independence from Mexico and established herself as a republic with Sam Houston as president. Already at this time there was a good number of German immigrants living in the Houston/Galveston area who were known for their appreciation of the arts. Shortly after the republic was established, professional dramatic theaters sprang up in Houston and Galveston, but it appears that the Texas public was not yet accustomed to the finer things of life, reported in this account of a performance at which President Houston was in attendance:

The front seats were reserved for ladies and school children, the next seats for the president, his staff, and the Milam guards. The school arrived early, found the reserved seats occupied, and was accordingly seated in the second seats. There was considerable confusion, as the house was crowded. As the president and escort entered, the orchestra played "Hail to the Chief," but there were no seats vacant to accommodate them. The stage manager, Mr. Corri, came out and requested the men in front, who were gamblers and their friends, to give up their seats. This they refused to do. Then the manager called for the police to put them out. They became enraged, and drawing weapons, threatened to shoot. The sheriff called upon the soldiers to arrest and disarm them. It looked as if there would be bloodshed, gamblers on one side, soldiers on the other, women and children between, everybody talking, women and children crying. The president got on a seat, commanded the peace, asked those in front to be seated, ordered the soldiers to stack arms, and said that he and the ladies and children would take back seats. This appeared to shame the gamblers. One man acted as spokesman and said that if their money was returned they would leave the house, as they had no desire to discommode the ladies. He said they would have left the house at first if the police had not been called. After the gamblers left, the evening passed very pleasantly. The president addressed the audience, particularly the children.[1]

Though the number of theaters and dramatic presentations increased throughout the state in the ensuing years before Texas was admitted to the United States in 1845, there is no record of an opera being staged and little evidence of public musical performances at all during the time. As mentioned before, however, the German immigrants who had settled mainly in central and southeastern Texas remained quite active with musical activities through church and community functions.

The first connection between opera and Texas involves these German immigrants. In 1846, Pastor Adolf Fuchs arrived in Texas with his family and settled in Austin County near Houston. Fuchs was a friend of the poet Hoffmann von Fallersleben. Shortly before Fuchs's departure for Texas, he spent time with von Fallersleben discussing his future in this new land. Based on these conversations and events, the poet wrote a series of thirty-one song texts dealing with Texas and German emigration to the state. These songs were published in 1846 without melodies, but from von Fallersleben's diary it is apparent that these texts were sung during his last visit with Fuchs.

After Fuchs's arrival in Texas, he continued to correspond with von Fallersleben describing his new surroundings with great praise and encouraging the poet to immigrate also. It appears that von Fallersleben became quite intimate with the subject of Texas and was even inspired to write an opera libretto based on his perceptions, entitled *In beiden Welten*. He completed the libretto in 1852 and presented it to several guests at a dinner party. The guests were most impressed with the text, but felt that it was "too good" for an opera. Von Fallersleben sent the libretto to several composers, including Robert Schumann. Schumann also agreed that the libretto was "too good," and he preferred not to deal with contemporary themes.

The libretto concerns a group of Germans in Schleswig-Holstein who flee to Texas from Danish military forces. Upon their arrival in Texas they are faced with Indian wars and the rescue of a young German girl who had been kidnapped to become the bride of the

Indian chief. The German girl, who had emigrated to Texas earlier, was the fiancé of one of the newly arrived German men.
The libretto concludes with the German lovers reunited and the
Indians defeated. Somehow, it seems appropriate that the first
opera to be associated with Texas would be a forerunner of the
many Western adventures that would follow, only with a German
"twist." It seems, however, that no music was ever composed for
the libretto, and *In beiden Welten* was forgotten.[2]

According to Lota Spell, the first musicologist to study systema-
tically the history of music in Texas, the first actual performance of
an opera in the state occurred in Galveston in 1856.[3] Galveston, at
the time, was becoming a truly international city because of the
port there. Trade between the city and New Orleans was extensive. Therefore, a large number of foreigners, particularly Germans and French, lived and worked there. Due to this foreign influence, Galveston became the center of fine arts entertainment in
the state and ranked second only to New Orleans in cultural arts
importance in the South for several years.

Spell states that a German opera troupe came from St. Louis to
Galveston and presented several acts from various operas. The
performance was in German, but this would have posed no problem for the audience because many were native speakers. Unfortunately, Spell does not provide any details about the works
performed or the performers. Another source verifies that such a
performance did take place in Houston, but efforts to locate a contemporary report of the event were unsuccessful.[4] The other early
occurrences of opera productions cited by Spell include an 1857
performance in Brownsville by an Italian opera company from
Mexico and a performance by a French opera company (probably
from New Orleans) in Galveston between 1857 and 1860.[5] Again,
Spell provides no details, and attempts to document these performances were unsuccessful.

Just as Texas was beginning to experience a growth in musical
activities and performances, including visiting professional artists,
the Civil War erupted. This brought an abrupt end to all such
amusements. The theaters stood empty, and traveling dramatic
and musical performers, whose tours originated primarily in the
North, did not hazard many trips, especially to the South. Galveston, the center of fine arts culture in Texas, became a strategic
military post for the Confederacy, and was thus attacked on several occasions by Union forces from the Gulf of Mexico.

At the conclusion of the war, renewed activity in the musical
arts began almost immediately. As early as 1867, Galveston audi-

ences were treated to performances of selections from *Ernani, La traviata, Martha,* and *La sonnambula* on 5 April, and apparently complete performances of the operas *Norma* on 10 April, *Lucretia Borgia* on 16 April, and *Un ballo in maschero* on 18 April. *La traviata* and *Il trovatore* were presented, presumably by the same group, in Houston on 11 and 12 April, respectively.[6] The works were presented by the Roncari Opera Troupe, featuring Elisa Tomassi, Pietro Fabri, Alexandria Ottaviani, Carlotta Cattinari, Friede deGebele, Alessandro Boetti, and Signor Rocco, complete with a full orchestra and chorus. Apparently the Galveston audiences were most supportive and appreciative of the performances. In Houston, a city with a smaller international population, however, the public's response was less enthusiastic, resulting in the opera troupe leaving the city without paying the newspaper for the promotional advertisements.[7] A review of the performance in Houston of *Il trovatore* provides not only insight into the quality of the performance, but also the level of musical criticism in the city at the time:

Last night a house just a little better than the night previous witnessed the excellent execution of Il Trovatore. The role of Leonora was sustained by Mlle. Carolina Cattinari in a most magnificient manner. This lady is rather large for a part like Leonora, but the sweetness of her bird-like voice, ascending in liquid measure through every scale, hides the want of harmony of feature, and conceals all faults of gesticulation and action. Her singing is superb. We know not what to like it to, save rare, good old wine that exhilirates the soul and steeps the senses in a dream of luxurious pain. The part of Azucena by Madame Frieda De-Gebele was dressed and acted to life, and the different music of the role was rendered as perfect as we have ever heard it done.

The tenor, Signor Alessandro Boetti, was at home evidently in the piece, and his voice is strong, lovely and melodious. The others in the cast were popularly rendered, and on the whole, [it] will be long before the citizens of Houston have again the opportunity of seeing so good a company of Italian Opera.[8]

The next major series of opera productions in Texas occurred in Galveston on 18–24 January 1869. On seven consecutive evenings, the visiting Marie Frederici Opera Company presented *Martha, Fra Diavolo, Der Freschütz, The Magic Flute* twice (21 and 23 January), *Faust,* and *Il trovatore.*[9] It is interesting to note that in the performance of *Magic Flute* the roles of both Pamina and Papagena were sung by Frederici. According to Spell, Partido's

Mexican opera troupe toured San Antonio, Austin, New Braunfels, Seguin, Brenham, Houston, and Galveston also during 1869.[10]

In 1870, Houston experienced another version of opera. The touring black minstrel group called Buckley's Serenaders appeared for three nights, beginning 8 March. Not only did the performers sing and dance, but they also presented burlesques of the operas *La sonnambula*, *Lucrezia Borgia*, and *Il trovatore*. The minstrels played to full houses.[11]

In the 1870s and 1880s, the railroad system in Texas was completed, connecting most of the major cities of the state as well as many smaller towns. The new railway network lessened the problem of distance in such a vast state. The trains allowed for shorter travel time between the various cities in the state that could support touring companies of all kinds. This resulted in an increased number of professional opera companies who added Texas to their itinerary. A concert circuit soon evolved, consisting of the cities of Dallas, Fort Worth, Austin, San Antonio, Houston, and Galveston, and often including numerous smaller towns along the way. Eventually, El Paso would be included in several of the opera troupes' touring engagements. Between 1870 and 1900, over fifty different opera companies visited the state, with some troupes such as the Emma Abbott Opera Company and the Grau Opera Company making consecutive appearances for numerous years. Appendix I lists the various opera companies that performed in Houston and Galveston during the nineteenth century, including the year of their initial appearance.

Another impetus that lured the opera companies to the state, beginning in the 1870s, was the building of several opera houses throughout Texas. The first such opera house was completed in Galveston in 1871 and came to be known as the Tremont Opera House. Galveston had long been the center of dramatic and musical activity in the state, and therefore it was only natural that the first such building in Texas to be erected for the purpose of stage entertainment was in that city. Prior to the opening of the Tremont, stage productions were given in various halls and theaters around the city. The Tremont was a beautiful theater with some of the latest innovations of stage equipment. The Tremont played host to many fine dramatic and musical productions, but the manager of the house complained that many well-known performers refused to come to Galveston because he could not guarantee their fees. Therefore, in an attempt to remain solvent, the Tremont was not immune to a less sophisticated form of entertainment, as reported by the Galveston historian, David McComb, in his account of one such performance on 8 March 1875:

> . . . Interest soared in 1875, at least for five days, while Mme. Rentze's Female Minstrels were in town. The male population from "banker to bootblack" jammed the Opera House to witness the variety show, which included the notorious Can-Can, "a lewd and voluptuous dance, in which a lot of depraved men and women throw themselves into all manner of lascivious motions." Feeling somewhat ashamed, men in the audience sat low in their seats with collars turned up, but the police refused to stop the show. After the group left town, the newspaper said, "It is understood that incense and olive oil will be burned in the Opera house throughout to-day to purify its atmosphere and make it a fit place once more for ladies." [12]

At the end of the month, the Tremont Opera House's reputation was restored by the appearance of the Emily Soldene Opera Company in a series of *opera bouffe* performances in English. The series lasted six days, from 22–27 March 1875, with a different work presented each day including *La Fille de Madame Angot, Geneviève de Brabant, La Grande Duchesse de Gérolstein, Chilpéric,* and *Madame L'Archiduc.* Miss Soldene spoke interestingly of her visit to Galveston:

> The theatre was not exactly Drury Lane, and stinging nettles grew up to the stage door. The public was pleased with us. The Press, rather chaste and faddy, found us "improper," which we were not, also "beefy," which perhaps we were. . . .Anyway, every night the theatre was crowded. We had a real good time, beautiful drives on the beautiful beach, and saw wonderful things and people.[13]

Though the Houston/Galveston area continued to be the center of opera activity in Texas during the 1870s, some of the other cities in the state experienced their first encounters with touring opera companies. In Fort Worth, an opera house called Evans Hall was built in 1876. The first operas to be performed in the city were at this house in 1878. The Adah Richmond English Opera Troupe presented two evening performances of *Les cloches de Corneville* and *La Périchole.* Although Fort Worth, the city known as "Cowtown," was some twenty years behind Galveston in hosting opera companies, apparently some of the citizens of the city were not completely ignorant of the art form of opera. Two years later in 1880, the Tagliapietra Grand Italian Opera Company visited Fort Worth. The troupe was scheduled to perform Donizetti's *La Favo-*

rite; but due to a small house and experiences with bad weather, Flotow' s *Martha* was substituted, but with sections being omitted. The Fort Worth audience was insulted, and the press later wrote, "Companies who do not intend to do their best are advised to stay away from Fort Worth."[14] Evidently, the cowboy spirit and attitude remained strong, regardless of the "refined trappings" that accompanied opera in the United States.

Dallas heard its first opera with an orchestra performed on 12 February 1875 at Field's Theatre. Unlike the other opera performances discussed thus far, the first opera to be presented in Dallas was not from a professional touring company, but rather from local talent. The opera given was *Martha*, and the entire cast and orchestra was composed of members from the two singing societies of the city, the Swiss Glee Club and the Turner Singing Association. The production was highly praised by the local press:

Field's theatre was crowded last night with the largest and most fashionable audience that ever assembled in the city. The occasion was the performance of Flotow's beautiful little opera "Martha" by a number of lady and gentlemen amateurs. It had been but a short time in preparation, and was given sooner than was originally intended. For a first performance by amateurs it was highly creditable to the lyric talent and musical culture of all who took part in it. . . . The production of "Martha" marks an era of musical history in Dallas which cannot but be a source of pride to all interested in the elevation of the standard of art.[15]

Another article in the same issue of the paper seemed to verify that Dallas had caught the opera "bug" and, in true Texas fashion, was ready to "take on" the rest of the state in its support of the arts:

The success of "Martha" was so great and so flattering to the taste, energy and musical culture of those who performed it, and their effort met with such appreciation, that it has been determined to put into rehearsal immediately, Verdi's grand opera "Il Trovatore." The cast will be a fine one, and will include additional amateur talent of a high order. Having eclipsed Galveston, Houston and San Antonio, we rest on our laurels. [16]

A performance of *Il trovatore* followed shortly thereafter. In 1876, the touring company of Saulsbury's Troubadours presented the comic opera *Patchwork* in Dallas. The grandest year of musical life in Dallas before 1900 was 1883, when the state Sängerfest held its biennial festival there. In this same year the new Dallas Opera House opened, and the inaugural production was Gilbert and Sullivan's *Iolanthe*.[17] The opera was probably presented by the St. Quintin Opera Company, who also gave the work in Galveston that same year. Other opera companies to visit Dallas during those years include Emma Abbott's troupe and the Boston Ideals.[18]

The earliest evidence of operatic activity in Austin dates from the late 1860s. Austin had a large German population that was extremely active in musical affairs. Various selections from numerous operas were presented by local talent on public programs, and the local conductor Julius Schutze directed a performance of the first scene from *Don Giovanni* and the first act of *Der Freischütz*.[19] On 21 September 1871, the newly opened Austin Opera House presented *La Fille du regiment* in English.[20] During the 1880s and 1890s, numerous operas involving small casts of local artists were performed under the direction of William Besserer, an Austin native who had received his musical education in Germany. These works included *Prince Wolfgang of Anhalt* in 1876 and *Stradella and Lorelei* in 1886.[21] Austin, however, also hosted several touring companies during the decades preceding the twentieth century. The Carleton Opera Company appeared there in 1887, and the Whitney Mockridge Grand Opera Company in 1900.

San Antonio's situation was similar to Austin's. The railroads were late in coming to the two cities; therefore, San Antonio, like Austin, had to rely on local talent for productions of opera. This presented no great problem for the city because of the large German and Mexican populations. Both groups valued the importance of music and made it a part of their everyday lives. Spell writes:

> In spite of the lack of transportation facilities, which made it difficult for musicians who visited other parts of the state to reach San Antonio, opera troupes from Mexico, and occasionally from Houston, came by stage and were always cordially greeted there by a music-loving audience. It was in the years before the coming of the railroads that the foundations for the cosmopolitan and music-loving city, which San Antonio has since been acknowledged to be, were securely laid.[22]

With the extension of the railroads to San Antonio in the 1880s, it became possible for the touring opera companies to visit the city. During the 1887–88 season the Emma Abbott and the Carleton Opera Companies performed there after completing engagements in Houston and Galveston. In 1889, the Faust Opera Company and Campanini's Opera Troupe appeared there after visiting Dallas and Austin. The professional groups performed in Turner Hall, while the local Germans used a small stage in a building called the Casino for their own productions of opera and operetta.[23]

There were, undoubtedly, other examples of opera activity in Texas during the nineteenth century, but the major centers of performance were in Fort Worth, Dallas, Austin, San Antonio, and above all in Houston and Galveston. El Paso did not receive train service until 1881, and the city's Myar Opera House was first built in 1890. Both Emma Abbott's and Emma Juch's opera companies visited the city shortly before the turn of the century.[24]

Texas was largely a rural state in the nineteenth century, and even those who had moved to the cities held firm to their rural values and customs, which usually did not include an appreciation for opera. However, because of the large foreign population in the state, especially in the cities, opera found a place in the "cowboy" society. Indeed, as Appendix II shows, almost six hundred performances of over one hundred different operas and operettas were performed in the Houston/Galveston area alone during those years. The appendix lists only works presented by professional touring companies with an approximate number of performances for each opera. Although the Lone Star State's association with the field of opera may be relatively short in comparison with many northern cities, it is apparent that the touring companies found their visits profitable enough to include Texas on their itineraries each year during the latter part of the nineteenth century and that there were Texans who were both knowledgeable and appreciative of the art form. Local amateur productions of opera would also increase in the ensuing years. With the advent of the twentieth century, Texas would experience increased activity in the field of opera, and certain segments of the population would become strong supporters of the genre, though not necessarily giving up their rodeos and other forms of native entertainment.

Appendix I
Opera Touring Companies Appearing in Houston/Galveston before 1900

Premiere

1867	Roncari Opera Troupe
1869	Marie Federici Grand German Opera Troupe
1871	Alice Oates Opera Company
1875	Emily Soldene Opera Company

1875	French Opera Bouffe Company
1876	Caroline Richings-Benard Opera Company
1878	Adah Richmond Opera Bouffe Company
1879	Hess Grand Opera Company (Emma Abbott)
1879	Saville English Opera Company
1879	Haverly's Juvenile Pinafore Company
1880	Miles Juvenile Opera Company
1880	Emma Abbott Opera Company
1880	Tagliapietra Opera Company
1881	Strakosh-Hess Opera Company
1881	C. D. Hess Opera Company
1881	Templeton Star Opera Company
1882	Ernest Stanley Comic Opera Company
1882	Max Strakosh Opera Company
1882	Winston and Stevens Comic Opera Company
1882	Charles E. Ford's Comic Opera Company
1883	Marie Geistinger Opera Company
1883	De Fossez Grand Opera Company
1883	Haverly's English Opera Company
1883	St. Quintin Opera Company
1883	Grau Opera Company
1883	Duff Opera Company
1884	Minnie Hauk Opera Company
1884	Brignoli and Godini Opera Company
1884	Chicago Ideal Opera Company
1884	Madame Theo Opera Company
1884	Grau's French Opera Company
1885	World John T. Ford Opera Company
1886	Bijou Opera Company
1886	Whitney Opera Company
1887	Carleton Opera Company
1889	MacCollin Opera Company
1889	Thompsom Opera Company
1889	Grau Comic Opera Company
1890	Henderson's Gondolier Opera Company
1890	Emma Juch Opera Company
1891	Conried Opera Company
1891	Reeve's Opera Bouffe Company
1892	Kimball Opera Comique Company
1893	Home Opera Company
1894	Algerian Opera Company
1895	Marie Tavary Grand English Opera Company
1897	Columbia Light Opera Company
1899	Sofia Scalchi Opera Company
1899	Wilbur-Kirwin Comic Opera Company
1899	Andrews Opera Company
1900	Lombardi Opera Company

Appendix II
Operas and Operettas Performed in Houston/Galveston through 1900

Premiere   = year of initial performance
Total   = approximate total number of performances in 19th century.
Title—Composer = advertised title and composer of opera/operetta; year of American debut for major works

Premiere	Total	Title—Composer
1881	34	*La Mascotte*—Audran
1876	29	*Bohemian Girl*—Balfe
1867	24	*Martha*—Flotow (1852)
1869	24	*Fra Diavolo*—Auber
1885	22	*Mikado*—Sullivan
1878	22	*Chimes of Normandy*—Planquette
1867	18	*Il trovatore*—Verdi (1855)
1889	17	*Said Pasha*—Stahl
1883	15	*Boccaccio*—Suppé
1877	14	*Giroflé-Girofla*—Lecocq
1887	14	*Erminie*—Jacobowski
1875	14	*Grand Duchess of Gérolstein*—Offenbach
1881	13	*Olivette*—Audran
1869	12	*Faust*—Gounod (1863)
1882	11	*The Merry War*—J. Strauss
1881	11	*Carmen*—Bizet (1878)
1883	10	*The Beggar Student*—Millöcker
1870	10	*Lucia di Lammermoor*—Donizetti (1841)
1888	9	*The Black Hussar*—Millöcker
1875	8	*La Périchole*—Offenbach
1889	8	*Amorita*
1879	8	*Fatinitza*—Suppé
1895	8	*Hendrick Hudson*
1868	7	*La Fille de Madame Angot*—Lecocq
1889	7	*Falka*—Chassaigne
1884	6	*The Queen's Lace Handkerchief*—J. Strauss
1871	6	*Mignon*—Thomas (1871)
1881	6	*Billie Taylor*—Solomon
1889	6	*The Brigands*—Offenbach
1890	6	*Gondoliers*—Sullivan
1892	6	*Cavalleria Rusticana*—Mascagni (1891)
1890	6	*The Gypsy Baron*—J. Strauss
1895	6	*The Tar and the Tartar*—Itzel
1879	6	*H.M.S. Pinafore*—Sullivan
1886	6	*Rob Roy*—De Koven
1867	5	*La traviata*—Verdi (1856)

1883	5	*Pirates of Penzance*—Sullivan
1884	5	*The Little Duke*—Lecocq
1895	5	*Paul Jones*—Planquette
1883	5	*Iolanthe*—Sullivan
1877	5	*The Princess of Trebizonde*—Offenbach
1886	4	*The Bridal Trap*—Audran
1887	4	*Nanon*—Genée
1882	4	*Evangeline*—Rice
1893	4	*Dorothy*—Cellier
1896	4	*Indiana*—Audran
1871	4	*William Tell*—Rossini (1831)
1877	3	*La Jolie Parfumeuse*—Offenbach
1867	3	*Norma*—Bellini (1841)
1880	3	*Maritana*—Wallace
1875	3	*Geneviève de Brabant*—Offenbach
1867	3	*Lucrezia Borgia*—Bellini (1844)
1867	3	*Ernani*—Verdi (1847)
1890	3	*The King's Fool*—Müller
1891	3	*Poor Jonathan*—Millöcker
1892	3	*Tannhäuser*—Wagner (1859)
1893	3	*Ship Ahoy*—Miller
1894	3	*The Algerian*—De Koven
1897	3	*The Two Vagabonds*—Ziehrer
1877	3	*Trial by Jury*—Sullivan
1871	3	*Rigoletto*—Verdi (1855)
1870	3	*Barber of Seville*—Rossini (1819)
1882	3	*Patience*—Sullivan
1882	3	*The Sorceror*—Sullivan
1884	2	*Don Pasquale*—Donizetti (1846)
1883	2	*Rip van Winkle*—Planquette
1867	2	*La sonnambula*—Bellini (1835)
1877	2	*Madame L'Archiduc*—Offenbach
1887	2	*Doctor of Alcantra*—Eichberg
1887	2	*Madame Boniface*
1888	2	*Ruy Blas*—Lutz
1889	2	*The King's Musketeers*—Lecocq
1889	2	*The Rose of Castile*—Balfe
1889	2	*Francois, the Blue Stocking*—Messager
1892	2	*Arcadians*—Monckton
1898	2	*New Boccaccio*
1895	2	*The Fencing Master*—De Koven
1883	2	*Les Huguénots*—Meyerbeer (1839)
1897	2	*Pretty Persian*—Lecocq
1869	2	*The Magic Flute*—Mozart (1833)
1874	2	*La Favorita*—Donizetti
1880	2	*Romeo and Juliet*—Gounod (1867)
1882	2	*Jolly Bachelors*—Darling

1882	2	*Babes in the Woods*—various composers
1881	2	*Mefistofele*—Boito (1880)
1875	2	*Chilpéric*—Hérve
1883	2	*Heart and Hand*—Lecocq
1885	2	*Three Black Cloaks*—Hellmesberger
1883	2	*Donna Juanita*—Suppé
1883	2	*Trompette*—Bazin?
1886	1	*Linda di Chamounix*—Donizetti
1883	1	*Girola, or the Miller's Bride*
1886	1	*Princess Ida*—Sullivan
1888	1	*Carnival of Venice*—Thomas
1889	1	*Mynheer Jan*
1889	1	*Virginia*—Solomon
1890	1	*Yeoman of the Guard*—Sullivan
1893	1	*Pocahontas*—Brougham
1895	1	*Pagliacci*—Leoncavallo (1893)
1899	1	*Semiramide*—Rossini (1825)
1867	1	*Un ballo in maschero*—Verdi (1861)
1869	1	*Der Freischütz*—Weber (1824)
1871	1	*La Dame Blanche*—Boieldieu
1883	1	*La Petite Marie*—Lecocq
1893	1	*Clover*—Suppé
1883	1	*Le tour et la nuit*—Lecocq
1875	1	*La timbale d'argent*—Vasseur
1879	1	*Le Duc Raol de Parthenay*
1880	1	*Grand Bill*
1880	1	*Paul and Virginia*—Massé
1880	1	*Long Branch*
1881	1	*Aïda*—Verdi (1873)
1875	1	*Le Petit Faust*—Hervé
1878	1	*Barbe-bleue*—Offenbach
1877	1	*Les Bavards*—Offenbach

Notes

1. Lota M. Spell, "The Theatre in Texas before the Civil War," *The Texas Monthly* 3 (April 1930): 294.

2. Copies of both the collection of songs (*Texanische Lieder*) and the libretto by von Fallersleben, along with other information regarding Fuchs and von Fallersleben, can be found in a special collection in the Eugene C. Barker Texas History Center located on the campus of the University of Texas at Austin.

3. Lota M. Spell, *Music in Texas* (1936; reprint, New York: AMS Press, 1973). p. 101.

4. Joseph Gallegly, *Footlights on the Border: The Galveston and Houston Stage before 1900* (The Hague: Mouton 1962), p. 72. The author provides the date of performance as 21 March 1856.

5. Spell, *Music in Texas*, p. 101.

6. Gallegly, *Footlights*, p. 177–178.

7. *Tri-Weekly Telegraph*, Houston, Texas (13, 15, and 17 April 1867). As cited in Donald W. Pugh, *Music in Frontier Houston*, 1836–1876 (D.M.A. treatise: University of Texas at Austin, 1970), p. 91.

8. *Tri-Weekly Telegraph* (13 April 1867). As cited in Pugh, pp. 91–92.

9. Gallegly, *Footlights*, p. 179. Pugh (pp. 93–94) states that the Frederici opera troupe also presented *Martha* (15 January), *Fra Diavolo* (16 January: matinee), and . *Magic Flute* (16 January: evening) in Houston.

10. Spell, *Music in Texas*, p. 104. The author provides no further information regarding the Partido tour.

11. Gallegly, *Footlights*, p. 90.

12. David G. McComb, *Galveston: A History* (Austin: University of Texas Press, 1986), p. 107.

13. Gallegly, *Footlights*, p. 107. The author quotes from Emily Soldene, *My Theatrical and Musical Recollections* (London, 1897), p. 163.

14. Leonard Sanders, *How Fort Worth Became the Texasmost City* (Fort Worth, Texas: Amon Carter Museum of Western Art, 1973), p. 100.

15. "The Opera—First Performance of One in Dallas," *Dallas Weekly Herald* (13 February 1875).

16. "The Next Opera," *Dallas Weekly Herald* (2 February 1875).

17. Spell, *Music in Texas*, pp. 79, 104.

18. Ronald Davis, *A History of Opera in the American West* (Englewood Cliffs, 1965), p. 114.

19. Spell, *Music in Texas*, p. 104.

20. Mary Starr Barkley, *History of Travis County and Austin 1839–1899* (Waco, Texas: Texian Press, 1963), p. 319.

21. Spell, *Music in Texas*, p. 76.

22. Spell, *Music in Texas*, p. 75.

23. Spell, *Music in Texas*, p. 105.

24. Samuel Freudenthal, *El Paso, Merchant and Civic Leader* (El Paso, Texas: Texas Western College Press, 1965), p. 25.

Part Four
Puccini's America

David Belasco and Giacomo Puccini: Their Collaborations

SHELBY J. DAVIS

In 1900, when Giacomo Puccini was in London to superintend the English premiere of *Tosca*, Frank Neilson, then stage manager of Covent Garden, convinced him to take a night off and see the Belasco play, *Madame Butterfly*, which was playing at the Duke of York's Theatre. Puccini had finished *Tosca* in 1899 and was looking for a fresh, new subject for another opera, so he was receptive to Neilsen's suggestion and went to the play. Although Puccini understood very little English, he nonetheless seemed able to follow even the most minute details of the play and found himself totally enthralled with the little geisha girl and her tragic story. It is questionable that Puccini "rushed backstage with tears in his eyes" and begged to secure the operatic rights,[1] but it is possible he was excited enough to go backstage after the performance and congratulate Belasco. "I never believe[d] he did see *Madame Butterfly* that night. He only heard the music he was *going* to write," averred David Belasco.[2]

When Puccini returned to Italy, he consulted Giulio Ricordi, his publisher, about obtaining the rights to adapt *Madame Butterfly* to an opera. Ricordi was reluctant, remembering his recent disaster with Mascagni's *Iris*, which was also set in Japan,[3] but he complied with Puccini's request and wrote a letter asking permission from Belasco. While waiting for an answer, Puccini managed to find a translation of the original short story by John Luther Long, which he sent to Luigi Illica in March 1901,[4] cautioning Illica that Belasco's ending was different from the short story,[5] but asking whether or not he considered this to be a possible subject for his next opera. Illica was very enthusiastic about it.

On 7 April 1901 the agreement between Puccini and Belasco was finalized. In May Puccini sent a copy of the Italian translation to Giuseppe Giacosa, a librettist with whom he had successfully collaborated before (Giacosa had worked on *La Bohème* and *Tosca*), and Puccini began his work with zeal.

In order for his new opera to be as authentic as possible, Puccini visited the wife of the Japanese ambassador to Milan, Italy. She gave him recordings of Japanese music and helped him with some of the chosen names. He also studied Japanese customs, architecture, and religion, and in the spring of 1902 he met the Japanese actress Sado Jacco, who spoke Japanese to Puccini so that he could assimilate the inflections and instill them into his music.

No opera is created without some measure of difficulties, but this particular opera was nearly doomed when Puccini almost lost his life in a car accident in February 1903. He had been to Lucca to see a doctor about a throat ailment and, after a lengthy dinner with some friends, started back home. However, the night was foggy and the roads were icy. Puccini's chauffeur took a curve too fast just four miles out of Lucca, and the car skidded and crashed fifteen feet into a field. The other passengers, Elvira, Puccini's soon-to-be wife, and Tonio, his son, were only in shock, and the driver suffered a fractured thigh. But Puccini was trapped under the car. He was nearly poisoned by gas fumes by the time he was rescued and he had fractured his right shin.

On 1 March 1903, he wrote Illica, stating, "Carissimo Illica, this is from my bed, where I will remain, I am told, two months."[6] He was actually unable to return to his writing for nearly eight months because he was unable to sit at the piano. The leg was imperfectly set and another surgeon finally had to be summoned to reset it. Unfortunately, that surgeon suffered an accident and fractured his own thigh, and so was unable to come. Another doctor reset Puccini's leg, but the additional delay resulted in an extreme wastage of muscle, thus, Puccini walked with a painful limp for the rest of his life. Because of the muscle waste, a tumor developed within the ligaments, which further slowed the healing process. It was also discovered, through a urine test, that Puccini was diabetic. The doctor put Puccini, still bedridden, on a diet of five sugar-free meals a day with Karlsbad water and small doses of strychnine, in the hopes of curing his diabetes.[7] It did not.

Despite these trials, Puccini was back composing by September, and *Madama Butterfly*, the opera, was finished in December 1903. As usual, Puccini fell in love with Cio-Cio-San, but this love was pure and ethereal, compassionate: "Manon suffered for her own follies, Tosca for her jealousy, and even the gentle little Mimi had deserted her Rodolfo for a rich nobleman; only Cio-Cio-San was without sin, and her tragedy stirred him even more deeply than had the fate of her more culpable sister."[8]

Madama Butterfly premiered at La Scala, 17 February 1904. Puccini was convinced this was his greatest masterpiece and was so optimistic that he invited his son Tonio and his sister Ramelde and her daughter to watch with him in the wings.

The cast was brilliant: Rosina Storchio sang the pathetic little geisha, Giovanni Zenatello was cast as Pinkerton, and Giuseppe de Lucca as Sharpless; Lucien Jusseaume, a French theatrical painter, designed the sets; and Cleofonte Campanini conducted. Unfortunately, an anti-Puccini claque organized complete mayhem and disorder during the performance.[9] Shouts of "That's from Bohème!" and "He stole that from Mascagni!" and jeers during such crucial moments as the melodramatic introduction of the child (Trouble) at the end of the Letter scene in Act II filled the opera house. Tito Ricordi (Giulio's son) aimed for atmospheric realism with chirping birds at the end of the Vigil Scene and the coming of dawn, which attempt was met with a cacophony of barking, braying, and mooing.[10] Puccini appeared onstage at one point to try to restore order and was promptly jeered off. And at the conclusion of the performance, there was only glacial silence: no applause, no cheers or jeers, no shouts. Giulio Ricordi wrote, in his 17 February 1904 musical review:

> Growls, shouts, groans, laughter, giggling, the usual single cries of *bis*, designed specially to excite the audience still more: these sum up the reception given by the public of the Scala to Giacomo Puccini's new work. After this pandemonium, throughout which practically nothing could be heard, the public left the theatre as pleased as Punch. And one had never before seen so many happy, or such joyously satisfied, faces — satisfied as if by a triumph in which they all shared. . . . The performance given in the pit seems to have been as well organized as that on the stage, since it too began punctually with the beginning of the opera.[11]

The opera closed the next morning, and Puccini and the producers returned the money invested in the opera.

Of course, Puccini's opera was revolutionary. In the first place, the opera had what Italians considered an exotic setting—Japan.[12] That and the intercultural love affair (between the American, lieutenant and the Japanese, geisha) did not appeal to Italian tastes. Also, unorthodox orchestration projecting background and atmosphere through music, accentuating dramatic tension through altered harmonies, suspensions, oriental pentatonic scales, piercing

dissonances, unusual rhythm, and instrument choices were un-
acceptable to Italian ears.

Puccini's friends convinced him to rewrite some parts of the
opera. He deleted the more objectionable and exotic passages, enlarged the tenor role by adding an aria, and cut the extremely long
Act II in half at the Vigil scene (Puccini's original draft of *Madama
Butterfly* was written in two acts, the first act just under an hour,
but the second act an intolerable eighty minutes. Puccini had written it thusly so as not to detract from the beauty of the scene and
the faithfulness of Cio-Cio-San's vigil).[13] He cut the wedding scene
by eliminating Yakasude's drunken stupor and Cio-Cio-San's other
relatives lunging at the free liquor;[14] cuts were made in the Flower
Duet (which was one of the only pieces in the entire original opera
that was well received), and the Vigil lost a berceuse. Three
months later, on 28 May 1904 at the Teatro Grande in Brescia,
Madama Butterfly made a second appearance and triumphed. Demands of encores of Cio-Cio-San's Second Act aria "Un bel dil"
filled the house, the scenery earned a special round of applause,
and roars for Puccini to come on stage and receive his acclaim
rose to near hysteria. This audience was as Milanese as it was Bres-
cian, which prompted Puccini to confirm his belief that the opening night fiasco had been organized by his professional enemies.
Successive triumphs followed in South America, Paris, Cairo,
Washington, D.C., Covent Garden in England, and the New York
Metropolitan (11 February 1907).

Puccini was in New York for a Puccini festival during the Metropolitan premiere of *Madama Butterfly*. Although he enjoyed the
spectacle the Met presented — David Belasco had loaned his models, drawings, and blueprints from his dramatic version of *Madame
Butterfly* and sent his electricians to help create the atmosphere—
he did not like the performance of his opera; he considered it to
be without poetry, lacking the lyrical qualities for which he had
become famous, and Geraldine Farrar, who played Cio-Cio-San,
sang out of tune and her voice did not fill the house satisfactorily.
But his visit to New York had a second reason: he was searching
for a new subject for another opera. He had been toying with
Louij's *Conchita* or the unsuccessful libretto written by Luigi Illica
about Marie Antoinette, *The Austrian Woman*. Then Belasco, with
whom he had by this time become good friends, took him to see
The Girl of the Golden West. Puccini viewed the first part of the
play with little enthusiasm:"I've found some good hints in Belasco,
but nothing definitive or solid or complete. The atmosphere of the
Wild West attracts me, but in all the plays I have seen I found only

good scenes here and there. Never a clear, simple line of development . . . and sometimes in very bad taste and old-hat."[15]

However, in April, he wrote Belasco asking for a copy of the play. It was one of Puccini's closest friends, Sybil Seligman, who presented him with solid arguments that his next opera should be *The Girl of the Golden West*. This heroine would break from his normal tragic ones. Seligman also did not like Puccini's alternate choice, *The Austrian Woman*, mainly because there was no role for a hero (and she always felt there must a good hero role, preferably for a tenor).[16] Seligman's clinching argument was that the author, Belasco, was the same source as *Madama Butterfly*, and she felt that a revival collaboration would be nothing short of equal success. However, it was the scenic splendor of the American West[17] that finally convinced Puccini to write "the first Grand Opera based on an American theme."[18]

Sybil Seligman graciously provided Puccini with a translation of *Girl of the Golden West*, but he had to find his own team of librettists. Giuseppe Giascosa had died in 1906, so Tito Ricordi bypassed Illica and found Carlo Zangarini, a promising young dramatist who wrote fluent English and whose mother was from Colorado. Although Zangarini was able to capture much of the American taste through the folksongs and spoken word, he lacked Illica's creative spark, sense of operatic construction, and theatrical flair. Therefore, Puccini added Guelfo Civinini, a Tuscan poet with the missing theatrical instincts. Civinini revamped Zangarini's first two acts and wrote his own third act, based on the translation of the play Puccini had supplied him with. Thus, the libretto of *La Girl* was completed. (Oddly enough, Puccini generally called this opera "La Girl" and never "Fanciulla." The last two syllables—"ciulla(o)" in slang—meant "stupid."[19])

David Belasco's *Girl*, which premiered in Pittsburgh on 3 October 1905, was taken from a real-life incident his father, Humphrey, had once related to him. Humphrey was involved in the California Gold Rush of 1848–49, and there was a shortage of food in the mining camp. Someone whose luck was the poorest stole some food to give himself strength to find his way back east to his home. He was tracked down, spotted, and shot. Wounded, he made his way to Belasco's father's cabin and begged to be hidden, which the father consented to do. The sheriff arrived, and a game of poker ensued. Belasco's father and his cabinmate let the sheriff win to put him in a better mood but, just as he was turning to leave, a drop of blood fell on his handkerchief. He looked up and saw the face wildly staring down from the loft through the cracks.

Without a word, he drew his gun, fired, and left the cabin. With minor adjustment, this is very like the scene in Act II of Belasco's *Girl* play (and Puccini's *La Girl* opera). However, the poker game in the play and opera becomes a bid for Johnson's life and an attempt to put Jack Rance (the sheriff) into a better mood (because he had shot and only wounded Johnson). The Girl wins, thus saving Johnson's life for another, later confrontation with the sheriff.

When he discovered that *La Girl* was to be premiered at the Metropolitan in 1910, Belasco volunteered to stage the opera. His goal was to transfer all of the realism he had carefully imbued into the dramatic version to the operatic version. His first realization of the size of the job before him was the amount of tact and patience that was needed to deal with the temperamental peculiarities of the opera stars.

Among the group of Metropolitan stars . . . Enrico Caruso, who sang the role of Dick Johnson, the Stranger, is an Italian; Pasquale Amato, who was cast as Jack Rance, the gambler and Sheriff, is also an Italian, and Emmy Destinn, who impersonated the title character, the Girl, is a Bohemian.

At the first rehearsal of the chorus I discovered it would be necessary to change my stage-directing methods. Men and women by the scores and fifties would troop out on the stage, range themselves in rows, and become merely a background for the principals. Then, for no clear purpose, they would all begin to shrug their shoulders, grimace, and gesticulate with their hands. I resolved to undo all this at once. I located the ones who shrugged too much and either backed them up against trees and rocks or invented bits of "business" by which they were held by the others. When a chorus-singer became incorrigible in the use of his arms, I made him go through entire scenes with his hands in his pockets.

To form some idea how the stars intended to interpret their roles, I allowed them to go through the first rehearsal almost undirected. I found that, according to the convention of grand opera, they would step to the front of the stage and sing the music allotted to them with very little effort to impersonate character, always using the scenery merely as a background. I wondered what the revolt would be when I let them know I intended to do away with all such formalities and introduce the absolute "business" of the play, even if it were necessary for them to sing with their backs turned to the audience.

I was relieved when all of them promised to attempt the innovation, though they seemed dubious as to how my plans would work out. So I put Emmy Destinn behind the bar of the Polka Saloon and directed her to sing while she was serving drinks to the miners. It was hard for her to adapt herself to this byplay, which took place far back on the stage, for she had to readjust her voice to the new distances, but she soon succeeded.

Meanwhile I was wondering how Caruso would comply with my orders. In the first scene he had to stride into the Polka Saloon, fling his saddle on the table, and call for drinks, and with his back to the audience sing his opening song. He was entirely willing to adopt this method of making his entrance, although he must have realized it would prevent him from acknowledging the applause which invariably greets him. Later, when, wounded, after leaving the cabin of the Girl, he staggers back inside and climbs the steep ladder to the cabin loft, meanwhile singing all the time, Caruso seemed a little reluctant.

"It is difficult, for I must sing," he said, shrugging his shoulder.

"But even if Puccini has given you a song at just this point, you must suit the words to the action and the action to the words," I explained.

"Let me see you do it," he replied.

So I pretended I was Dick Johnson, staggered in with my wound, listened to the approach of the Sheriff's posse, and then climbed up the ladder, singing in a voice that must have made the very walls of the Metropolitan groan with agony.

Caruso saw the value of the realism in a flash. A dozen or more times at each rehearsal after that, in response to my directions, he would go through the scene and end by climbing up the ladder, all the time pouring forth tenor notes which were worth bagsful of gold. He was full of enthusiasm and was not content until he could play the scene as well as could reasonably have been expected of any accomplished actor on the dramatic stage. The prodigious amount of wasted song he poured into the dark recesses of the big, empty Metropolitan, as he good-naturedly toiled up and down the almost perpendicular ladder during these long rehearsals, would have sent his worshiping public into transports of delight.

I had more misgivings over the . . . scene in which the Girl, when she is insulted by the Sheriff, seizes a whisky-bottle to defend herself. Puccini . . . had given Emmy Destinn a very difficult aria to accompany it. I wondered what would happen when I had to tell her that, in order to carry out my conception of the realism of the scene, she would have to sing and struggle at the same time. I knew it was contrary to all the traditions of the grand-opera stage . . . [and] was not unaware of the temperamental idiosyncrasies of grand-opera stars when they are asked to changed their established methods. So I was . . . delighted to find her keen to adopt every suggestion I made.

I must have been exceedingly trying to them [Destinn, Caruso, and Amato] to change abruptly the operatic technique which had become almost second nature to them. But they seemed actually to enjoy making the experiment. Over and over again they would go through the [gambling] episode until they completely conquered it. . . . All the while Toscanini was scolding them from the conductor's stand and making them repeat the music.[20]

Puccini's *La Girl* was very innovative for its day, not only because it was the first grand opera set in America, but because of his integration of bits of American music ("Old Dog Tray," "Camptown Races"; the plaintive Native American lullaby sung by Wowkle, Minnie's Indian girl "housekeeper") and his new experimental composition techniques. The opera has no memorable arias because they are integrated into the surrounding music. It was considered "through-composed" like Wagner's operas, but *La Girl* sounded nothing like Wagner; Puccini used impressionistic elements such as Debussy's harmonizing techniques and Richard Strauss's orchestration, but it didn't sound like Debussy or Strauss. His tempos were violent contrasts in his attempt to depict the physical and emotional violence of the California Gold Rush days, and the orchestra supporting the composition was the largest he had ever written for in his attempt to embrace the entire panorama of the American West through music.

The 10 December 1910 premiere of *La fanciulla del West* was a great success. There were fifty-two curtain calls, which included separate bows from the composer, the author (Belasco), the conductor (Toscanini), and the Metropolitan general manager (Gatti-Casazza). Despite the enthusiasm of the opening night and equally successful premieres in Covent Garden (29 May 1911) and Rome (12 June 1911), this opera is considered one of Puccini's lesser works today. With the cast (Caruso, Destinn, and Amato) and Toscanini, the opera could not fail to be successful with the public, but the critics were guarded. Technically it was a masterpiece: Debussian in the treatment of harmonies and Straussian in orchestration, but lacking what Puccini was most noted for—the incandescent lyrical phrase. Richard Aldrich of the *New York Times* praised the production, but missed "the melodic lustre, outline, point and fluence" of Puccini's earlier works. He also noted the elaborately scored choral scenes of Act III (which anticipated *Turandot* in harmonic discord and emotional peak) and heard echoes of the sensuous magic of *Madama Butterfly* and *La Bohème*, but the opera was never wholly American nor wholly Italian and lacked memorable arias.[21] It was always a public pleaser, although after seeing it once or twice people's curiosity was satisfied. The music was either over-familiar or unrecognizable to the American ear, but "the illusion of opera stage was best when action was in another country and another age and another language."[22] Vincent Seligman expounded on his personal theory in *Puccini among Friends*. He stated that perhaps the opera did not succeed because it had a happy ending. The traditional "love story" with a "happy ending" denied Puccini's ability for his power of suggestion. Minnie did not touch Puccini's heart — he did not fall in love with her — therefore, he felt no sorrow or justification, which was Puccini's very essence of life.[23]

The collaborations of David Belasco and Giacomo Puccini united two very different geniuses from two different genres with similar ideas of what to present and how to present drama. Puccini believed "the basis of an opera is the subject and its dramatic treatment," and to be "sparing with words and try to make the incidents clear and brilliant to the eye rather than the ear."[24] His librettos were very stage-worthy and offered him opportunities to use the full power of his imagination. He did not aim for the Wagnerian music-drama, but rather *musical drama*, and he felt strongly that all aspects of the stage (singing, acting, declamation, facial expression, gesture and movement, costumes, scenery, and lighting) should be used throughout to create the maximum effect. Puccini held the story line almost reverently as his chief means of holding the spectator's attention through music. He insisted on *l'evidenza della situazione*, the enabling of the spectator to follow the drama without understanding the words. (*Tosca and Madama Butterfly* were two plays Puccini saw in foreign languages before adapting them to the opera stage. Although he knew almost no other language outside of Italian, the plays were spectacular enough, physically and emotionally, to make him understand nearly every detail and nuance).[25] He was truly considered a man of the theater.

David Belasco was also truly considered a man of the theater. He attempted at all times to give the audience a sense of the period of the play on the stage. Settings were created to make the audience feel they were in the place and to feel the passage of time. Lighting was not just lighting, it was specific. For example, in the play *The Girl of the Golden West*, he did not want just sunlight but California sunlight. In *Madame Butterfly*, the vigil scene lasted fourteen minutes, so that night, complete with a star-filled sky, passing into day, with early songbirds, would be so gradual as to make the audience actually feel part of the scene. His drama of emotion was depicted on the physical stage first, and through the actors second, to open the heart as well as the eye, just as Puccini worked for emotion through spectacle for the eye first, then through his music to open the soul.

Both of these men attained their goals through *La fanciulla del West*: Belasco, through his transfer of realism from the dramatic stage to the opera stage, and Puccini through his transfer of the spoken word to the sung word. Both of these men attained a lasting friendship and working relationship because, although neither spoke the other's language, each nevertheless spoke the same tongue through his chosen art. Belasco and Puccini's collaboration on *La fanciulla del West* prompted future opera stage directors and composers to strive for more realism of character, both in the physical presence and in the evolution of the character through music.

Notes

1. Stanley Jackson, *Monsieur Butterfly: The Story of Giacomo Puccini* (New York: Stein & Day, 1974), p. 110.

2. Ibid.

3. Vincent Seligman, *Puccini among Friends* (New York: Benjamin Blom, 1971), p. 100.

4. Luigi Illica was onehalf of the libretto team, the other being Giuseppe Giacosa, that Puccini used up through *Madama Butterfly*, when Giacosa died.

5. In the short story by John Luther Long, Cho-Cho-San does not die. Her maid enters right after she has attempted suicide, binds up the wound, and with the child and Cho-Cho-San leaves the house before Pinkerton comes back. In the adapted play by David Belasco, Cho-Cho-San manages to succeed in slitting her throat just as Kate, Pinkerton's wife, drags him in. Puccini, ever the melodramatic one, found the music composing in his head to be much more receptive to Belasco's ending than the original.

6. Jackson, *Monsieur Butterfly*, p. 112.

7. Ibid.

8. Seligman, *Puccini among Friends*, p. 52.

9. Puccini's rivals Leoncavallo and Mascagni, although not jealous, had claques who were of Puccini's fame and genius. Puccini also made the supreme mistake of coldshouldering these particular claques, which resulted in the fiasco of opening night. Jackson, *Monsieur Butterfly*, p. 119.

10. Ibid., p. 120.

11. Giuseppe Adami, *Letters of Giacomo Puccini* (New York: AMS Press, 1971), pp. 137–138.

12. Only three known operas were set in the Far East: Mascagni's *Iris*, which is rarely sung today, was set in Japan, as was Puccini's *Madama Butterfly*. The third opera, also written by Puccini, *Turandot*, was set in Peking, China. David Ewen, *Encyclopedia of the Opera* (New York: Hill & Wang, 1955).

13. Maestro Toscanini, when looking over the manuscript, believed Puccini had made a dreadful blunder by making his opera only two acts long: the first was weak and long, the second stronger but nearly an hour and a half. "I thought at once this length is impossible. For Wagner, yes! For Puccini, no!" Jackson, *Monsieur Butterfly*, p. 117.

14. These scenes were not in David Belasco's play. Puccini found them in his translation of the short story by John Luther Long. John Luther Long, *Madame Butterfly, Purple Eyes, Etc.* (New York: Garrett Press, 1968).

15. William Weaver, *Puccini: The Man and His Music* (London: Hutchinson, 1977), p. 73.

16. Puccini often teased Sybil Seligman, saying that she liked *Girl of the Golden West* because there was a perfect part for her idol, Caruso. Seligman, *Puccini among Friends*, p. 131.

17. In August 1907 Puccini wrote to Giulio Ricordi: "This is it! *The Girl* promises to become a second *Bohème*, but stronger, bolder, vaster. I have an idea for a grand scene, a clearing in the California forest with colossal trees, but requires eight or ten horses as supers." Weaver, *Puccini, the Man and his Music*, p. 73.

18. Lise-Lone Marker, *David Belasco: Naturalism in the American Theatre* (New Jersey: Princeton University Press, 1975), p. 139.

19. Adami, *Letters of Giacomo Puccini*, p. 180, Letter 104, Footnote 2.

20. David Belasco, *The Theatre through Its Stage Door* (1919, reprint, New York: Benjamin Blom, 1969), pp. 101–104.

21. Jackson, *Monsieur Butterfly*, p. 191.

22. Seligman, *Puccini Among Friends*, p. 199.

23. Ibid., p. 202.

24. *Grove's Dictionary of Music and Musicians* (London: Macmillan, 1980), 15: 435–36.

25. Ibid., p. 435.

Uncle Giacomo's Cabin: David Belasco's Direction of *La fanciulla del West*

ROXANA STUART

It has become accepted in theater history to praise David Belasco as a great innovator in directing and design while downgrading his contribution as a playwright; and in musical circles Puccini is often regarded as a composer with an undeniable instinct for theater but with a crude musical palette—"not one of the greats, but within his own limits . . . he worked honorably."[1] It will be the contention of this paper that both men have been underappreciated, perhaps as a direct result of their wide popular appeal. Belasco's play *Girl of the Golden West*, now dismissed as melodramatic hokum by most critics, became one of Puccini's so-called lesser operas, *La fanciulla del West*. An analysis of the stage history of both works, with particular emphasis on Belasco's methods as the stage director of the premiere productions of both *Girl* and *Fanciulla*, will at the same time explore the fine qualities of each work and suggest that both deserve higher niches in the current theatrical and operatic canons.

Melodrama itself is an undervalued genre—indeed the word has become a pejorative—although it is acknowledged that Belasco, one of the last practitioners, raised the form to new heights of naturalism and subtlety. *Girl*, which opened in Pittsburgh at the New Belasco Theatre on 3 October, 1905 and in New York at the Belasco on 14 November, 1905, was one of the last and most sophisticated. It is considered the best of the Western melodramas, obviously a peculiarly American genre. Some precursors were Belasco's own *Rose of the Rancho* and *The Girl I Left Behind Me*, Augustus Thomas's *Arizona*, Alonzo Delano's *A Live Woman in the Mines*, and Bret Harte's *Two Men of Sandy Bare* and his short stories "The Luck of Roaring Camp" and "Miggles," which, like *Girl*, features a woman bartender and is based on a real person who ran the Polka Saloon in Marysville in 1853.

Belasco, who was often sued for plagiarism but never lost, was quite resentful of any suggestion that his plot was unoriginal: "My youth surged on me while I worked," he wrote. "Why, I know the period of Forty-nine as I know my alphabet, and there are things in my *Girl of the Golden West* truer than many of the incidents in Bret Harte."[2] Like his character Dick Johnson, Belasco claimed to have been nearly hanged after being mistaken for a horse thief in Virginia City, where he was acting at Piper's Opera House during the Comstock Lode boom; and the incident of the dripping blood that closes Act Two was an adventure of his father's when he worked at the Cariboo Mines in British Columbia. Whatever the truth is, he clearly drew upon his experiences and memories to create the atmosphere and romance of his native California, and for Belasco, atmosphere was the soul of a production. The main function of a director, in his view, was creating atmosphere:

> One must treat the play as a human being; it must laugh at certain points, at others it must be sad; lovers must come together in certain lights: and all its changing moods must be blended harmoniously. For the completed play is impressive and fulfills its purpose only to the extent that it carries an audience back to its own experiences. If my productions have had an appealing quality, it is because I have kept this important fact constantly in mind and have tried, while concealing the mechanism of my scenes, to tug at the hearts of my audiences.[3]

The Girl, Minnie (Smith or Falconer, she isn't sure which), was played by Blanche Bates, a seasoned veteran of Belasco's company, who had created his Madame Butterfly, Yo-San in *Darling of the Gods*, and Cigarette in *Under Two Flags*. Johnson was played by Robert Hilliard, and Rance by the great character actor Frank Keenan. Outstanding features of the production were the opening panorama, the Act Two blizzard, and the sunrise that closes the play. Many writers have commented on the cinematic quality of the opening device: several hundred yards of canvas which rolled vertically on drums placed across the proscenium, showing first the Sierra Nevada, then Cloudy Mountain, the Girl's Cabin, and finally the Polka Saloon; a dissolve (by back-lit scrim?); and we are in the interior of the saloon. This remarkable sequence served as a visual prologue and is the theatrical equivalent of a cinematic pannng shot.

Every melodrama has a sensation scene, and the realism Belasco achieved with his snowstorm was so meticulously detailed that the more usual effects of trains and buildings aflame paled in comparison. He used thirty-two stagehands working various machines (blowers, snow bags, gauzes, salt sprayers, wind machines, air tanks, thunder, and set shakers) who were led by a technical director who functioned like a conductor. The powerful presence of nature thus evoked, the snowstorm assumed the importance of a character in the play. As described by William Winter:

> Throughout the progress of the action, intensifying the sense of desolation, dread and terror, the audience heard the wild moaning and shrill whistle of the gale, and, at the moments as the tempest rose to a climax of fury, could see the fine-powdered snow driven in tiny sprays and eddies through every crevice of the walls and the very fabric of the cabin quiver and rock beneath the impact of terrific blasts of wind— long and shrieking down the mountainsides before they struck—while in every fitful pause was audible the sharp click-click of freezing snow driving on wall and window.[4]

Belasco wrote that he spent $5000 and worked three months on a sunset effect, only to discard it and try again: "It was a good sunset, but it was not Californian. Afterward I sold it to the producers of *Salomey Jane* and it proved very effective.[5] Daniel Gerould, in many ways a great admirer of Belasco, pokes some good-natured fun at this passage: "Here we have a fine illustration of American ingenuity and enterprise in the fabrication of melodramatic illusion. Every sunset has its pricetag! . . . If the final product fails to match the precise hues of the sun as it sinks below the Sierra Nevada, it can be sold to a competitor for use in another play."[6] (If I may add a facetious note, I would point out that perhaps the first sunset effect looked wrong to Belasco because his script actually calls for a sun*rise*.)

Verisimilitude—realism carried to such a degree that it becomes a form of spectacle, masterful and innovative lighting, meticulous attention to details of costuming, stage business, grouping and ensemble work, and authentic music—was one of the marks of Belasco's directorial style. Popular songs of the Gold Rush era—"Old Dog Tray," "Camptown Races," "Rosalie the Prairie Flower," and "Coal Oil Tommy"—played not by the customary pit orchestra but by onstage musicians and singers, and woven believably into the action, not only contributed powerfully to the atmosphere but served to underscore the themes of loneliness and exile, the evils of gambling, and the redemptive power of love.

Although he spoke no English, perhaps Giacomo Puccini was filled with a longing for home by the songs of the lonely cowboys and inspired to create an opera: "Che faranno i vecchi miei / Là lontano, là lontano, / Che faranno?" is a melody that breaks one's heart with homesickness, wherever that home may be.

In January 1907, six years after the collaboration on *Madama Butterfly*, Puccini was in New York to supervise several productions at the Metropolitan Opera and saw a performance of Belasco's *Girl*. He told reporters of his enthusiasm and wrote to the playwright asking him to write the libretto himself.

Puccini's longtime librettist Giuseppe Giacosa had died in 1906, and in 1908–1909 his wife Elvira suffered a psychotic episode, accusing a servant girl of seducing Puccini. The girl committed suicide, and Elvira was tried and convicted of defamation of character. This and other sorrows prevented him from commencing work on *La Girl*, or *mia Girl* as he usually called it, until 1909. The score was completed in July 1910.

Whatever Belasco had sent to the composer by way of a libretto, something rather different and inferior to the stage play emerged from the hands of the new librettists Guelfo Civinini and Carlo Zangarini, who reduced the script to a much more conventional, sentimental, and artificial work. Belasco's Polka had become a Waltz. Belasco's Girl loses her rough exterior and becomes sweet, innocent, and much too motherly. One glaring example is the Act One curtain "Ha detto . . . Comme ha detto? Un viso d'angelo! . . . Ah! . . . ,"[7] contrasted with the play's "He says . . . he says . . . (*Sentimentally*) I have the face of an angel. (*A little pause, then turning her face away*) Oh, Hell!"[8]

Belasco's reaction, when he saw the "improvements" in his script, has not been recorded. As a practical man of the theater he held his opinions close and proceeded to stage the piece at the Met using the naturalistic methods he had developed in the theater. Giulio Gatti-Casazza, the Met's manager, had assembled a spectacular cast under Arturo Toscanini's musical direction. Emmy Destinn as Minnie (the Girl), Enrico Caruso as Johnson, and Pasquale Amato as Rance. The polyglot company included ten Italians, two Germans, one Czech, one Pole, one Spaniard, one Frenchman, one American, and several unclassified. Assisted by an interpreter, one Signor Viviani, Belasco proceeded to assign bits of realistic business to the singers, who were accustomed to turning front and delivering every aria in direct address, and who seldom condescended to impersonate anyone but themselves.

The problem of teaching singers to act is a complex one; Stanislavsky became fascinated by the mechanical and psychological difficulties involved and spent the last years of his life trying to solve them. Many singers feel that as soon as they start to feel emotion, the voice chokes up; others lack the self-confidence to tear their eyes from the conductor and feel the *only* task is to send the voice to the back of the house, resisting any temptation to turn profile and glance at their scene partners. For *Fanciulla* Caruso was asked to sing his opening phrases entering with his back to the audience (an unnatural proceeding few tenors today would accede to), and to climb a ladder during one aria. Destinn had to sing while she tended bar and washed out glasses, probably for the first time in her life.

The greatest difficulties, however, were in dealing with the chorus; the problem, amusingly enough, was hamminess and un-motivated gesticulating:

> Men and women by the scores and fifties would troop out on the stage, range themselves in rows and . . . then for no clear purpose they would all begin to shrug their shoulders, grimace, and gesticulate with their hands. I resolved to undo all this at once. I located the ones who shrugged too much and either backed them up against trees and rocks or invented bits of "business" by which they were held by the others. When a chorus-singer became incorrigible in the use of his arms I made him go through entire scenes with his hands in his pockets. Little by little I tamed this wriggling crowd until they themselves began to understand the value of repose.[9]

There is no record of whether Belasco was able to maintain an amiable atmosphere at rehearsals, but he had two strong suppor-ters in Toscanini and Puccini. Toscanini told a reporter from the *New York Times*, "The music of the opera is Italian, and that we understand, but the play is American and not only American but Mr. Belasco's. We want every detail to be correct, because other theatres in the future must copy this production. And Mr. Belasco is the man to initiate us into these details."[10]

Puccini, who upon his arrival insisted on the use of eight horses for the finale, wrote to his wife, "The opera emerges splendid-ly. . . . Belasco has attended all rehearsals with great love and in-terest. Caruso is magnificent in his part, Destinn, not bad but she needs more energy. Toscanini, the zenith! . . . But how difficult it is, this music and the staging!"[11]

The premiere took place on 10 December, 1910 and was one of the great nights in the history of the house. Ticket prices had been doubled and, despite efforts to thwart scalpers, were resold at thir-ty times their printed value. There were fifty-three curtain calls, and when the composer, the conductor, and the director appeared, the ovation was tremendous and Puccini was crowned with a silver wreath.[12] One critic remarked, "The result of Mr. Belasco's work was apparent, for a more realistic production has never been seen on the Metropolitan stage. Never has an operatic mob acted with such spirit as did this gang of miners and cowpunchers in the last act: and all through the production there were just those little touches that stamp a Belasco production."[13]

The English premiere followed in a few months on 29 May 1911 at Covent Garden with Emmy Destinn repeating the role of Minnie. The first Italian performance was in Rome at the Costanzi Theatre on 12 July 1911, again with Toscanini and with Amato as Rance and Eugenia Burzio as Minnie.

Despite its auspicious premiere, *Fanciulla* has become the most neglected of Puccini's mature operas (excepting *La rondine*, which is more nearly an operetta). The first large-scale grand opera on an American theme, it has never been popular here, and the derisive phrase "horse opera" is an apt description of the low esteem in which it is held by many. Belasco, courtesy of the Italian librettists, is held to have written an old-fashioned, almost funny melodrama, full of crude passion and violence.

But the play is admirable in many respects: believable, colloquial dialogue full of flavorful regionalisms and rhythms, subtlety, irony, and folksy comedy. For example, melodrama is well-known to be full of mother reverence, but the Girl's earliest memory of her mother is fond but not pietistic: her mother is dealing a hand of poker and playing footsie under the table with her husband. Belasco's use of irony here is unusual, and the sexual knowingness is years ahead of its time.

Most melodramas have a villain, and the characters are either purely good or purely evil. *Girl* has a villain who *is* the hero, a man with a double identity; Ramerrez/Johnson is a divided person, full of self-doubt and self-contempt, a wonderful part for an actor with imagination and depth. The play even takes a condemning look at the racist laws against foreign miners in California during the 1850s Gold Rush, which forced many Mexicans, Indians, Blacks, and Orientals to become outlaws to live. The "racial" taboo that the Girl violates in choosing Johnson is completely lost in the opera.

Finally, Puccini's Girl is a very watered-down version of Belasco's, who is an American-style New Woman—she drinks, swears, rides a horse, carries a gun, runs a business, plays cards, and cheats when she has to. Sexually aware and book-ignorant, tough-minded and tough-talking, she sees what she wants and goes after it, a true female protagonist who initiates the action at every turn, controls her destiny, and wins the male love-object. This was fresh

and new when Belasco wrote it, and has only become cliche by
repeated stealings from it through the years.

Even the more pallid version of the character in Puccini's opera
is an extraordinary contrast to the typical operatic heroine, whose
mental resources seldom suggest any course of action to her but to
kill herself. Renata Tebaldi, the beloved golden voice who was
never noted for her acting, called Minnie her favorite role. She
must have enjoyed surviving the final curtain for a change. But
plays and operas with female protagonists have notoriously been
marginalized by the critics; they are almost as disreputable as
female authors and composers.

And lest we begin to denigrate the opera in order to praise the
play, let us admit *Fanciulla* has its own distinct magnificence.
"Ch'ella mi creda libero e lontano" is a tenor aria which ranks with
"Nessun dorma" and "E lucevan le stelle" in its power to tear out
the hearts of hearers. Under the influence of Debussy's *Pelléas et
Mélisande*, Puccini in this period was experimenting with the
whole-tone scale, which permeates the score beginning with the
first notes and paints atmosphere with a mastery that matches Belasco's. The musical handling of the poker game is thrilling,
psychologically acute, and full of dramatic tension. The much-
despised librettists quite rightly cut most of the weak third act, and
the farewell chorus that ends the opera is beyond praise, except to
say that this purportedly happy ending evokes in this listener
mysterious bittersweet emotions of homesickness, the sorrow of
parting with old friends, a haunting sense of nameless loss, hope
and fear of the unknown, and just "riding off into the sunset."
Minnie loved her independence: now she grows up, becomes an
adult woman, takes on care and the pain of love—"Mai piu ritor-
nerai, / Mai più, mai più . . . "[14]

Bill Nye has written of Wagner's music that it is better than it
sounds: Donald Grout write that Puccini's music "often sounds
better than it is, owing to the perfect adjustment of means to ends.
He had . . . the Italian gift of knowing how to write effectively for
singers, an unusually keen ear for instrumental colors . . . and a
poetic imagination excelling in the evocation of dreamlike, fantas-
tic moods."[15]

Finally, Catherine Clément suggests some reasons for *Fanciulla*'s
popularity and unpopularity:

> [Let us] look beyond the movie screen where the steely blue gaze and
> phallocratic chins of American heroes parade in your memory [of

Western movies]. Listen with your inmost heart. Look: she is playing cards with her lover. She almost shouts when she lays her cards on the table. Then she grabs her wounded lover by the waist and, in a sublime gesture, while the music writhes in pain, she drags him to the hideout. But above all . . . she does it when she has won the hand—three aces and two of a kind—finally, we have the flawless exception, and happiness dearly won. They go, the bandit and the girl, off into the rising sun, and the sky resounds with the cheers that go with them.

Is it because this opera . . . shows a woman out to win her love, a woman who wins painlessly, without defeat, without coming undone? This opera is not particularly popular. It would take the greatest sensibility to women's defeated soul to manage to succeed with this masterpiece. It would take someone intimately accustomed to feminine pain to love a woman to the point of transforming her into a tender and victorious warrior woman. It would take, oh, role reversal, Giacomo Puccini, and Mimi's revenge. Minnie, the girl, is the rising sun: contrasted to her nocturnal sisters, she is the day that does not close on an act of mourning. Opera lovers do not like this antiheroine. She is made for tomorrow. Tomorrow she will set out, lit by the brilliance of her victory.[16]

Notes

1. Donald J. Grout, *A Short History of Opera* (New York: Columbia University Press, 1947), p. 441.

2. William Winter, *The Life of David Belasco* (New York: Moffat Yard, 1918), II: 205.

3. David Belasco, *The Theatre Through Its Stage Door*, ed. Louis V. Defoe (New York: Harper and Bros., 1919). Reprinted in *Directing the Play*, eds. Toby Cole and Helen Krich Chinoy (New York: Bobbs-Merrill, 1953), p. 99.

4. Winter, *Life of Belasco*, pp. 206–7.

5. Belasco, *Stage Door*, pp. 65–67.

6. Daniel C. Gerould, "The Americanization of Melodrama," in *American Melodrama* (New York: Performing Arts Journal Publications, 1983), p. 24–25.

7. Guelfo Civinini and Carlo Zangarini, libretto. *La fanciulla del West* by Giacomo Puccini, translation uncredited (London Records A4338, undated), Act I.

8. David Belasco, *Girl of the Golden West*, in *American Melodrama*, ed. Daniel C. Gerould (New York: Performing Arts Journal Publications, 1983), p. 209.

9. Belasco, *Stage Door*, p. 103.

10. *New York Times*, 5 December 1910.

11. George Marek, *Puccini* (New York: Simon and Schuster, 1951), p. 263.

12. Craig Timerlake, *David Belasco, the Bishop of Broadway* (New York: Library Publishers, 1954), p. 292.

13. Montrose Moses, *The American Dramatist*, quoted in Lise-Lone Marker,

David Belasco: Naturalism in the American Theatre (Princeton: Princeton University Press, 1975), p. 158.

14. *Fanciulla* libretto, Act II.

15. Grout, *Short History of Opera*, p. 441.

16. Catherine Clément, *Opera, or the Undoing of Women*, trans. Betsey Wing (Minneapolis: University of Minnesota Press, 1988), pp. 94–95.

Puccini's *Fanciulla* as Exemplar for American Composers

THOMAS WARBURTON

Having mounted the Met's first world premiere with Puccini's *La fanciulla del West* late in 1910, Giulio Gatti-Casazza labored earnestly for the next quarter century to promote opera by American composers.[1] It may well be that it was Gatti-Casazza's willingness to produce many new works that accounted for the fact that so many American composers "tried their hands" at opera during the period of his management. Gatti-Casazza's years also saw a period of zeal to define a special category to be called American opera. Journalists recognized early that the presence of English-language and American singers in productions was essential to give opera an American identity.[2] Already in 1911, a group whose leaders included Charles Henry Meltzer and the baritone David Bispham had formed the National Society for the Promotion of Grand Opera in English. The group not only advocated the composition of new works to English librettos, but it also pressed for translating existing works into English. Eventually, characters, subjects, and locale would prove to be significant enough national qualities in opera to give rise to a book by H. Earle Johnson entitled *Operas on American Subjects*.[3] Johnson lists all operas with ties to the Western Hemisphere, including *Fanciulla*, whether the works are by American composers or not. In addition to setting and subject, the quotation of native tunes also was recognized as a means of imparting an unmistakable American identity to a work.

An article from *The Nation* in 1911, on the other hand, offers an important caution to American composers of opera. In the opinion of the anonymous writer, *Natoma* possessed two of the quintessential qualities of an American opera—a native atmosphere and familiar national melodies. Then the writer raises the inevitable question: "But, is it a masterwork?"[4] The writer here wants the work to be both an American opera *and* a good opera. Many native composers during Gatti-Casazza's years may well have associ-

ated their works with the United States as they used the English
language or as they quoted familiar native tunes; however, many
of them lacked fundamental experience in writing for the stage.
Because the operas lacked essential dramatic strength, the works
were frequently ignored, some even unproduced even when considering the possible interest of American elements.

Despite the seeming ease with which many writers were setting
down the criteria for an American opera, nationality in opera was
actually not so simple a quality to define. In 1911, less than six
months after the premiere of *Fanciulla*, a writer for *The Nation*
noted, "The most German of all operas, 'Tristan and Isolde,' has
an Irish subject, and Gounod's choice of Goethe's 'Faust' and
Shakespeare's 'Romeo and Juliet' did not prevent his best two
operas from being as French as French can be."[5] That same writer
might well have added that *La fanciulla del West*, even with its setting in America's golden west of the mid-nineteenth century, remained as Italian as any of Puccini's other operas. It then may
seem at first surprising that an ostensibly Italian opera by Puccini
might be an exemplar for American opera.

Puccini's use of American elements in *Fanciulla* was not simply a
mannerism of national quality; rather, that use became essential to
the dramatic effect, as will be shown. It is the dramatic context for
native elements that helps establish Puccini's *Fanciulla* as exemplar
and enables us through comparison to comprehend the dramatic
strengths of American operas. Indeed, in many cases the lack of
dramatic substance is revealed. After reviewing the dramatic and
national qualities of *Fanciulla*, it will be my purpose to examine a
number of American operas to assess their significant dramatic use
of native materials and their resulting dramatic effectiveness.

The images of miners and the "occidente d'oro," the "terra
maledetta" of David Belasco's play *The Girl of the Golden West*,
are established clearly by musical associations at the very beginning of Puccini's opera. The seductive dotted rhythms at the close
of the brief prelude suggest the Spanish habanera. As the miners
enter the Polka Saloon and light the lamps, the orchestra plays a
hearty ragtime. The speech of the miners is colored with occasional
English words, "Goodby" or "All right." They even sing "Do-
dah," syllables associated with Foster's "Camptown Races." These
syllables sound against the ragtime music, which actually is similar
in rhythmic quality and spirit to Foster's own song. This is a frontier music hall. Later, in the opening of the second act, Puccini
mimics Indian music in Wowkle's lullaby to her baby.

Beyond these outward native symbols of words and music types is a native element that is more fundamental to the drama. Also early in the first act, Jake Wallace sings a song of longing that is taken up at length by all the miners present. The title of the nostalgic song has been identified variously as "Echoes from Home," or "The Old Dog Tray." It is not Foster's song of the same title, although Jake's melody is similar in musical character to the one by Foster. As demonstrated by Allan Atlas, it is actually a Zuñi melody used by Carlos Troyer in his composition "Festive Sun-Dance," which had been published in 1904 by the Wa-Wan Press.[6] The song of nostalgia and longing is a foil for the roughness of the miners who join with Jake. The lyrical quality heard here recurs through the opera to underscore the more intimate and nostalgic moments of the opera. For example, we hear this lyric quality later in Act I as Rance himself sings of having left his own home. We hear it as Minnie first greets Dick Johnson or when she reads to the miners from the Bible.

The very melody itself returns at the very end of the opera as the miners bid farewell to their beloved Minnie. This song, with its lyric, folklike qualities becomes an even larger symbol for the miners and their devotion to Minnie, who has been their "mother," who has kept them in touch with their home by helping them to write letters home. It is quite possibly their loving devotion to Minnie that has allowed them to be dissuaded finally by her from hanging Dick Johnson, alias the bandit Ramerrez. Their longing for home and their consequent devotion to Minnie become united, expressed in a lyric, nostalgic folklike melody both in the beginning and at the end of the opera. What may have been initially a self-conscious reference to locale, an American remembrance, in the end achieves a larger significance as it seems to impel the action of the drama.[7]

Puccini's adoption of native elements may well be through assimilation more than by actual quotation. Both Ernst Krause and Mosco Carner have suggested a possible source for the Indian melody, but no specific melody has indeed been discovered. While Krause, Carner, and others have identified the title "Echoes from Home" for the miner's melody, a purposeful search for such a song has been unsuccessful despite Krause's assertion that its origin is around 1850.[8] Indeed, the melody recalls Foster's nostalgic melodies such as "Old Dog Tray" or "Old Folks at Home." However, Puccini may have actually created a subtle conceit by only suggesting the quality of a remembered tune, not quoting one directly. There may be no specific melody that is remembered; the miners may be remembering a melody inaccurately, one that has been corrupted by loss of time and place and thus not really identifiable. Thus, Puccini's native symbols merge into his larger musical fabric.

While it is not the best-known of Puccini's operas, it is surely an understatement that the survival of *La fanciulla del West* stems from its essential dramatic effect no matter what its national setting. We remember the drama borne of the love triangle—Minnie, Rance, and Dick Johnson. Having defined briefly the role of American characteristics in Puccini's opera, we will now examine a small number of the American operas whose settings are specifically Western. The purpose of this examination will be to describe the role of American setting and to evaluate the essential dramatic structure, whether as *part of* or as *apart from* that American setting. Such a set of comparisons may help explain why these and other operas failed to survive while Puccini's opera has survived.

Of all the operas with Western settings, the one with a subject closest to Puccini's opera is Quinto Maganini's opera tetralogy *The Argonauts*, written between 1920 and 1934. Maganini's opera portrays the lives of mid-nineteenth-century California gold miners, inspired in general by Bret Harte's stories.[9] The first opera introduces the characters as they board the stagecoach at Sutter's Mill to travel to the mines in the mountains of Calaveras County, California. Here, Maganini confirms national identity with frequent quotations from Stephen Foster's songs, usually complete tunes, sometimes even several verses. In the first and fourth operas, new words are written for the tune of "Oh, Susannah" to introduce each of the main characters, the chorus repeated as each character is welcomed by the crowd. Kentucky Jack sets the scene in Act II of the second opera *Tennessee's Partner* as he sings "Oh, Susannah" still to new words. "Oh, Susannah" returns in the fourth opera as the crowd gathers on Christmas Eve in the "Blazing Star" at Angels. In the third opera, Kentucky Jack remembers his home by singing "My Old Kentucky Home." Are we far from Puccini's Jake Wallace here? But these familiar tunes are just that, part of the scenery, the local color. In fact, the tunes cover significantly large sections of each opera, making the whole a series of tableaux, more a musical pageant than an opera.

Moreover, the quoted music does not consist only of native materials. In the first opera, when Maria introduces herself, she reveals her devotion to Christ. Her melody is appropriated from the top line of one of one of Josquin des Prés's four-part settings of the "Ave Maria." Finding himself in love with Maria, Loran asks that Maria teach him to pray, and he follows her in canonic imitation with one of the other voice lines from Josquin's motet. These two chief characters of the tetralogy are united not by a familiar American music, but rather by a music well removed from national identity in time and place. Here, in an American opera, it is not an "American" tune that brings focus to the drama, rather it is an ancient one.

Not only is the American identity of the opera cycle perhaps weakened by the quotation from Josquin, but the profusion of quotations, whether foreign or native, signals the lack of central, pervasive development of character in the operas as a whole. For example, we see Loran and Maria only briefly again in the fourth opera and then scarcely long enough to see Maria jilt Loran. These characters are part of the scene, not really a focal element in it. Like so many of his compatriots, Maganini was inexperienced in affairs of the stage, and his urge to create an American work here perhaps overshadowed the more fundamental urge to involve the characters in a fundamentally dramatic way.

Ernst Bacon's opera *A Tree on the Plains* may well be the most self-conscious American opera from the first half of this century. It was originally commissioned by the League of Composers and completed in 1940.[10] Unlike the other operas discussed here, Bacon's opera does contain passages of spoken dialogue both accompanied and unaccompanied. According to Paul Horgan's libretto, published fully in the *Southwest Review* in 1943, none of the characters should "sound like 'opera' singers. There are no arias; plenty of songs; much declarative melody for dialogue; some crooning."[11] In centering on the maturing of Corrie Mae, the daughter of the homesteaders, it parallels the setting of Copland's *The Tender Land* composed some fifteen years later. The "tree" of the title becomes a symbol for Corrie.

Each of the four parts of the opera represents a different part of a single day as well as a stage in Corrie's life. Morning (God and Death) is the time of her grandfather's funeral and features a spiritual. Noon (The Earth) introduces us to Lou, the cowboy in love with Corrie, and Buddy, Corrie's brother who has returned briefly from his wanderings to the city. Evening and Night (The Lovers) centers on Lou and Corrie and features both an evening hymn and a bluesy love song. Buddy and Lou sing "Frog went a-courtin'" early in this part. Daylight (The Next Morning) sees the lovers married. Like Maganini's *The Argonauts*, Bacon's opera is a series of tableaux.

One of the important Americanisms in the opera is the presence of jazz. It is associated principally with Buddy, who, having come in contact with urban life, also plays the clarinet. In fact, he actual-

ly plays the clarinet himself on stage. Near the end of the third part
are two brief musical numbers for Buddy, one a bluesy nocturne
with clarinet solo. Just as jazz permeates Buddy's music, it becomes a symbol of his persona and his alienation from his family.
It also represents the lure for Corrie Mae of life beyond the
farm. The selection "Buddy's Vamoose" at the end of the third part
is a lively, brief jazz number. This personification of a character
through jazz reminds one of the much more sinister Michel in
Harling's *A Light from St. Agnes*, who introduces himself in that
opera with a seductive fox trot. Bacon does link jazz to a dramatically significant context here; however, the opera, conceived as a
series of glimpses of Corrie Mae, perhaps fails in the end to
achieve a larger, more fundamental dramatic structure.

All of William Grant Still's operas have North American settings: *Troubled Island* in Haiti; *Blue Steel* and *A Bayou Legend*
both in the deep South, with hints of voodoo; *Minette Fontaine* in
Louisiana; and *Highway No. 1 U.S.A.* in the Southeast. *Costaso*,
Mota, and *The Pillar*, all dating from the years 1949–54, are set in
the Southwest, reflecting perhaps the composer's domicile in Los
Angeles during those years.[12] The latter two deal with Indian subjects. *Costaso*, which like so many operas by aspiring American
composers has never been performed, is set in the Southwest of
the nineteenth century dominated by the Spanish Dons.

In the opera, Filipe Armona sends his principal rival Ramon
Costaso to the desert on a search for a nonexistent city of gold, a
search that Costaso and his companion Manuel indeed survive. In
the meantime, Armona's wife has warned Costaso's wife Carmela
of Armona's intentions to seduce her. In the end Costaso triumphs
because Carmela reveals Armona's treachery to the Governor of
the region. When Armona hears that the Governor will punish him
by banishing him to the desert, he shoots himself.

Still is not particularly preoccupied with locale as an element
closely linked with the drama. Here and there are hints of a Spanish musical idiom, such as the rhythm of the malagueña or the timbre of the guitar. Costaso himself sings a ballad, called a *corridó* at
the beginning of the first act. When Costaso and Manuel find their
way out of the desert, they end the second act with an "Ave
Maria," reflecting the Catholic influence in the region. Nevertheless, the music is predominantly in Still's lyrical, mildly dissonant
style; a waltz that fills much of the first act, for example, is more
generically of the nineteenth century than it is specifically of Spain.
The temperament in the characters is developed more through the

contour of the vocal lines than through appropriating an associated national musical idiom.

Still and his librettist Verna Arvey, his wife, reveal the heart of the drama in Armona's aria "Songs of the Desert" in the first scene of the second act. Here Armona considers how he will show Costaso the lure of the desert and thus be rid of him. After a brief recitative, the aria develops three stages in Armona's thought. The mystery and the romance of the desert is evoked in the first section. A more sinister picture of the desert unfolds in the second section, a place strewn with dead men's bones and a scene of struggle against thirst and hunger. A return to the opening music of the aria reveals how the allure of the desert described in the first section will bring Costaso's ruin, which in turn has been portrayed in the second. In Still's opera, the locale provides a particular color for the drama, but, especially in this aria, the locale is not integral to the drama to the extent achieved by Puccini with his folklike melody. Of all the American operas under our consideration here, the dramatic line is perhaps clearest and most effective in Still's opera. Unlike Puccini's opera, however, the national element is not a factor central to the development of the plot.

Charles Wakefield Cadman's *Shanewis* was the first opera with a contemporary American setting to be produced by the Metropolitan Opera Company, in 1918. It was also the first of the American works at the Met to be heard during a second season. The name of the opera is a phonetic approximation for the name of the Indian princess Tsianina Redfeather, whose life is the basis of the opera. The plot begins with actual incidents in the life of the Indian princess. Mrs. J. Asher Everton has become interested in the vocal talents of the princess Shanewis, who is living with her in her California home near the sea. Mrs. Everton gives a dinner party in honor of Shanewis and her own daughter Amy, who has just returned from a European trip after graduation from Vassar. Lionel Rhodes, who is betrothed to Amy, is also attracted to the Indian maiden. When at length Shanewis retreats to her Indian reservation in Oklahoma, Lionel follows her secretly. In the meantime, Shanewis learns of Lionel's unfaithfulness to Amy and rejects his advances. When she is unable to kill Lionel for his deception, her brother Harjo kills Lionel himself as Amy looks on.

Cadman achieves a dramatic result by contrasting Indian melodies with "white" melodies. Shanewis introduces herself with a "spring song." Lionel makes advances to her and calls her "My sweet enchantress! My Robin Woman! Calling the springtime to my heart!" Then he sings to her a more "cultivated" melody with functional harmonies. As if infused by her beauty, when he reaches the word "magic," the three-note descending figure—a second plus a third—subtly alludes to the more pentatonic nature of the Indian melodies. When Lionel and Shanewis join in duet at the climax of their scene, she adopts the style of the more cultivated melody, thus revealing musically her attraction to him.

The brief opera *Shanewis* points the way that would be followed by many a composer later in the twentieth century. It is brief; it has few characters; it is, like all the others, in English. It has an American subject.[13] It is perhaps the opera's temporal context that explains its ultimate oblivion. First, in its musical style it represents the musical taste of its era, particularly the fascination with Indian materials that was strong at the turn of the century. Its overripe, rich harmonic language also represents an idiom, associated with composers such as Henry Hadley, Frederick Shepherd Converse, Victor Herbert, and Henry Louis Reginald De Koven, whose operas were also produced at the Metropolitan in the early years of the century. The opera seems in idiom and subject too specific for its era to attain a larger relevance. On the other hand, in its reduced dimensions, it was indeed perhaps ahead of its time. It anticipates the more modest lengths of works by Menotti, Moore, and Copland that would be composed in the thirties. On the other hand, it simply may be that the preoccupation with native materials obviates a more fundamental dramatic substance required by the critic of Herbert's *Natoma* cited in the beginning.

In this brief survey of five operas, the attempt has been made to show how a given national subject or context can be the basis of dramatic fulfillment in an opera. Despite a certain pretension to the dramatic in all four of the American operas surveyed here, only one of them, William Grant Still's *Costaso*, actually focuses consistently on the dramatic unfolding of the plot with the national context remaining secondary. The others are simultaneously so brief and so preoccupied with their national identity and allusions that they scarcely have time to allow their characters to develop lives of their own. Despite their lack of lasting relevance to the stage, these works represent a prevalent search for an "American way of opera" in the first half of the present century. By acquainting ourselves with these operatic experiments, we see some American composers coming to grips with their own integrity as composers with a possible American stamp on their music. In their use of Western settings we are also watching the efforts of Americans to make their important first steps to adapt the hallowed tradition of opera for their own culture.

Notes

1. The Met had actually produced its first American opera—Converse's *The Pipe of Desire*—in March 1910, but that production was not a premiere. Converse's opera had already been performed in Boston in January 1906.

2. See especially Lawrence Gilman, "An American Opera," *Harper's Weekly* 54 (9 April 1910), p. 25, and Frederic Dean, "The Opera—By, for, and with Americans," *Bookman* 46 (November 1917), pp. 260–66. Besides English librettos and American singers, these would add the stipulation that the composers be native Americans.

3. See H. Earle Johnson, *Operas on American Subjects* (New York, 1964).

4. "Victor Herbert's 'Natoma,'" *The Nation* 92 (2 March 1911), pp. 223–24.

5. "American Operas," *The Nation* 92 (11 May 1911), pp. 486–87.

6. I am grateful to Allan Atlas for sharing this information with me prior to the publication of his article "Belasco, Puccini, "Old Dog Tray," and the Zuñi Indians," *Musical Quarterly* 3 (1991), Atlas demonstrates the orgin of the label "Old Dog Tray" as well as the significance of music at this point in the Belasco play. The melody appropriated by Puccini occurs in the section titled "Chorus of the Maidens."

7. For this interpretation I am indebted in large part to Spike Hughes, *Famous Puccini Operas* (London: Dover, 1959), p. 146. He points out that not only is the lyricism of the nostalgic melody a unique quality in the otherwise declamatory, dramatic opera, it also draws attention to the longing of the miners for their home and their resulting attachment to Minnie.

8. See Ernst Krause, *Puccini* (Berlin: Siedler, 1984), pp. 235–53. Krause identifies Alice Cunningham Fletcher, *Indian Story and Song from North America* (Boston: Small, Maynard, & Co., 1900) as among Puccini's possessions and thus the source of the Indian melody sung by Wowkle. Wowkle's very simple melody is not an exact replica of any in the Fletcher work, but its oscillation about two pitches a step apart or the skip of the fourth are indigenous to many of the melodies in the Fletcher collection. Mosco Carner, *Puccini* (London: Knoff, 1974), p. 406, cites a melody from Natalie Curtis, *The Indian's Song Book* (New York: Harper & Bros., 1917) as similar. Obviously, Curtis's work was issued seven years after Puccini's opera premiered. Krause claims that the melody "Echoes from Home" is a folk tune from about 1850, but he does not identify the source.

9. *Tennessee's Partner*, the second opera in the series and the only one actually based on a story by Bret Harte, received some attention when, in May 1942, it was broadcast by New York radio station WOR, conducted by Alfred Wallenstein, the station's music director. Wallenstein produced radio versions of seven operas, each lasting one hour, during the spring of 1942. The other six were *Porgy and Bess, Four Saints in Three Acts, The Devil and Daniel Webster, The Old Maid and the Thief, The Second Hurricane,* and *The King's Henchman.* Since the opera had not yet been performed, Maganini had to orchestrate the opera for Wallenstein's performance. As a result of the broadcast, he was awarded the David Bispham Memorial Medal by the American Opera Society of Chicago.

10. As Professor of Music at Converse College in South Carolina in the 1940s, Bacon had founded the New Spartanburg Festival, billed as a new plan: "No imported stars; No guarantors and no debts; No barriers to local talents; No performances of hackneyed works; No predjudices [sic] against the American in music." The opera was performed as part of the festival in Spartanburg in May 1942.

11. See *Southwest Review* 28 (1943): pp. 345–376.

12. Still composed *Costaso* very rapidly between May and November of 1949, having just seen *Troubled Island* performed in March of that year at the New York City Center.

13. In his preface to the opera, Cadman has indicated how the brief opera is in some ways a kind of pageant. For the musicale at the home of Mrs. Everton, Cadman has suggested that the characters could be costumed so as to represent "various phases of America in the making." Mrs. Everton could be Queen Isabella of Spain; Amy, Evangeline; Lionel, John Alden; and Shanewis, Pocahontas. Members of the chorus could be attired each as a different figure from American history. Likewise, the second part is set in the context of a large Indian "pow wow."

Part Five
European Influences

Parsifal Performances in America, 1886–1903: Changing Tastes and the Popular Press

MICHAEL SAFFLE

The performance of Wagner's *Parsifal* given by New York's Metropolitan Opera Company on 24 December 1903, the first complete stage performance presented anywhere outside Bayreuth, remains one of the most notorious events in American opera history.[1] A triumph for Heinrich Conried, in 1903 the Met's new General Director, *Parsifal* proved an artistic as well as a financial success. Unfortunately, the notoriety resulting from Bayreuth's outspoken opposition to Conried's production has for a long time obscured other important aspects of that event. Conried's *Parsifal* was a victory not only for American ambition and artistry; it was also a victory on behalf of Wagnerian music-drama and *Gesamtkunstwerke*. Objections by American newspapers to *Parsifal* of the 1880s and 1890s included the representation of religious events and issues on stage. Concert performances of Wagner's work during those years, however, helped dispel these and other objections, and they demonstrated the necessity of staging that work—whether or not Bayreuth objected—if it were to be understood by American audiences.

Concert *Parsifal* performances were given in Manhattan in 1886, in Brooklyn in 1890, and in Boston and New York in 1891–92; and for the most part they achieved considerable success. Indeed, these performances won praise from more than a few critics *because* they were concert performances. On the other hand, reports published in American newspapers and music magazines during the 1880s, 1890s, and early 1900s reflect the gradual acceptance of Wagner's art as drama on this side of the Atlantic. Only after decades of familiarity with the music of *Parsifal* were American critics and audiences able to accept the necessity of staging that work in order best to realize Wagner's ideals.

Performances of *Parsifal* excerpts in America before 1903 were almost as numerous as they are little known. The *Parsifal* Prelude, for example, was presented by the Musical Society of Milwaukee as early as 31 October 1882; the same piece was performed subsequently by the Brooklyn Philharmonic under Theodore Thomas on 3 November 1882, and the following spring the Boston Symphony Orchestra presented it and other Wagner excerpts on several occasions. Another *Parsifal* fragment—the "Transformation and Closing Scene" from Act I—was first heard on 4 November 1882 at a Brooklyn Philharmonic concert, again under Theodore Thomas. (By coincidence, the New York Symphony Society under the direction of Leopold Damrosch presented the same scene on the same evening at Steinway Hall in Manhattan.) Philadelphia heard the first performance of the "Good Friday Spell" music by the Thomas Orchestra on 2 December 1882. All these performances, except a memorial program presented by the Boston Syrnphony, took place before Wagner's death.[2]

Complete concert *Parsifal* performances began in America in 1886, when the Oratorio Society of New York City, under the direction of Damrosch, presented that work twice at the Metropolitan Opera House on 3 and 4 March of that year. Five years later, on 31 March 1890, Anton Seidl led the "Seidl Society" of Brooklyn, a pro-Wagner musical group, in an abbreviated concert *Parsifal* production (without chorus) at the Brooklyn Academy of Music. The following year Seidl led his own orchestra and singers from the New York City area in *Parsifal* performances at the Met on 15 February 1891, and at Boston's Music Hall two months later on 15 April. The Boston production was so successful that a repeat performance was given in that city on 4 May 1892. Notices, reports, and reviews of the 1886 New York, 1890 Brooklyn, 1891 Boston, and 1903 New York *Parsifal* concert performances tell us a great deal about American attitudes toward Wagner, his music dramas, the subject of *Parsifal*, and musical theater in general.

By 1886 enthusiasm for German opera and especially for Wagner was widespread.[3] In describing the New York opera scene of the 1880s, the New York *Evening Post* praised Seidl (who directed the 1890–92 Brooklyn, Boston, and New York *Parsifal*s and the Met company: "The repertory has become more Wagnerian even than it was last year [1885], when 28 out of 58 performances were devoted to his works. This year Wagner got 28 out of 52 performances—'Die Meistersinger' having been given 8 times, 'Rienzi' 7, 'Lohengrin' 5, 'Tannhaüser' [*sic*] 4, [and] 'Walküre' 4".[4] (These figures did not take the March 1886 *Parsifal* concert performances into account.) Nor did the newspapers overlook the costs of Wagnerian productions. Just before the Damrosch *Parsifal* was presented in Manhattan, the New York *Times* observed that "[t]o convey an imperfect idea of the cost of giving opera on the scale of magnitude that has characterized affairs at the Metropolitan it is worth while stating that as many as 700 persons have occasionally been under pay in connection with one performance; that 405 persons are on the regular [1886] payroll of the establishment, and that the monthly expenses, not including rent or outlays for music, scenery, or dresses, approximate $50,000."[5]

In a word, Wagner was popular with New York audiences before the turn of the century.[6] Yet his works were often ridiculed, occasionally attacked in the most unenlightened manner imaginable, and regularly misunderstood. Sympathetic statements like those of Charles Dudley Warner were comparatively rare:

> Whether Wagner is successful [in making his theories work] is still in dispute; but he attempts [in *Parsifal*] a production which has purpose and unity, and which excludes everything not consistent with the effects he aims at. A story is to be told, a lesson is to be taught, an impression is to be produced on the hearer and spectator; and to this impression the orchestra, the scenery, and the singing are of almost equal importance. . . . The effort is made to impress and stimulate the imagination, and to engage the attention in the work "as a whole" rather than in certain lyrical and melodic details.[7]

Warner's views were not extraordinary, but they were unusually sensitive to the integrity of Wagner's art. Most American critics of the 1880s and 1890s saw nothing wrong with "doing Wagner" as they thought fit, or at least "doing" *Parsifal* on the concert platform when objections from Bayreuth or high production costs made stage performances problematic. As a consequence, concert *Parsifal*s were praised—as often as not—for aesthetic reasons as well as reasons of practicality or because Bayreuth forbade staged productions.

Reviewing press notices for the 1886, 1890, 1891, and 1903 *Parsifal* productions proves these points. Some critics complained that concert *Parsifal*s just wouldn't do. In March 1886, for example, the New York *Herald* stated that "'Parsifal' is essentially a dramatic work," and that "[t]he adjuncts of the stage are as indispensable to it as to any of the other works by the same composer."[8] Yet the *Herald* implied that a little *Parsifal* was better than none when their critic praised Damrosch and company for successful musicmaking. A somewhat firmer line was taken by the New York *Even-*

ing Post: "Wagner would have been the last person to thank Mr. Damrosch for producing his latest music-drama in the form of a [concert work]."[9] The *Times*, on the other hand, ignored stage-vs.-concert arguments and described the Damrosch performance as if none other were possible, or at least preferable:

> Those who have fully believed the dictum of certain German critics that to know music one must devote his days and nights to the study of Wagner unquestionably found themselves [on 4 March 1886] moved to deep emotion by this most marvelous dream of that most perfect and transcendental dreamer of modem dreamers. . . . The performance was perhaps not fully up to the requirements of the work; and to reach that point would be difficult indeed, for the music is full of appalling difficulties. Nevertheless, taken as a whole, it was highly commendable and merited the hearty applause which it received.[10]

The anonymous reporter for the *Times* considered only musical issues. Other critics went further when they suggested that staging *Parsifal* would be wrong on moral if not aesthetic grounds. Writing in 1886 for the *Keynote*, a popular New York City music magazine, Frederic Archer stated that "[t]he presentation of some of [the incidents of *Parsifal*] on the stage, notably the celebration of the Eucharist, is certainly open to objection. The age of 'miracle plays' has passed, and their revival for the mere purpose of providing entertainment for the cultured opera *habitué* is both unjustifiable and offensive."[11] Archer went on to describe the music of *Parsifal* as "weak" and to claim that "Wagner, in his 'Parsifal,' appears almost exclusively as a scene painter, his music being avowedly only a stage accessory intended to heighten the effect of the drama." Archer's conclusion that "dramatics" lower "the dignity of musical art" ignores the essential alliance in Wagnerian music-drama between stage *and* music, an alliance missing in concert productions of stage works.

Boston and New York newspapers and magazines of 1890–91 passed over Bayreuth's claim to sole ownership of *Parsifal* stage productions. Instead, they had more to say in favor of concert performances than 1886 New York papers. Louis Henry Elson represented this "Bostonian" point of view and did much to promulgate it. In evaluating the 15 April 1891 *Parsifal* performance, Elson stated:

> "Parsifal" is a peculiar work and requires peculiar surroundings; although written as a sacred opera . . . it is, in certain parts, suitable for concert performance as an oratorio. . . . The loss of stage acces-

sories [in the Boston performance] was not without some small gain, for the presentation of the episode of Mary Magdalen at the feet of the Savior, even though disguised under the veil of an action of Kundry and Parsifal, could not have failed to shock those who revere the scene; even in Beyreuth [*sic*] this has seemed a defect to many, although there the whole musical drama has taken on the character of a memorial service and has become to some degree a cult.[12]

Here religious sentiment reared its head. It is not the music or even the story of *Parsifal* Elson objected to, but the representation of religious action and subject matter on stage. Other journalists preferred a concert *Parsifal* to none at all. In reviewing the 1890 Brooklyn production conducted by Seidl, the New York *Times* observed that

[t]he music-drama of "Parsifal" was constructed by Wagner with a special view to the possibilities of the stage of the Wagner theatre, and with a regard for such surroundings as are possible only at Bayreuth. . . . The question will naturally arise whether it is possible to give a satisfactory rendering of this music-drama without the accessories of scenery and action which Wagner held to be inseparable parts of his "art-work of the future." And the additional question may be asked whether it is not a mistake to set aside the purposes of the poet-composer in order to hear his music, which is necessarily at a disadvantage when presented in concert form. But perhaps, as we are denied the privilege of a complete performance of "Parsifal," we would better be as well satisfied as we can with what we receive, and not "look the gift horse in the mouth."[13]

Elson was joined by some of his colleagues on the issue of Wagner presenting "sacred" subjects on stage. Other critics felt *Parsifal* should be banned even from the concert platform. An article entitled "'Parsifal' as an Oratorio," which appeared in March 1886 in the New York *Daily Tribune*, epitomized this position. "The adoration of the Holy Grail, which is the real business of the drama," wrote the *Tribune* critic, "becomes a piece of superstitious relic worship which is certainly foreign to the religious as well as scientific thought of the time."[14] Only a staged production of *Parsifal* could have discredited objections like these and demonstrated once and for all that Wagner was anything but sacrilegious.

Some Boston newspapers presented thoughts closer to Wagner's own. In April 1891, for example, the Boston *Daily Globe* raised the following issue: "To see and hear the religious opera [*Parsifal*] as Wagner designed it to be produced on the stage, one must go to

Bayreuth. This is as Wagner himself wished; and it will be long, in all probability, before *Parsifal* can be heard elsewhere by the public."[15] The *Globe* did not deny the suitability of *Parsifal* for the American stage, only the likelihood of a production in the face of Bayreuth's objections. The *Evening Transcript*, on the other hand, argued that a concert *Parsifal* was the only appropriate *Parsifal*, at least for American audiences:

> A more complete production of Parsifal [than that presented in Boston in 1891] it would be unwise to give, and everyone who has heard it in Bayreuth must devoutly hope that so long as the present temper of the public may endure and present social and religious conditions also, it may be utterly impossible to give "Parsifal" in a complete form. Like the Passion Play it is far too sacred a thing to be given under the conditions which would now alone be possible. . . . The dawn is not yet. The [United States] isn't ready for genuine art.[16]

Still other papers ignored the concert-vs.-stage issue altogether and praised the Boston performance on musical grounds, the *Herald* among them. Only the *Post* complained about the performance as such, to a considerable extent because of the character of Wagner's work. In an article entitled "Parsifal," Philip Hale wrote: "[In *Parsifal*] there is hardly any dramatic action. . . . We find this same restlessness, this eternal shifting and gliding [in the music that we do in the libretto]. Long drawn out monotony is the result of the frantic efforts to rivet the attention and inflame the imagination. This limits of the hearer's capacities are ignored. Every episode is treated at too great a length."[17] Yet Hale also pointed out that concert productions of *Parsifal* were unsatisfactory as well as "in defiance" of Wagner's wishes. For some turn-of-the-century American critics there was no right way to give *Parsifal*, nor was there anything right about the work itself.

Finally came the Conried production of December 1903, and the New York newspapers. In reviewing that event—despite the brouhaha over legal issues and Bayreuth's outrage—we find in virtually every press report greater understanding of Wagner's work and aims (not to mention greater praise for the production itself) than in reports of the previous decades. Among more than a dozen contemporary reviews, that of Richard Aldrich for the New York *Times* remains the best known. Published originally on 25 December 1903, it has been reprinted and quoted from frequently.[18] Aldrich's review need not be cited here; it is enough to state that it was highly favorable and applauded Conried for his efforts. What deserves to be mentioned instead is that anti-Wagner sentiments had not vanished entirely from American papers in 1903. The New York *Sun*, a somewhat more sensationalist publication than the *Times* and *Tribune*, ran a series of *Parsifal* articles during the weeks immediately preceding Conried's production—articles that, for the most part, capitalized on the news of religious (or quasi-religious) spectacle scheduled to be sumptuously staged and shown to anyone who could afford the outrageous ticket prices. Among *Sun* notices was a lengthy complaint entitled "Mr. Mayor, Stop 'Parsifal,'" written by one Rev. David J. Burrell (no relation, apparently, to the Mrs. Burrell of Wagner document and reminiscence frame).[19] Yet the following day the *Sun* ran a long article explaining "The Music of 'Parsifal'"to its readers—an explanation illustrated with fourteen musical examples.[20] And when the *Sun* reviewed Conried's production—a review, despite its title, that was far from entirely favorable—it did so without suggesting that the music-drama might better have been produced in concert form or even omitted altogether from the repertory of a respectable house like the Met.[21] Clearly, the 1903 Metropolitan opera performance of *Parsifal* was preceded by seventeen years of some form of exposure to Wagner's opera in America.

Notes

The author would like to thank Virginia Polytechnic Institute and State University for research and travel monies that facilitated the preparation of this article.

1. Many accounts of the 1903 Metropolitan Opera *Parsifal* production have appeared in print. Two of the most widely available are Paul E. Eisley, *The Metropolitan Opera: The First Twenty-five Years* (Croton-on-Hudson, N.Y.: North River Press, 1984), pp. 258–62; and Irving Kolodin, *The Metropolitan Opera, 1883–1966: A Candid History* (New York: Knopf, 1968), pp. 161–63.

2. See Julius Mattfeld, *A Hundred Years of Grand Opera in New York, 1825–1925* (New York: New York Public Library, 1927), p. 69; and H. Earle Johnson, *First Performances in America to 1900: Works with Orchestra* (Detroit, 1979), pp. 386–87. Additional information is available in M. A. DeWolfe Howe, *The Boston Symphony Orchestra: An Historical Sketch* (Boston: Atlantic Monthly Press, 1914), pp. 83, 97, and 273–74; David Ewen, *Music Comes to America* (New York: Allen, Towne & Heath, 1947), pp. 107–9 (the only one of these sources that mentions the 1890 Brooklyn *Parsifal* production); and Johnson, *Symphony Hall, Boston* (Boston: Little, Brown, 1950), p. 396.

Other sources of information about early American *Parsifal* performances are sometimes incorrect. For example, one source gives "1896" (instead of "1886") for the New York concert performance by Damrosch. See Howard Shanet, *Philharmonic: A History of New York's Orchestra* (Garden City, N.Y.:

Doubleday, 1975), p. 443. The New York *Times* article by Joseph Horowitz cited below gives 30 March 1890 for the "Seidl Society" Brooklyn production; the correct date is 31 March.

3. America's love-affair with Wagner during the last decades of the nineteenth century has been chronicled in several places Among the most important of these is Anne Dzarnba Sessa, "At Wagner's Shrine: British and American Wagnerians," in *Wagnerism in European Culture and Politics*, ed. David C. Large and William Weber (Ithaca: Cornell Univ. Press, 1984), pp. 246–77; and Burton W. Peretti, "Democratic Leitmotivs in the American Reception of Wagner," *Nineteenth Century Music* 13 (Summer 1989) 28–38. Peretti's article, like the article by Horowitz cited below, appeared in print after the present study had been drafted and submitted for presentation at Hofstra University's "Opera and the Golden West" conference.

4. "German Opera," New York *Evening Post*, 5 March 1886. Like most of the articles cited below, this one appeared anonymously.

5. "Record of Amusements—Metropolitan Opera House," *New York Times*, 3 March 1886.

6. See Joseph Horowitz, "Wagner's American Emissary," *New York Times*, 10 March 1991, sec.2. The author wishes to thank Mr. Horowitz for drawing this article to his attention.

7. Charles Dudley Warner, "Wagner's Parsifal," *The Atlantic Monthly* 51 (1883): p. 76.

8. "The First American Production of 'Parsifal' by the Oratorio Society," New York *Herald*, 4 March 1886.

9. "Music and Drama—'Parsifal' as an Oratorio," New York *Evening Post*, 4 March 1886.

10. "The Oratorio Society," *New York Times*, 5 March 1886.

11. Frederic Archer, "Parsifal," *The Keynote* 10 (13 March 1886), p. 3.

12. Louis Henry Elson, "'Parsifal' in Boston," Boston *Advertiser*, 16 April 1891. Reprinted under the title "Parsifal as Concert Music" in the [Boston] *Musical Herald* 12 (May 1891), pp. 81–82.

13. "'Parsifal' in Brooklyn," *New York Times*, 1 April 1890.

14. "'Parsifal' as an Oratorio," New York *Daily Tribune*, 5 March 1886.

15. "'Parsifal' Music," Boston *Daily Globe*, 16 April 1891.

16. Ralph Adams Cram, "The Spiritual in Wagner," Boston *Evening Transcript*, 14 April 1891.

17. Philip Hale, "Parsifal," Boston *Post*, 16 April 1891.

18. Reprinted in Richard Aldrich, *Concert Life in New York, 1902–1923*, ed. Harold Johnson (Freeport, New York: Books for Libraries, 1971), pp. 46–53. Quoted in Eisler, p. 261, and in many other sources.

19. David J. Burrell, "Mr. Mayor, Stop 'Parsifal,'" New York *Sun*, 19 December 1903.

20. "The Music of 'Parsifal,'" New York *Sun*, 20 December 1903.

21. "A Great 'Parsifal'—The Metropolitan Production Better than Bayreuth's," New York *Sun*, 25 December 1903.

Gustav Mahler and Opera in America, 1907–1910

ZOLTAN ROMAN

Aside from the surpassing excellence and lasting influence of his productions, and in addition to the role his presence there undoubtedly played in nurturing New York's reputation as an important city on the international operatic map, Mahler's time at the Metropolitan Opera appears interesting to us today for a largely fortuitous circumstance: his two seasons straddled what was arguably the most critical change in management in the history of the theater. Also, the total of four seasons during which Mahler worked in New York witnessed that most significant—if dearly bought—achievement of the new regime at the Metropolitan: elimination of the damaging financial and artistic competition represented by Oscar Hammerstein's Manhattan Opera House. As the necessary limitations on this study preclude a full examination of Mahler's activities at the Metropolitan Opera, the focus of the following essay is a comparison of his two seasons in light of the noted management change, concluding with some remarks on possible connections between Hammerstein's departure from the New York scene and Mahler's work at the Metropolitan. In order to understand fully the personalities and events discussed here, though, an introductory look at the importance and conditions of opera in turn-of-the-century America (in fact, chiefly New York) is essential.

The prefatory "Chronological Table" in the 1912 edition of William J. Henderson's *Story of Music* begins with the birth of St. Ambrose in 333 and ends with the 1910 world premiere of Puccini's *La fanciulla del West*.[1] Moreover, of the twenty-seven first performances of music listed in the table from the years between 1831 and 1910, all but four are operas—and *those* four (Mendelssohn's two oratorios and the Faust-settings of Schumann and Berlioz)—are dramatic works of the first order in everything but name. Clearly, for Henderson "music" was well-nigh synony-

mous with "opera," at least as concerned much of the Romantic
and—for him—contemporary periods This, together with the fact
that in 1912 Henderson was one of New York's most respected and
widely read music critics, tells us a great deal about the position of
opera in American musical life earlier in this century.

Although the reasons for the popularity of opera in America at
the turn of the twentieth century are many and varied,[2] its true
position is perhaps most strikingly reflected in the flood of European artists to these shores. Other fields and types of organizations
certainly attracted some outstanding musicians from time to time:
it is sufficient to mention conductor Arthur Nikisch, who led the
Boston Symphony Orchestra from 1889 to 1893, or violinist Fritz
Kreisler's regular American concert tours and lengthy residence in
New York. There is no doubt, however, that the majority of eminent overseas musicians to settle in, or make annual pilgrimages
to the "New World" were connected—in one way or another but
more or less exclusively—with opera.[3] In keeping with the nature
of the art form, and aside from the orchestral musicians, singers
are the most heavily represented group; stellar names such as Lilli
Lehmann, the de Reszke brothers, or Caruso readily come to
mind. The impresario-entrepreneurs who arrived around 1900,
such as Maurice Grau, Oscar Hammerstein, and Heinrich Conried,
were soon followed by the best of the European director-
managers, starting perhaps with the Metropolitan's Giulio Gatti-
Casazza. And inevitably in what was then the first high plateau in
the age of the virtuoso orchestral leader, an emerging international
coterie of celebrated conductors began to command increasing
attention even in the world of the opera house. The Hungarian-
born Anton Seidl, Wagner's erstwhile assistant, had been a towering, early representative of the type; but the arrival in New York
of the Bohemian-Austrian Gustav Mahler and of the Italian
Arturo Toscanini in virtually the same year overshadowed all previous arrivals.

I see this phenomenon as a necessary precondition for the one
further development that was to formalize, as it were, what had
been achieved slowly and in the face of much European skeptic-
ism, namely, America's (but especially New York's) place among
the leading homes of first-rate opera. That final step was the willingness of the foremost European composers to introduce their
new operas in North America. The first *and* second such occasions
took place during an amazingly short time span of eighteen days,
in a season that is, in some significant ways, intimately connected
with the period that is the subject of this study. I refer, of course,

to the 1910 world premières of Giacomo Puccini's *La fanciulla del West* (on 10 December) and Engelbert Humperdinck's *Die Königskinder* (on 28 December), both at the Metropolitan Opera.

But to begin, it seems quite reasonable to assume that in 1910 Puccini was attracted by the Metropolitan at least in part because of the presence there of a new and stable regime under his countryman, Gatti-Casazza. Nevertheless, the real credit for laying the foundation for the rapid rise to pre-eminence of New York's leading music theater must go to the always quixotic, frequently controversial, yet occasionally brilliant and daring Heinrich Conried. It is safe to say today that the last masterly stroke of his administration (the first one had been the engaging of Caruso) was the hiring of Gustav Mahler in 1907. Though Toscanini's fortunes had clearly begun to rise by the time he came to the Metropolitan in 1908, in those days Mahler was the unequalled (if no longer the unchallenged) star in the international world of opera. Having recently resigned his post of ten years as all-powerful head of the leading operatic institution of the time, the Imperial Court Opera in Vienna, Mahler was ready to listen to "the well-known siren song, accompanied by an astute impresario on a golden lyre with golden strings," as one regretful Viennese critic phrased it upon learning of the events leading to Mahler's engagement by Conried.[4]

Though we are not, and likely never will be, wholly informed about the complex of reasons behind Mahler's decision to exchange a world in which he was at home as man and artist for one that must have seemed distant and alien in every respect, the lure of the "golden lyre with golden strings" must have played a most important role. In order to grasp fully the quality of the contract Mahler made with Conried, we must compare it, at least in gross terms, with the circumstances of his employment in Vienna. His highest total annual income at the Imperial Opera (comprised of basic salary as conductor, plus directorial and other honoraria) amounted to 36,000 crowns, or about $7,200 equivalent—This for a season of some ten months, during which he conducted several dozen performances, personally coached many of the solo singers, and carried out his largely onerous duties as director.[5] Now, following minimal bargaining with Conried, he had a contract that (in its amended form) assured him of $20,000 for roughly four months, plus very generous traveling and living expenses; for this, he was obliged to conduct not more—and very likely fewer—than two or three opera performances a week, and possibly an occasional orchestral concert.[6] Most importantly to Mahler, as was to become evident from his letters and from his actions following

Conried's departure, he was to be "merely" one of the conductors at the Metropolitan, without (certainly ultimate) responsibility for repertoire, staff, and financial decisions.

While Mahler was presented with many and varied possibilities for conducting assignments, especially for his second season in New York,[7] the contract is silent on this matter. It is from his letters to Alma that we find out how the question of repertoire figured in his negotiations with Conried: not surprisingly in light of his established reputation as well as on the basis of the faint yet clearly discernible impression we gain throughout those negotiations of a man looking for a sinecure rather than for new challenges, the two composers specifically mentioned are Mozart and Wagner.[8] In fact, during the two seasons which provide the central time-frame for this study, only Beethoven's *Fidelio* and Smetana's *Bartered Bride* joined some half dozen works by those two composers. (In the spring of 1910—that is, after he had ceased to be permanently associated with the theater—Mahler undertook to mount and guest-conduct Tchaikovsky's *Pique Dame* at the Metropolitan.)

Nothing in the foregoing should imply, however, that Mahler was motivated only by the prospect of financial gain and ease of working conditions during his two seasons at the Metropolitan Opera. His letters—especially to Alfred Roller, the famed stage designer, his devoted associate in Vienna—are eloquent testimonials, both as to the missionary zeal with which Mahler approached his self-set task of "educating" the naïve but eager and well-meaning American public—as he saw them—in the high art of Continental opera production, and as well to his undiminished need to meet his own high standards to the extent that it was possible to do so under the prevailing conditions.[9]

Although Heinrich Conried was a man of the theater he was not a musician or even an experienced opera producer. Accordingly— as is abundantly clear from the press—Mahler (the new "chief conductor," as the critics were wont to refer to him, although no particular title is found in his contract) was given virtually free rein to realize his musical aims, while matters of the stage remained securely under Conried's control. Consequently, Mahler's first three productions in New York (*Tristan und Isolde* on 1 January, 1908, *Don Giovanni* on 23 January, and *Die Walküre* on 7 February) received unstinting praise almost universally for the quality of the music, while the staging came in for much negative criticism.[10] Such a result was virtually assured by the management system in effect at the Metropolitan at the time. The theater was leased to

Conried by its owners, the Metropolitan Opera and Real Estate Company, through his own producing firm, the Conried Metropolitan Opera Company. Thus, his direct financial interest in the theater inevitably caused him to wish to keep major expenditures, such as those that would have been required by new sets and costumes, to a minimum. In any case, his "investment" in Mahler appeared to be paying rich dividends.

As it turned out, Conried's enjoyment of Mahler's initial critical and popular success was to be rather short-lived. Already unhappy with him because of a number of controversial managerial decisions, the stockholders took swift advantage of Conried's rapidly worsening physical condition (he had been ailing for some time) and convinced him to resign from the lease that was otherwise effective until 1911. In point of fact, rumors concerning Conried's departure had been circulating in New York even before the Mahlers arrived there on 21 December 1907. Then, some four days after Mahler's first appearance at the Metropolitan, *The World* declared him to be "the man who just now is most likely to be chosen for the place of Heinrich Conried when he vacates it at the close of the present season.[11] But as early as 12 February the press, officially disclosing Conried's resignation, announced a "sweeping change of management" for the Metropolitan Opera: it was to continue under the joint management of the tenor Andreas Dippel (at the theater since 1898) on the administrative side, and of Giulio Gatti-Casazza, artistic director of La Scala since 1898, in artistic matters. (Arturo Toscanini's appointment to conduct the Italian works was announced at the same time.)[12] Perhaps most importantly, the "sweeping change of management" also put an end to the leasing of the Metropolitan; starting with the 1908–1909 season, the theater was to be under the direct control of the shareholders of the Metropolitan Opera and Real Estate Company, through the Metropolitan Grand Opera Company, a holding group formed chiefly from the Executive Committee of the parent firm. Now "the policy of the institution [was to] be to give opera for art's sake only"; all profits were to go into a pension fund.[13]

That rumors of Mahler's possible succession to Heinrich Conried had not been merely flights of journalistic fancy is made evident by some of his letters from around this time: clearly, he had been offered some sort of managerial or directorial position by the incoming regime; equally clearly, he turned them down decisively and without hesitation.[14] But there is another, curiously incongruous complex of events to consider that may well shed additional light on this question; if nothing more, it may hint at the lengths to which the new directors of the Company (headed by Otto H. Kahn, a wealthy and highly cultivated immigrant from Germany) were at first prepared to go in order to tempt Mahler into renouncing his decision never again to take on the overall responsibilities of an artistic director. The events in question concern, directly and indirectly, the fifth and final production of Mahler's first season at the Metropolitan Opera, that of *Fidelio* on 20 March.

As indicated above, under Conried's management the Opera's patrons often had to suffer through shoddy stage presentations. So, presumably, had Mahler[15]—at least up to and including *Siegfried*. For on 20 March, *Fidelio* was given with completely new costumes and scenery; moreover, both were precise replicas of those designed by Alfred Roller for his and Mahler's revolutionary production of the opera in 1904 in Vienna. It is reasonable to ask at this point: why did the habitually parsimonious Conried decide to loosen the purse strings for just this opera—and at a time when his own departure into a less than promising financial future was already a foregone conclusion? I wish to suggest that he may not have done so at all. It seems entirely possible to me that, barring the chance that Conried was coerced, the directors of the leasing company—all affluent shareholders—had themselves secretly put up the necessary funds. This may have been done in order to tempt Mahler by making it—or appearing to make it—possible for him once again to present the well-rounded, fully controlled productions for which he justly became famous during his tenure at the Imperial Opera. If this suggestion seems somewhat specious on its own merit, it cannot but gain credibility from one of Mahler's letters to Roller. It dates from 20 January 1908—that is to say, two months before the *Fidelio* production, and some three weeks before Conried's resignation and the new management's appointment had been officially announced. Yet, in this letter Mahler as good as assures Roller (albeit privately) of the chief stage manager's/designer's job at the Metropolitan, on financial terms quite as generous as were his own.[16] (The *Fidelio* sets and costumes are not mentioned in the letter; but, given the lead-time needed for the construction, that matter would have been concluded some time earlier, and then through official channels.) My contention is that if the incoming directors were anxious to secure Mahler's services as something more than a mere conductor, assuring him of a renewed collaboration with Roller (an introductory act of which could have been the joint re-staging of *Fidelio* in New York) would have seemed, to all concerned, like an eminently promising avenue to pursue.

In any event, Mahler resisted the directors' blandishments. My reading of the Roller affair (including the unexpectedly lavish new production of *Fidelio*) finds added support in the fact that already on 27 February (that is, only two weeks after the announcement of the new management) Mahler was dejectedly advising Roller about the sudden collapse of his plans.[17] It seems likely that Gatti-Casazza's appointment, his intention to import stage scenery from his former institution,[18] and the disappearance of the need to please Mahler, combined to put an end to his attempts to have Roller hired by the Metropolitan.

It quickly became obvious on other fronts as well that the new regime at the Metropolitan was not compatible with Mahler's aspirations. To be sure, the beginning was promising: the contract negotiated with the new directors (with the personal participation of Otto Kahn) was every bit as generous as the earlier one;[19] Dippel was expert in all areas of music theater and was genuinely willing to support Mahler's artistic aims; and the new management immediately embarked on a program to expand and improve the Metropolitan's orchestral and choral forces. However, Dippel was soon relegated to non-managerial status (as had been forecast by some observers), leaving the arena to be dominated by the Italians. This appears to have had a number of unhappy consequences for Mahler, and for German opera in general.

Already before the 1908–1909 season began, it had become clear that Toscanini was bent on making his mark in New York not only in the Italian repertoire but also by conducting Wagner's works, including the ones that had been most recently presented under Mahler's baton. Of those, Mahler (as he had in Vienna) considered *Tristan* as his "personal" vehicle. Though his vehement protestations carried the day at first, following Dippel's demotion it was only a matter of time before Toscanini was to conduct this work—and then with scenery imported from Milan.[20] While such a personal matter was no doubt intensely irritating for Mahler, more injurious still to his artistic integrity must have been the programming decisions made by Gatti-Casazza. *Don Giovanni*, a critically successful and popular work under Mahler, was taken off the schedule altogether, while the wholly new and expensive Mahler-Roller production of *Fidelio* was given but once in the entire season. Even in general terms, the initial optimism and exuberance caused by the change of management and the consequent importation of fresh foreign expertise proved to be short-lived. Already in December of Gatti-Casazza's inaugural season, the press felt obliged to raise many of their former complaints (such as the inadequacy of even the lead singers, frequent changes in casts and programming, and so on). But now an ominous new grievance was added to the list, namely, that direct control of the theater by the shareholders was reducing it to a plaything of the rich. An editorial in *Musical America* summed it up well:

> To-day, the situation at the Metropolitan is rapidly tending to duplicate the situation in the latter part of Mr. Conried's term. We have . . . the same conditions in the front of the house. . . . We have had unquestioned deterioration in the performances that are being given. . . .
> One of the causes for this would appear to be the fact that the powers behind the management of the Opera House are less concerned in promoting musical culture and satisfying the public, than they are concerned in maintaining a certain social prestige.
> . . . The result of this will be that the public will gradually lose interest, or will confine itself to sustaining Mr. Hammerstein, who is doing splendid work at the Manhattan. . . .[21]

If there was a message in all of this for Mahler, he did not fail to get it. Although it was officially confirmed only in February 1909, for several months by then he had been fully committed to assuming the musical directorship of a reorganized New York Philharmonic in the 1909–10 season. Ironically in the light of the new Metropolitan management's apparent indifference to his earlier achievements, it seems that Mahler himself considered precisely the *Fidelio* production as the turning point in this development. He wrote this to Anna Moll towards the end of March 1908 (!): "Fidelio was a total success, completely altering my prospects from one day to the next . . . things are moving towards the formation of a Mahler Orchestra entirely at my own disposal. . . ."[22]

Eventually, the owners of the Metropolitan also got the "message" they had been reading in the press for some time, and were soon seeing in concrete terms at the box office: the competition posed by Hammerstein was becoming a genuine threat to the financial well-being of the Metropolitan, not to mention to their personal prestige. Characteristically, a solution to the problem was sought not in improving artistic standards in their own theater but in eliminating the competition. Although it is clear that negotiations got under way considerably earlier,[23] in April 1910 it was announced officially that a certain "Edward T. Stotesbury, of the City of Philadelphia" (fronting, of course, for the stockholders of the Metropolitan Opera and Real Estate Company) bought out Oscar Hammerstein for the very considerable sum of $1,200,000, obliging him to refrain from producing "grand opera" in New York, Boston, Philadelphia, or Chicago for a period of ten years.[24]

While the large sum of money he was being paid no doubt helped to induce Hammerstein to abandon opera production for what must have seemed to him as a very long time at his age of sixty-four years, he had often (and publicly) declared himself to be a very rich man who, at least by implication, was in the business of opera for the love of it; and, in fact, he had proved himself to be a passionate, full-blooded man of the theater (especially of the music theater) for a very long time. Thus, it would seem reasonable to suspect that other considerations may have entered into—and perhaps even carried the day in making—his decision. I believe that, at the very least, one of those considerations was the undeniable (and, perhaps, to Hammerstein seemingly irreversible) success the Metropolitan Opera was beginning to have in attracting the first performances of operas by famous European composers. Furthermore, it is possible that it was the pending première of Humperdinck's *Die Königskinder* that caused Hammerstein to conclude that his days of successful competition with the Metropolitan were numbered. Having failed at one time to secure Mahler's services for his own theater,[25] Hammerstein may have seen one result of that failure in that Mahler's prestige was now attracting even the German composers to the Metropolitan.[26] The Italian composers, such as Puccini, had probably been conceded to the Metropolitan earlier because of the new Italian regime being established there. While Mahler had already resigned there as a full-time conductor, his successful return in March 1910 to produce *Pique Dame* could well have confirmed in Hammerstein's mind what had, in any case, existed as a rumor all along, that is, that Mahler would remain associated with that theater in some capacity.

Thus, while Mahler probably felt compelled to look to a more congenial arena for his music making because of the conditions that were brought about by the new management at the Metropolitan,[27] it would seem that his two brief seasons at the Opera may have had an effect on that theater's fortunes—and on opera in America in general—that was out of all proportion to the actual length of time or to the very few productions that had been presented under him. A fully objective analysis and evaluation of Mahler's influence in this area was made impossible then, and is still hindered today, by the turbulence and controversy that marked his time at the head of the New York Philharmonic; moreover, before the end of his second season with them, and a short two years after he left the Metropolitan Opera, Mahler was

dead. The most appropriate—and perhaps the only possible—
summary, then, may well be one that was expressed in a particularly sensitive commemorative column among the many that were
published in America in May 1911:

> Art has suffered an incalculable loss with Mahler's death. . . . The
> extent to which one man leaves his imprint on his time can never be
> expressed in words; . . . but that which was the very essence of his
> being—the titanesque humanity, the infinite wisdom, borne of good-
> ness and understanding, with which he was able to see beyond the
> limits of our own time—is no more.[28]

Notes

1. William J. Henderson, *The Story of Music*, rev. ed. (New York: Longmans, Green, 1912), pp. xiii–xix.
2. Aside from the more obvious reasons—artistic and economic—Irving
Kolodin believed that the growth of the foreign-born population in New York between 1900 and 1910 (some 700,000, or more than half of the total population
growth) was especially pertinent to this situation (*The Metropolitan Opera 1883–
1966* [New York, Knopf, 1967], pp. 184f.)
3. This is not to say, of course, that this was a new phenomenon around the
turn of the century. Lorenzo da Ponte, for example, spent the last three decades
of his life in America where, among other undertakings, he was active in producing and underwriting opera. His most important venture in this field was no doubt
the role he played in the first American production of *Don Giovanni* by the
traveling troupe of Manuel Garcia, at the start of their extended tour of North
America in 1825.
4. *Neue Freie Presse*, 16 June 1907, quoted in Kurt Blaukopf, *Gustav
Mahler*, trans. Inge Goodwin (London: Allen Lane, 1973), p. 215.
5. Franz Willnauer, *Gustav Mahler und die Wiener Oper* (Wien-München,
Jugend und Volk, 1979), pp. 209 and 48.
6. The original text of Mahler's contract with Heinrich Conried, together
with a somewhat later addendum, was first published in my book, *Gustav
Mahler's American Years 1907–1911—A Documentary History* (Stuyvesant, N.Y.:
Pendragon Press, 1989), pp. 498–501 and 501f.; English translation, pp. 26, 30–
33, and 39f. (Hence cited as *GMA*.)
7. See the detailed letter written by Dippel to Mahler in preparation for the
1908–1909 season (*GMA*, pp. 144f., 148–51 and 510–15.)
8. Alma Mahler, *Gustav Mahler—Memories and Letters*, trans. Basil Creight-
on, ed. Donald Mitchell and Knud Martner (London: Cardinal/Sphere Books,
1990), pp. 289f. (Hence cited as *AMM*.)
9. For some of these letters to Roller, Carl Moll (his father-in-law and a noted
artist) and others, see *GMA* passim.
10. Beginning with the fourth production (*Siegfried*, 19 February), some of the
critics sounded increasingly critical of certain aspects of Mahler's interpretation of
the music. Though this is a topic altogether beyond the scope of this paper, it may

at least be said here that this development undoubtedly played a role in Mahler's decision to leave the Metropolitan at the end of the 1908–1909 season.

11. *The World* (New York), 5 January, 1908, 2d. ed.

12. *The World* (New York), 12 February, 1908.

13. *Musical America* 7, no. 14 (15 February, 1908), p. 1.

14. For an example of such a letter (to his concert agent, Emil Gutmann), see *GMA*, p. 62.

15. Knowing Mahler's absolute insistence on the perfection and harmony of all details of an operatic presentation (whenever and wherever he was in a position of sufficient authority to so insist), it is difficult to have much faith in Alma Mahler's memory (if not her veracity) when she writes that, at the Metropolitan, Mahler "could devote himself exclusively to the music, which was a blessed change from Vienna in recent years," and "all was wonderful, and even if the settings . . . were often . . . abominable, Mahler did not care" (*AMM*, pp. 128, 129).

16. Gustav Mahler, *Selected Letters*, trans. Eithne Wilkins et al, ed. Knud Martner (New York: Farrar Straus Giroux 1979), pp. 309ff. (Hence cited as *MSL*.)

17. *MSL*, pp. 317f. An ironic footnote to the Roller affair is provided by the information that by June Roller had still not been paid for the *Fidelio* production by the Metropolitan (*MSL*, p. 320).

18. This is clear from Dippel's letter to Mahler, cited in n. 7 above.

19. Although the contract between Mahler and Conried's successors seems to have disappeared, three letters to Mahler (two from Kahn and one from Dippel) preserve all essential details; the letters were published for the first time in *GMA* (original texts on pp. 505–8; English translations on pp. 102, 108f., and 127f.).

20. For Mahler's reaction to the suggestion that Toscanini may conduct *Tristan* before the former's return to New York in 1908, see *AMM*, pp. 316f. Though the presentation of this opera with new scenery was certainly to be welcomed (it had been the target of critical barbs for a number of seasons), had things turned out differently in the Roller affair, the new sets at the Metropolitan could well have been those from Mahler's first collaborative venture with Roller in 1903 in Vienna.

21. *Musical America* 9, no. 5 (12 December 1908), p. 16.

22. *MSL*, p. 319.

23. Even the amount of what may have been the initial offer (one million dollars) had been leaked to the press by December (*The World* [New York] 31 December, 1909). It seems equally clear that the offer of money had been preceded by a period of mutual harassment; frequent press reports speak of the actual or alleged raiding of each other's contracted singers, and of the Metropolitan's machinations to keep Hammerstein out of new markets, such as Pittsburgh (*New-York Daily Tribune*, 2, 3, 5 December 1909).

24. The complete text of the agreement is published in John F. Cone, *Oscar Hammerstein's Manhattan Opera Company* (Norman: Oklahoma Univ. Press, 1966), pp. 356–64.

25. Although precise details are not known, an undated letter from Mahler to his agent, probably written while he was negotiating with Conried in May-June 1907, implies that Hammerstein was also interested in hiring Mahler at the same time. The letter was published the first time in *GMA* pp. 10, 496f.

26. While there is no evidence known to me that Mahler had been personally

involved in convincing Humperdinck to introduce *Die Königskinder* at the Metropolitan Opera, it is clear from Dippel's letter to Mahler, cited in n. 7 above, that plans for the premiere were being made already for Mahler's second season at the theater; the question of a conductor, though, is left open in that letter. At any rate, Mahler had admired *Hänsel und Gretel* ever since he heard it in Richard Strauss's premiere production in 1894 (Blaukopf, pp. 110f.), and conducted no fewer than thirty-three performances of it in Hamburg in the very next season (Henry-Louis de La Grange, *Mahler*, vol. 1 [Garden City, N.Y.: Doubleday, 1973], p. 318). On the other side, as is evident from a letter written in 1909 (the salutation reads "Honoured Master"), the older Humperdinck virtually revered his younger colleague (*AMM*, pp. 324f).

27. At the same time, it would be grossly misleading to imply that Mahler had not welcomed the opportunity to move to the Philharmonic also for another reason. He put it so in a letter to his friend, the musicologist Guido Adler, written on 1 January, 1910:

> . . . This very conducting of a concert orchestra was my life-long wish. I am happy to be able to enjoy this once in my life. . . . Why has not Germany or Austria offered something similar? (Quoted in Edward R. Reilly, *Gustav Mahler and Guido Adler—Records of a Friendship* [Cambridge: Cambridge Univ. Press, 1982], p. 110.)

28. *Sonntagsblatt der New-Yorker Staats-Zeitung*, 21 May 1911 (my translation).

Selling *Salome* in America

NADINE SINE

The reception accorded Richard Strauss's *Salome* in the United States in the first decades of this century remains unequaled in our opera history. During its brief stay on the boards of the Metropolitan Opera and the Manhattan Opera, it generated tremendous amounts of publicity, grabbed headlines on almost a daily basis, spawned furious protest, both alienated and attracted the wealthy classes on whom the production of opera was dependent, infuriated the clergy, and sold out the house. Though the specific combination of elements makes the story unique, it may also serve as a case study in salesmanship and censorship with implications for the arts today.

A brief overview of the chronology of the work prior to its appearance in New York appears in Figure 1. In 1893 Oscar Wilde wrote the play entitled *Salomé* in French rather than his native English, expanding upon and altering the biblical episode in which John the Baptist was martyred. Salome, unnamed in the Bible, danced at the request of her step father Herod only when he promised to give her whatever she might ask. In Wilde's version, the young virgin had conceived a passion for the Baptist who had loudly rejected her advances. Thus, out of spite and revenge, she demanded that his head be delivered to her on a silver platter. Having given his word, Herod, though horrified at her request, ultimately had to accede. The execution accomplished and the head delivered, Salome addresses it in a long speech betraying a range of emotions, finally kissing it. Herod, aghast at what he has just witnessed, orders his soldiers to kill her.

Wilde interested Sarah Bernhardt in the play but she was prevented from doing it because of censorship difficulties. By the time it was first produced Oscar Wilde was behind bars, having been condemned to hard labor because of his homosexual relationships. Although translated into many languages, the play was performed rarely, and usually in private performances, until Max Reinhardt

Figure 1. *Salome* **Chronology**

Year	Work	Published	Performed
1893	Wilde, *Salomé* (French)	Librairie de l'Art Independent	
1894	Wilde, *Salome* (Eng. tr. Douglas, Beardsley drawings)	Mathews & Lane	
1896	Wilde, *Salomé* (in French)		Paris: Théâtre de L'Oeuvre-Feb. 11
1902	Wilde, *Salome* (Ger. tr. Lachmann)		Berlin: Reinhardt–Nov. 15 premiere
1903	Wildre, *Salome* (Ger. tr. Lachman, Behmer drawings)	Insel-Verlag	
1905	Strauss, *Salome* (Ger. tr. Lachmann)	Fürstner	
1905	Strauss, *Salome* (Ger. tr. Lachmann)		Dresden: Court Opera–Dec. 9
1906	Strauss, *Salomé* (original French text)	Fürstner	

began producing it in Berlin in 1902 where it received over one hundred performances. According to his memoirs, when Richard Strauss saw the Reinhardt production, he was already at work on the opera, setting the German translation to music, word for word. Upon finishing the score in June 1905 Strauss immediately started to prepare the French version of the piano-vocal score himself, because he wanted to remain faithful to the language of Wilde's original text. Doing that necessitated rewriting large segments of the vocal line to accommodate the French words, accents, and declamation. Mahler, then conductor of the Vienna opera, desperately wanted to produce the work but was forbidden by the censors of that city. The premiere of the opera took place in Dresden in December 1905. Despite troubles with censors in several European cities, or perhaps because of them, the opera, like the Reinhardt theatrical production, was soon a hit. Warned that the opera might damage him, Strauss later remarked: "The damage enabled me to build the villa in Garmisch."[1]

The stage is now set for the arrival of *Salome* in the United States. (Figure 2 gives a chronology of early American performances, including productions of the play and of the opera.) It was the opera that caught the attention of a wider public: in New York, Philadelphia, Boston, Chicago, and Milwaukee protests arose among different groups with varied results.

Figure 2. American Performances of *Salome*

Date	Work	Company	City	Lead role	Dancer
13–16 Nov. 1905	Wilde	Progressive Stage Society	New York		
15 Nov. 1906	Wilde	Astor Theatre	New York	Leigh	
22 Jan. 1907	Strauss	Metropolitan Opera (German)	New York (1)	Fremstad	Froelich
28 Jan 1909	Strauss	Manhattan Opera (French)	New York (10)	Garden	Garden
Feb. 1909	Strauss	Manhattan Opera (French)	Philadel-phia (5)	Garden	Garden
25 Nov. 1910	Strauss	Chicago Grand Opera (French)	Chicago (2)	Garden	Garden
March 1918	Wilde	Washington Square Players (English)	New York	Yorska	

Much of the discomfort had less to do with *Salome* than with the playwright's sexual orientation. In a 1905 review Winter said:

> "progressive" movements take the direction of muck. . . . Oscar Wilde was a person of slender talent and of no lasting importance, and considering the baleful associations that hang about his name, it would be "progressing" to allow his works and all memory of him to pass at once into the oblivion that surely awaits them.[2]

Throughout this period mention of Wilde's name immediately brought with it references to decadence and unnatural vice—words that were then directly applied to his work. Another review in 1906 claimed that the play was "a repulsive composition called 'Salome,' written by that vulgar dramatist Oscar Wilde. . . . It is decadent stuff, and unworthy of notice."[3] And similarly, at a meeting of ministers assembled to denounce all Sunday performances, one Dr. Burrell declared:

> When you think of such productions as 'Salome,' written in the interests of sensuality by a man whose very name is infamous as the representative of unnatural vice, I wonder that any pure-minded woman could sit in that opera house and listen to that performance.

By acquiring the rights to Wilde's text Strauss thus acquired
much more than the words of his libretto; the notoriety came with
it. That the composer might knowingly have taken advantage of
that notoriety occurred to more than one observer. Even before
the Metropolitan production Hermann Klein noted:

> it matters little what the underlying purpose of Richard Strauss was in
> choosing for his theme Oscar Wilde's 'Salome'! . . . Attract your pub-
> lic, make them bite freely, and what does it signify whether the bait
> consists of a decomposed grub or a nauseous worm?[4]

In his review of the lone performance at the Metropolitan,
Krehbiel suggested:

> Strauss is a sensationalist despite his genius, and his business sense is
> large, as New Yorkers know ever since he wound up an artistic tour of
> America with a concert in a department store.[5]

The play and hence the opera offended on several fronts. The initial obstacle was that a biblical, or sacred, subject was staged, an
activity long banned in many European cities. Thus, quite apart
from the treatment of the subject, the subject itself was prohibited
from representation, and for that reason Mahler was denied permission to give the work in Vienna. In the United States, however,
it was the treatment of the subject that proved difficult. Before the
Philadelphia performances by Oscar Hammerstein's Manhattan
Opera Company in 1909, several groups of clergy and of socially
prominent Philadelphians adopted resolutions calling on the mayor
to prohibit the production, in part because it was "a profanation of
a sacred theme."[6] Resolutions from individual denominations protested the opera "was a perversion of Scripture," claiming that
it was "sacrilegious," that "it perverts the Gospel narrative and
degrades the character of the forerunner of Jesus Christ."[7] To de-
fuse criticism, Hammerstein's representative offered a special performance for the clergy, reminding them that

> some months ago he gave a performance of 'Samson and Delilah,' an
> opera which once attracted criticism, to which he invited six hundred
> ministers. That occurred in this city. The next day the clergymen
> praised the opera and said it was uplifting in nature and that there
> was nothing objectionable in it.[8]

One letter by a founder of the Philadelphia Orchestra supported
the production:

The objection that "Salome" is sacrilegious and blasphemous cannot be advanced by one who has intelligently read the play. The character of the saint is ennobled and glorified by contact with his surroundings. The fact that the Scriptural narrative is slightly departed from cannot affect any but the extreme adherents of realism. Whether Salome or Herodias caused John's death is of no material importance whatever. The artist has always license in the use of his material. . . . That sensual love is depicted is undoubted—that it could not be made more repulsive and revolting is still more undoubted. The ethical lesson is, therefore, sound.[9]

The "Dance of the Seven Veils" distressed another segment of the populace. In a column titled "How the Audience took it," the *Times* claimed that at the Metropolitan performance:

there was no sensation until the dance began. It was the dance that women turn away from, and many of the women in the Metropolitan Opera House last night turned away from it. Very few men in the audience seemed comfortable. They twisted in their chairs, and before it was over there were numbers of them who decided to go to the corridors and smoke.

Bianca Froelich, who executed the dance in place of Fremstad at the Metropolitan, said later, "as done all over Europe, it was ten times worse. I did it in the European way at rehearsal," she declared, "but was told to tone it down."[10]

In the *Tribune* Krehbiel remarked:

The dance is old. . . . But it is not to be seriously thought that from those days to this there was ever any doubt as to its significance and its purpose, which is to pander to prurient appetites and arouse libidinous passions. Always, too, from those days to this, its performers have been the most abandoned of the courtesan class.[11]

Just two years later, when Mary Garden appeared as Salome, the reaction to her dance was quite different. She had insisted on doing the dance herself rather than send in a substitute, and to prepare for it, she spent the preceding summer working with the ballet director of the Paris Operá. This time Krehbiel said:

Her dance is remarkable for its grace and voluptuous charm. She does not present the libidinous dance invited by the music at its outset, but a pantomime in rhythmical movement and pose, which is as varied as the terpsichorean play of Miss Duncan, though with less plasticity and eloquence. Through it all she is a vision of loveliness.[12]

According to *Theatre Magazine*:

> And when she danced she raised her audience into the seventh heaven
> of the seven veils. She postured and posed, and she struck a thousand
> attitudes that informed the audience of the beauteous lines of her con-
> tour. It was not sensational, this dancing, nor was her costume merely
> an excuse for unveilings.[13]

In fact, in the intervening two years, Salome dances had become
standard fare. Just two days after the Metropolitan performance,
the *Times* announced

> The Dance of the Seven Veils is immediately to be seen in vaudeville
> beginning next Monday at the Fifth Ave. Theatre. Mme. Pilar Morin,
> the pantomimist, is to do the dance to the strains of Massenet's music.
> Baroness von Elsner is to describe the movements of the acting, ex-
> plaining the meaning of each of the seven veils as they are discarded.[14]

In its review of Garden, *Theatre Magazine* lamented that current
protesters:

> should have begun their campaign last summer when the name
> "Salome" covered a multitude of nakedness and when, for the sheer
> excuse of exposing undraped ladies in public accompanied by non-
> sensically bad music wretchedly performed, almost every vaudeville
> sttage boasted its own "Salome". . . . The greater the expanse of bare
> skin, and the more suggestive the movements of 'dancing', the grea-
> ter the public clamor. . . . There was no excuse under the sun for
> those "Salomes," save that of depravity. . . . But there is some excuse
> for Richard Strauss's "Salome," for it is a musically dramatic
> masterpiece.[15]

Strauss's vivid depiction of lust also provoked comment.
Hermann Klein commented on European performances preceding
the Met's production: "Salome greedily seizes it [the head], and
forgetting every decent womanly instinct, defiles the dead lips with
her foul, voluptuous kisses."[16] At the first Metropolitan performance Krehbiel claimed:

> Mme. Fremstad accomplished a miracle. A sleek tigress, with seduc-
> tion speaking in every pose, gesture, look and utterance, she grew
> steadily into the monster which she was when she sank under the
> shields of the soldiers while the orchestra shrieked its final horror

and left the listeners staring at each other with starting eyeballs and wrecked nerves.[17]

The same critic said of Mary Garden in 1909:

> Miss Garden has realized a conception of incarnate bestiality which has so much power that it is a dreadful thing to contemplate. She has developed the stages from a wilful maiden to a human hyena, with wonderful skill.[18]

W. J. Henderson of the *New York Sun* was perhaps most graphic in his description:

> The whole story wallows in lust, lewdness, bestial appetites and abnormal carnality. The slobbering of Salome over the dead head is in plain English filthy. The kissing of dead lips besmeared with blood is something to make the most hardened shudder.[19]

One begins to sense that the critics were taking no small pleasure in composing these lurid passages.

Descriptions of audience reactions appear in unsigned articles accompanying the reviews. At the Metropolitan, the *Tribune* reported:

> the effect of horror was pronounced, many voices were hushed as the crowd passed out into the night, many faces were white almost as those at the rail of a ship. . . . The grip of a strange horror or disgust was on the majority. It was significant that the usual applause was lacking.[20]

The *Times* described the same scene:

> when . . . Fremstad began to sing to the head, the horror of the thing started a party of men and women from the front row, and from Boxes 27 and 29 in the Golden Horseshoe two parties bumbled precipitately into the corridors and called . . . to get their carriages. But in the galleries men and women left their seats to stand so that they might look down upon the prima donna as she kissed the dead lips. . . . Then they sank back in their chairs and shuddered.[21]

In *Theatre Magazine*, however, Ziegler said reports of the exodus during the opera were exaggerated, amounting to no more than the usual last act departures. And one letter to the editor of the *Times* declared:

Every man or woman who "assisted" at this performance knew exactly what he or she was going to see and went there to see it. Why, then, these wild cries of indignation?[22]

At the Manhattan Opera performance, the reaction was less marked, according to *Theatre Magazine*, because:

between the two productions of the "Salome" music drama, the city and the public have been deluged with vaudeville "Salomes"—girls of various weights and curves, in all manner of undress cavorting, sighing, yearning, and even heaving after the possession of the papier-maché head of John the Baptist. Don't smile at the suggestion that vaudeville has anything to do with the public's grand opera taste—for there is more than a modicum of truth in it. In a word, the great public had grown hardened to the decadent longing of the daughter of Herodias.[23]

We might now consider the size and makeup of the various audiences. At the Metropolitan Conried had made the decision to premiere *Salome* at a non-subscription, gala performance which preceded the one-act opera with a potpourri of arias sung by such Met luminaries as Caruso, Farrar, and Sembrich. Ticket prices were doubled for the event and long lines formed at the box office. According to the *Tribune*, since it was not a subscription performance, "many boxes were occupied by outsiders, and all over the orchestra were strange faces."[24]

The *Times* reported that "ten extra policemen were required last night to handle the crowds who flocked to the Metropolitan Opera House."[25] At the first performance at the Manhattan Opera, where ticket prices were again doubled, the *Times* informs us that "the curtain did not go up until 9:25 o'clock, as the line of carriages was so long that it was impossible for them to arrive quickly enough to discharge their occupants in time."[26]

There follows a long list of socially important persons who attended with detailed descriptions of the gowns worn by several prominent women.

In Philadelphia the capacity audience of five thousand attended while outside another five thousand clamored to gain admission, pressing against police barriers and forty-five patrolmen. In the days preceding the first Philadelphia performance Mrs. Frederick Thurston Mason, "the high priestess of society" was first in a long list of society women to sign a protest against the production. Nonetheless society was very well represented, and gossip columnist Phyllis recognized many faces and found many gowns to describe. And, she said, "approval of the performance was voiced by scores of the persons prominent in the city's social, professional, financial and industrial life who attended the performance."[27]

The *Inquirer* was at pains to quote a number of those people, including a judge and the mayor's wife, all of whom had only praise for the work and for the production. The same page of the paper reports the continued efforts of Rev. Charles H. Bond to have the Philadelphia Opera House license revoked since Hammerstein had refused to "accede to the wishes of the better class of citizens of this city in not suppressing the performance.[28] Throughout the descriptions of the audience there is the marked implication that members of society, "the better class of citizens," had more refined sensibilities than those of the people in the galleries who would leave "their seats to stand so that they might look down upon the prima donna as she kissed the dead lips." Yet, at the same time, there are indications that society was ambivalent about this display, or as Ziegler noted, that the shows on vaudeville stages were not without impact on grand opera audiences. In Philadelphia, where old money and blood lines were highly valued and where society women worked to stop the opera, "Interesting Social Gossip" columnist Phyllis saw the ambivalence in terms we now call the generation gap.

> Salome! Salome! That has caused a social war. Salome that divided the house of society, that divorced the gray-haired mothers and grandmothers from their youthful sons and daughters and filled the new million-dollar temple of music to the very doors, who caused men to pay $50 for a $5 seat—for what?. . . .
>
> Sixty women, whose names stand for real Society, . . . petitioned Hammerstein not to give "Salome", and hoped by their very position to shame their sex from going!
>
> What was the result! Half past eight o'clock found every box occupied (with three exceptions), every seat filled. . . . Men and women of culture, who were unable to purchase seats for money, crowding the exits, the stairways, standing on chairs, on tables, on anything that would command a view of shameless Salome! . . .
>
> Men and women who came prepared to blush, looked inquiringly at one another and said: "I find nothing to blush for." . . . "Huh!" said a well-known society man, "twenty-five dollars for two seats, and there isn't a show in town that was as moral. I wish I had my money back."[29]

While the gray-haired socialites of Philadelphia failed to rid the city of *Salome*, in New York, it apparently took just one woman offended by the first performance at the Metropolitan to get the opera removed. A brief look at the institutions involved will show how this could happen.

In 1903, when Heinrich Conried became manager of a newly organized producing group, the Metropolitan Opera had been in operation for a full twenty years. The financial base was a private company whose members occupied the boxes in the Golden Horseshoe. The Metropolitan Opera House and Real Estate Company thus owned the building and simply left production to another group: at the time of *Salome*, the Conried Metropolitan Opera Company. In 1906 Conried acquired the rights to premiere Strauss's work in the United States with multiple performances, but he made two miscalculations which, while not fatal in themselves, did not help his cause. First, he scheduled the public dress rehearsal for the work, which had encountered difficulty on religious grounds, for Sunday morning at precisely the hour of services. Secondly, although he gave subscribers the chance to abstain by putting *Salome* on a non-subscription concert, he failed to see that by coupling it with a gala potpourri, the audience would not be in the right frame of mind for the difficult nature of the piece. Or as Ziegler put it in *Theatre Magazine*:

> Its introduction to the American public was a misguided affair. . . .
> The varied bill of this concert served to waft into thin air any attempt
> at seriousness that might have possessed this audience, and, as a result,
> the "Salome" shudders were intensified.[30]

At the performance, J. Pierpont Morgan's daughter was aghast and appealed to her father. Morgan lobbied other members of the Metropolitan Opera House and Real Estate Company with the result that within a week *Salome* was pulled against the wishes of Conried's producing company and despite heavy advance sales for three further performances. Conried, ill during the whole episode, was not able to make his own case. His board protested, saying that the other board had ample notification, that they had all received copies of the play, that they had all been invited to, and some had actually attended rehearsals, all of which had transpired without a hint of opposition. The appeal was denied, nonetheless, and Conried withdrew the opera recognizing the difficulty and expense of trying to present it in another venue. Censorship in this case came from the inside, from a Board of Directors censoring its own productions.

Meanwhile, according to the *Times*, Boston was hesitating. The manager of the Boston Theatre, McCarty, said, "if I thought the

people of Boston did not want it I would not present it, but I have
never received so many requests for an opera so far in advance as I
have today for 'Salome'."[31]

Mayor Fitzgerald of Boston said, however:

> It looks to me that if the opera is considered unfit by the managers of
> the Metropolitan Opera House . . . it will hardly come up to the stan-
> dard for Boston. Of course, this office grants the licenses, and if the
> opera is of the offensive kind we can revoke the license of the Boston
> Theatre if anything immoral is produced there. . . . I don't think,
> though, that anything more will be necessary than to have a conference
> with Mr. McCarty and he will see the right side.[32]

Salome was not performed in Boston, apparently without an official act of censorship. Just the threat of a revoked license sufficed.

During the week of Metropolitan controversy, there was
talk for and against replacing Conried with Oscar Hammerstein.
Hammerstein, who had recently opened the Manhattan Opera,
was quoted at length in the *Times*.

> As the sole owner of the Manhattan Opera House and as the sole
> director of a grand opera company which within a few weeks has estab-
> lished itself firmly as one of the greatest musical institutions of the
> world, I am not apt to be looking for a job in the Metropolitan Opera
> House under several of these directors. . . . The doubt as to my ability
> or inability is probably based upon my refusal to accept for production
> at my Opera House such immoral musical and dramatic masterpieces
> as "Salome."[33]

This "outburst," as the *Times* called it, contains several pertinent
issues. First, Hammerstein, who owned the Victoria vaudeville
house, but whose passion was opera, had just opened his own
opera house the previous season in deliberate competition with the
Metropolitan. Second, he was the sole owner, director, and producer, and he therefore was not accountable to a Board of Directors. During one of the controversies he inspired, he held a mock
board meeting in which he conferred with himself in all his various
roles.[34] Third, the whole "outburst" is characteristic of Hammerstein's knack for gaining publicity at every turn.

Conried and the Metropolitan were feeling the competition since
Hammerstein's first season was considered musically and financially successful, even though his galaxy of subscribers did not shine
quite as brightly as at the Met. He had decided to concentrate on
Italian and French operas and leave the German repertoire to the

Met, probably the real reason he had not considered doing
Salome. For the next two seasons he continued to apply pressure
by signing on star singers: Nellie Melba, Tetrazzini, and then Mary
Garden, a great interpreter of French roles and the first
Mélisande.[35] Barely a year after the *Salome* debacle at the Met,
Hammerstein told Garden he was planning to do the opera at the
Manhattan, but in the French version Strauss had made. Otto
Kahn, financial advisor to the new director at the Met, Gatti-
Casazza, got wind of Hammerstein's negotiations with Strauss and
immediately wrote and implored the composer not to favor Ham-
merstein and punish the Met for the disaster wrought by Conried
and Morgan, but Strauss wanted revenge.

Krehbiel did not let Hammerstein's changed attitude toward
Salome go unremarked:

> The reason for his change of heart since is not far to seek. . . . The
> curiosity which was potent enough to fill the theatre at doubled prices
> was directed . . . to Mary Garden, and to her chiefly in the lascivious
> dance.[36]

Hammerstein must have sensed that New Yorkers had indeed become inured to dropping veils and papier-maché heads. He therefore did not have to worry about the opera being censored, but
neither would it gain him needed publicity. In any case, the impresario found other opportunities for headlines besides moral outrage in the month before *Salome* opened. His name, or that of his
company, or that of Mary Garden, appeared on page one of the
Times no fewer than nine times in the month of January 1909.
Every episode gave him the chance to plug *Salome*. In fact two
front page stories arose from the physical assault on Hammerstein
in front of the Hotel Knickerbocker by reporters of the *New York
Press* which had called the impresario, "king of press agents,"
accusing him of staging a row with Mary Garden. They only helped
him get more headlines. Just two days before *Salome* opened, a
letter to the editor of the *Times* lamented:

> Ten percent music and ninety percent notoriety seems to be about the
> ration that is being served out, and the public gulps it down. . . . It
> does not appear to me that the cause of real music was ever much ad-
> vanced anywhere in the world by tactics which combine the methods
> of a Coney Island barker and those of the manipulator of a "corner"
> in wheat or pork. Away with this whole cacophonous mob.[37]

In Philadelphia Hammerstein's name was constantly before the public prior to the opening of *Salome* there. He had just built an opera house in that city, and while the first performances were successful, he needed a mortgage to cover operating expenses. The ordeal of getting that mortgage made front-page headlines in New York as well as Philadelphia, with Hammerstein threatening to stop the season if it were not forthcoming. No sooner had that crisis passed, and Hammerstein's ruffled feathers been smoothed by an unprecedented banquet honoring his contributions to Philadelphia with speeches by Mayor Reyburn, than the cry went up in protest of *Salome*. Hammerstein appeared five times on page one of the *Philadelphia Inquirer* during the first two weeks of February. Here, where clergy and society matrons loudly protested to the mayor, they were unsuccessful in getting the opera canceled. Mayor Reyburn, unlike the mayor of Boston, declared that he did not feel it was in his power to stop the production. Further, he was an opera lover and intended to go. He probably did not want to alienate Hammerstein, who had just erected a million dollar building in the city. So in Philadelphia protests fell on deaf ears.

Back in New York, however, Hammerstein found he could not keep up the pace and the finances needed to support both his houses and the travel of the company. In 1910 he sold for $1,250,000 his performance rights to the Metropolitan Opera, which had been increasingly frustrated by the strength of the competition he had mounted.[38] The dissolution of the Manhattan Opera came at an opportune moment for the city of Chicago which was ready to have its own company. Many of the singers, including Garden, and the conductor Campanini packed up and went to Chicago where they presented *Salome* in their first season. A very positive review by Percy Hammond in the Chicago *Tribune* said about Garden's performance: "She is a fabulous she-thing playing with love and death—loathsome, mysterious, poisonous, slaking her slimy passion in the blood of her victim."[39]

In advance of the performance the Chicago Law and Order League sent a protest to the chief of police. Following the first performance a war of words began between the police, the Law and Order League, and Mary Garden, with the result that the third scheduled performance had to be withdrawn. Again, *Salome* was shut down, not by an official act of censorship, but by the company feeling it had no recourse.

Salome was not the only object of attempted censorship. In January 1907 ministers in New York gathered to denounce all Sunday performances which, they declared, "the courts have upheld as being against the law."[40] In 1909 the first in a series of arrests in vaudeville houses which had stage action on Sunday was made at Hammerstein's Victoria theatre. Once again, the impresario provided the press with good copy. He remarked:

> My son tells me that it if keeps up they are going to hire from fifty to a hundred detectives. They will go everywhere in New York where an audience is made to laugh and lay the evidence before the Mayor . . . they will demand an arrest if the audience laughs on Sunday.[41]

The same day police raided a penny arcade in the Bowery. Captain O'Connor said that he saw seven pictures in a penny slot machine that he considered immoral and charged the manager with a violation of the Penal Code.[42]

Mayor McClellan of New York attempted to shut down all of the city's five hundred movie theatres in an order that Supreme Court Justice Blackmar in Brooklyn declared invalid in January 1909. Blackmar held that "the Mayor was without the power to make the revocation of licenses; that he could not close up both the good and the bad shows indiscriminately."[43] Still, later in January two actors were arrested in Brooklyn because while they sang "Strolling through the Park," they strolled across the stage. Police, who were the censors of the performance, "determined that this came within the definition of 'dancing' and arrested them."[44]

Meanwhile, the New York Theatre Managers Protective League began to protest the closings, forming its own resolutions, noting that the city itself violated the laws by hiring musicians to play in the parks on Sunday. They wanted the opera houses to close as well if the prohibition against vaudeville continued.[45]

The spirit of Anthony Comstock was alive and well in New York, Boston, Philadelphia, and Chicago. In the 1880s Comstock and his New York Society for the Suppression of Vice had initiated hundreds of complaints primarily on charges of immorality. Even though many of these cases were overturned, the threat was ever present. *Salome* was never actually brought to court where injunctions against it would probably have been overturned, yet self-censorship, relinquishing the work in the face of the threat of losing a license or financial support, held sway more than once.

By 1918 when Wilde's play was presented by the Washington Square Players the mood had changed. The *Times* declared that "it was hard to realize that this was the minx whom the chaste directors of the Metropolitan drove out of doors—and into the shameless, welcoming arms of Oscar Hammerstein."[46]

Indeed, the mood of the country never stays the same for long. The homophobia underlying the rhetoric of a few vocal, elected officials set the tone for much of the Mapplethorpe debate just as it did for Wilde's play. The self-censorship undertaken by the Corcoran Gallery resembles cases discussed here. The critic of *The Nation* suggested in 1907 that "to insure an enormous vogue for a work of art or a book, nothing more is needed than that some responsible censor should forbid it on moral or religious grounds."[47]

Just as *Salome* had thousands clamoring for tickets, so the Mapplethorpe exhibits, which would have been seen by a few thousand, have drawn hundreds of thousands. The indictment of Barrie and the Cincinnati Contemporary Art Center may be likened, at a certain level, to the arrest of the manager of the penny arcade whose machines held seven pictures the police captain found to be immoral. And the courtroom acquittal echoes the judicial rebuttal of the Law and Order Leagues, although in Cincinnati a jury acquitted Barrie rather than a judge.

But perhaps more disturbing than public trials where juries and judges hear the evidence is the unofficial censorship surrounding us. In 1990 in Dedham, Massachusetts town officials forced the closing of *Henry and June*, the film that prompted the NC-17 rating, much like the mayor of Boston kept *Salome* out of his town in 1907. Meanwhile Blockbuster Video, the largest rental chain in the world, has quietly pulled Madonna's video, among others, and will not carry *Henry and June*. Blockbuster has evidently bowed to pressure from a conservative Southern group with financial clout that does not want anyone to witness male nudity or two women engaged in sex. At the same time, the chain continues to stock shelf upon shelf of slasher films whose violence is primarily directed against women, and dozens of violent movies of the *Die Hard* variety under the heading of adventure. Millions go to their local Blockbuster not knowing that choices have been made for them—a hidden censorship that forbids them to see nude bodies but allows them to witness bodies being cut up, blown up, shot, or burned. These unpublicized choices will not go unnoticed by the film industry, however, and will surely have a chilling effect on films yet to be made. Producers can not afford to ignore the practice of the largest video rental chain: exploration of adult sexual themes is out, blood and violence is in. Perhaps we have become used to the gore, just as New Yorkers tired of papier-maché heads.

Do these images simply not bother us, do they merely reflect society, or do they ultimately contribute to the documented increase in violence, a subject addressed in the 1 April 1991 cover story of *Newsweek*? Can a society reach a point where it should consider placing limits on what appears in public? Would an official censorship, as opposed to the current practice of self-censorship in response to pressure from vocal minorities, change anything? And who, by what authority, decides what we should not see?

Notes

1. Richard Strauss, *Recollections and Reflections*, ed. Willi Schuh, trans. L. J. Lawrence (London: Boosey, 1953), 152.

2. William Winter, "A Needless Affair," *New York Daily Tribune*, 14 November 1905, p. 7.

3. "The Drama: Astor Theatre," *New York Daily Tribune*, 16 November 1906, p. 7.

4. Hermann Klein, "Is Richard Strauss the Evil Genius of Modern Music," *Theatre Magazine* 6 (March 1906): 80.

5. H. F. K[rebhiel]., "The 'Salome' of Wilde and Strauss," *New York Daily Tribune*, 23 January 1907, p. 7.

6. "Want Salome Prevented by Police Power: Authorities Urged to Prohibit Production of Opera," *Philadelphia Inquirer*, 9 February 1909, p. 1.

7. Ibid., p. 2.

8. Ibid.

9. "Mayor Declines to Move Against Salome: Tells Protesting Citizens He Doubts Power to Interfere," *Philadelphia Inquirer*, 11 February 1909, p. 2.

10. "What It Means to Present 'Salome'," *New York Times*, 24 January 1909, sec. 5, p. 3.

11. Krebhiel, "The 'Salome'," p. 7.

12. H. F. K[rebhiel]., "Manhattan Opera House: A Second Production of 'Salome'," *New York Daily Tribune*, 29 January 1909, p. 7.

13. "'Salome' at the Manhattan Opera House," *Theatre Magazine* 9 (March 1909): 78.

14. "Salome's Dance: To Be Seen Immediately in Vaudeville with a Baroness Explaining," *New York Times*, 26 January 1907, p. 9.

15. "'Salome' at the Manhattan," p. 76, 78.

16. Klein, "Richard Strauss," p. 79.

17. Krebhiel, "The 'Salome' ," p. 7.

18. Krebhiel, "Manhattan," p. 7.

19. Quoted in "'Salome'—The Storm-Center of the Musical World," *Current Literature* (March 1907): 294.

20. "'Salome' Disgusts Its Hearers," *New York Daily Tribune*, 23 January 1907, p. 7.

21. "How the Audience Took It: Many Disgusted by the Dance and the Kissing of the Dead Head," *New York Times* 23 January 1907, p. 9.

22. Sancta Simplicitas, letter, *New York Times*, 26 January 1907, p. 8.

23. "'Salome' at the Manhattan," p. 78.

24. "'Salome' Disgusts," p. 7.

25. "How the Audience Took It," p. 9.

26. "Strauss's 'Salome' at the Manhattan," *New York Times*, 29 January 1907, p. 9.

27. "Interesting Social Gossip: Phyllis Tells Susie Secrets of Opera 'Salome'," *Philadelphia Inquirer*, 14 February 1909, p. 4.

28. "Brilliant Throng Greets Salome After Weeks of Battle," *Philadelphia Inquirer*, 12 February 1909, p. 2.

29. "Interesting Social Gossip," p. 4.

30. Edward Ziegler, "'Salome' at the Metropolitan Opera House," *Theatre Magazine* 7 (March 1907): 70.

31. "Boston Hesitates: Great Call for 'Salome' Seats, but the Mayor Not Sure It's Moral," *New York Times*, 4 January 1909, p. 3.

32. Ibid.

33. "No Decision on 'Salome'; Seats are Still on Sale," *New York Times*, 28 January 1907, p. 3.

34. "Opera Stars and 'Roman Candle' Roles," *New York Times*, 24 January 1907, sec. 5, p. 2.

35. "Kahn, Morgan, and 'Salome'," *Saturday Review*, 30 May 1964, p. 60.

36. Krebhiel, "Manhattan," p. 7.

37. W.C.T., letter, "The State of Opera," *New York Times*, 29 January 1907, p. 8.

38. Vincent Sheehan, *Oscar Hammerstein I* (New York: Simon, 1956), pp. 296–303.

39. Edward C. Moore, *Forty Years of Opera in Chicago* (1930; New York: Arno, 1977), p. 73.

40. "To Ask Mayor to Stop Sunday Performances, "*New York Times*, 29 January 1907, p. 5.

41. "All Sunday Shows Must Stop, They Say: Vaudeville Houses Will Agree to Close If All Amusements Be Forbidden," *New York Times*, 4 January 1909, p. 3.

42. Ibid.

43. "Moving Picture Shows Win: Court decides Mayor Cannot Close All on a Sweeping Order," *New York Times*, 7 January 1909, p. 18.

44. "Two Actors Arrested: Vaudeville Team Accused of Dancing at a Brooklyn Theatre," *New York Times*, 11 January 1909, p. 6.

45. "All Sunday Shows," p. 3.

46. John Corbin, "The Classics that Bloom in the Spring: Out-Heroding Salome," *New York Times*, 28 April 1918, sec. 4, p. 8.

47. "Richard Strauss's 'Salome'," *The Nation*, 24 January 1907, p. 89.

Debussy's Unfinished American Opera:
La Chute de la maison Usher

JEAN-FRANÇOIS THIBAULT

T*he Fall of the House of Usher* and *The Devil in the Belfry*, the two one-act operas after Poe which occupied Debussy after *Pelléas*, roughly between 1903 and his death in 1918, have been the object of much critical conjecture. Among all the numerous unfinished projects of Debussy, this one seems the most intriguing: first, because the preoccupation of Debussy with Poe stems from a deep personal fascination, but also because the double bill that might have been Debussy's *Cav & Pag* appears as a commission from the Met, as is shown in this letter in the form of a contract from Debussy to the newly appointed Giulio Gatti-Casazza:

Monsieur le Directeur   Sunday 5 July 1908
   Following our conversation earlier today, I confirm my undertaking to give first refusal on the two works herein mentioned:
La Chute de la maison Usher
La Diable dans le beffroi
to the Metropolitan Opera and to its affiliated theatres in the United States of America, including the Boston Opera Company.
   This agreement is made in return for a payment of 10,000 francs for the two operas, of which sum I already have received 2,000 francs, the balance to be paid on delivery by my editor of the complete music.
   Further I demand that the two works in question should always be given on the same evening, whether in New York or in the affiliated theatres and that no work of any other composer should appear on the same programme.
   I also confirm that I give the Metropolitan Opera the first option on my future works, and in particular on the "Légende de Tristan."[1]

Little does it matter that Debussy had also promised the works to the Opéra-Comique, which even announced performances of the double bill for its 1911–1912 season. According to Gatti-Casazza's *Memories of the Opera*, Debussy had warned him that he was engaging in "a bad piece of business," adding: "I do not believe that I will finish any part of this. I write for myself alone and do not trouble myself at all about the impatience of others."[2]

Debussy, at the time, did seem interested in the reception of his work in the United States. *Pelléas* had been received favorably the year before in New York. An interview given to Emily Frances Bauer and published in *Harper's Weekly* of 29 August 1908 announces the two works based on Poe's subjects and has Debussy state:

> I do not want to write anything which in any way approaches *Pelléas*. I cannot understand the object of a writer who creates a second work along the same lines which made the first successful. I should no more want to repeat myself than I should want to copy someone who had written before me. Therefore when I have nothing to say I do not attempt to write. The inspiration I have through E. A. Poe is totally different in its elements from that which I felt through Maeterlinck, and I believe that it will be equally successful and when I say equally successful I mean that it will find the same number of enemies and the same number of friends.[3]

Of *The Devil in the Belfry*, little need be said. All that remains is Debussy's notes for a libretto in two scenes and a few musical sketches in the Meyer Collection in Paris. The main originality of Debussy's very free adaptation is to add to the Poe story a tableau set in an Italian Village, in total contrast to the setting in the Dutch village of Vandervotteimittis (Debussy, like Baudelaire, keeps Poe's original denomination.) The critic Antoine Goléa recognized traces of the musical sketches in Debussy's first *Images pour orchestre*, "Gigues."

In 1911 he was working toward "an extremely simple and yet extremely mobile kind of choral unity" for *Devil in the Belfry* which in his mind must have been very different from anything in *Le Martyre de Saint Sébastien*.[4] He also mentions how this choral writing would differ from Mussorgsky's or Wagner's in *Meistersinger*.

The case of *The Fall of the House of Usher* is much more interesting, mostly because the fragments left by Debussy are substantive enough to have permitted two attempts at a reconstruction of partial scores: one by Carolyn Abbate and Robert Kyr, which received a staged performance at Yale University on 25 February 1977, and one by the Chilean composer Juan Allende Blin, which was staged by Nikolaus Lenhoff in Berlin on 5 October 1979. By all accounts, both performances were unsatisfactory from the staging point of view, although musically the Allende-Blin reconstruction is clearly the preferred one.[5] It is this version which was re-corded in 1984 by the Monte-Carlo Philharmonic under Georges Pretre.[6]

Robert Orledge, in his *Debussy and the Theater*, meticulously analyzes the different fragments left by Debussy and the attempts at reconstructing and orchestrating the work, without actually com-pleting it. There are three successive and complete versions of the librettos elaborated between 1908 and l916.[7] Only after completing this third version did Debussy really set out to write the music, that is during the period when he knew he was dying from the cancer which finally killed him in 1918.

What is left of the unfinished music is the particella, or short score, for the whole of scene 1 and the beginning of scene 2 of De-bussy's third libretto. Robert Orledge identifies thirteen fragments for the rest of the opera, most of which have been used in the Abbate-Kyr and Allende-Blin reconstructions, the latter amount-ing to four hundred bars of music, about twenty-nine minutes in performance, representing only a quarter of the final Debussy lib-retto. The actual reasons why Debussy never completed the score are, in my opinion, best left alone. Was it expediency, putting the realization of such major undertaking as *Jeux* or the three Sonatas ahead of this project, or even the composition of such commissions as *Khamma*, the ballet written for the sensational Maud Allan? Or was it, at the psychological level, the impossibility of completing a work whose very subject lay so close to his own preoccupation with death? Or simply the war? We will never know.

And yet the deep involvement of the composer with the theme at the center of Poe's story is, from the autobiographical point of view, overwhelming. In his correspondence Debussy was wont to quote the works (poems, plays) which he was setting to music, or had already set to music. To *The Fall of the House of Usher*, the references are almost as many as to *Pelléas* in its composition stage. The sincerity of these letters is unmistakable and they read like a personal diary, darker as the years pass.

[18 June, 1908, to Jacques Durand]
These last few days I have been working solidly on *La Chute de la Maison Usher* . . . it's an excellent means of strengthening the nerves against all kinds of terror.[8]

[25 August, 1909, to André Caplet]
[. . .] I've been spending my days lately in *La Maison Usher*, which isn't exactly a house to calm the nerves, quite the opposite. . . . You get into the strange habit of listening to the dialogue of the stones and

expecting houses to fall down as though they were a natural, even necessary phenomenon. What's more, if you press me to, I'd admit to a greater sympathy with that house's inhabitants than with. . . . many others.[9]

[15 July, 1910, to Jacques Durand]
As you say, I'm spending my time in *La Maison Usher*. . . . Not exactly a nursing home and sometimes I emerge with my nerves stretched like the strings of a violin.
At moments like that, I'd be capable of giving the Good Lord Himself a rude answer, except that his divine personage long ago chose the path of eternal anonymity![10]

Perhaps more striking even than this personal involvement is the feeling of inadequacy which Debussy experienced while trying to compose music for a subject that was both new and close to his heart. In words which seem to offer a comment on Poe's text, he writes to Caplet, in December 1911:

For every bar that has some freedom about it, there are twenty that are stifled by the weight of one particular tradition. . . . The fact that this tradition belongs to me is hardly relevant. . . .
In fact, we ought to destroy what devours the best of our thoughts and reach a position where we love nothing but ourselves with a fierce attention to detail.[11]

It is as though Debussy had been dragged down by the weight of his own enterprise, had drowned in the tarn that eventually engulfs the house of Usher, while seeking the means to express its fall.
Yet it seems that Debussy found in his Poe projects a last link with life which enabled him to face illness and his many anxieties, as demonstrated in his letter to Jacques Durand of 21 July 1916:

It's enough to drive one to suicide at the least. If I didn't have the desire as well as the duty to finish the two Poe operas, I'd have done it already.[12]

The thematic link between Poe's tale and *Pelléas* has often been stressed. Beyond the direct influence of Poe on Maeterlinck and on his two translators, Baudelaire and Mallarmé, two poets frequently set to music by Debussy, the common feature most often mentioned by critics is that of location. A dim and obscure castle or manor, set in an imprecise landscape, besieged by dark woods or forests, surrounded, permeated by water. In *Usher*, the dynamic sea of *Pelléas* has been replaced by Poe's stagnant tarn. In both works, the house or castle itself embodies the fate of its inhabitants, although in Poe this theme culminates in the engulfing of the house and its inhabitants in a final cataclysm. The flawed structure, the "barely discernible fissure" of the house, is emphasized at the beginning and the end of Poe's tale, but repeatedly Poe returns to the very nature of the stones themselves, of which the house is built, and to the elements that surround it. This, Debussy adapts in most dramatic terms in his libretto:

> Ancient stones! Ghostly stones! What have you made of me? From the day that departs to the day that returns, I belong to you. My thoughts gnaw away at me just as you are gnawed away by winter's rains.

It is significant that while describing his efforts to write music for this central monologue of Roderick Usher at the beginning of scene 2, Debussy links the image of the stones to his own music. Quoting himself, or rather Maeterlinck's words for Golaud in the fifth act of *Pelléas*, he writes in a letter to Jacques Durand, on 26 June 1909:

> I've been working on *La Chute de la Maison Usher* recently and have almost finished a long monologue for Roderick. It's sad enough to make the stones weep for what neurasthenics have to go through. It smells charmingly of mildew obtained by mixing the sounds of the low oboe with violin harmonics.[13]

It seems that Debussy had made the final jump and that the musical texture and language he was looking for had become an integral part of the imaginary structure of the house.

Debussy, writing his own libretto, generally follows the story line furnished by Poe, with some important modifications. The narrator, a childhood friend of Roderick Usher, has been called to visit the house where this rarefied race of intellectuals and artists is slowly dying. The last male offspring, Roderick Usher, is absorbed in the inner contemplation of his soul and obsessed by his ailing sister, Lady Madeline, his twin and spectral double. During the friend's visit, she is found dead and her corpse is buried in a vault under the castle. To assuage Roderick's grief and progressive withdrawal from the world, the friend reads a story from a romance of chivalry which they used to read as children. Against the background of a raging storm and at the violent action of the romance, sounds are heard from the innermost recesses of the castle. As the romance climaxes with the dramatic fall of a shield, Lady Madeline appears, dishevelled and bloody: she had been buried alive and now falls on her brother, dragging him to his death. As the friend flees, the house collapses and a red moon rises.

The principal change effected by Debussy in his libretto also has strong musical implications. In Poe's tale the narrative voice belongs almost exclusively to the friend through whose eyes and memory the story is told. In a way nothing exists outside his consciousness and voice. The voice of Roderick himself, his fears, his musical and poetic creations are revealed through this voice. In his libretto Debussy, writing in a dramatic form, had to give a voice to Roderick, who, according to Debussy, resembles Poe. He has also developed the sinister figure of the Doctor, only a silhouette in Poe. In Debussy's libretto he is the agent of death, Roderick's rival for the love of the Lady Madeline, ultimately responsible for her being entombed alive.

One does not know what exact baritone ranges Debussy would have used for his three male characters, or if, as in *Pelléas*, he would have graduated them from Deep Bass, to Bass-Baritone, to Bariton-Martin. The assignation of the three roles to baritones of the same range is significant in that it opens up the strong possibility that the characters are three incarnations of one single consciousness.

Lady Madeline, a silent apparition in Poe, is heard at the outset of the opera singing the first verse of Roderick's poem "The Haunted Palace." A metaphor for the deranged creative mind, this poem, which is at the heart of Poe's tale, becomes for Debussy a strong dramatic and musical motif. It sets the drama in its proper location, the house itself, since the unique setting is the interior of Roderick's study. It is also the means to establish from the very beginning Lady Madeline as a voice in the opera, her role as inspirator and victim of Roderick's obsessions. Musically this "song" plays very much the same role as Mélisande's song in act 3, scene 1, of *Pelléas*, establishing the musical and poetic climate which surrounds the character. As a motif, Debussy had planned to have Roderick sing a reprise of the song in the second scene of the opera, adding "this is what she sang" and therefore intimating that Roderick is conscious of his sister's death.

In the Allende-Blin version, this reprise is clumsily attributed to Lady Madeline's voice, not Roderick's, and is a florid setting of the forth stanza of the poem, an early sketch by Debussy that he seems to have discarded at an early stage of the composition of the piece.

Debussy emphasizes the motif of Lady Madeline's voice further by having the Doctor exclaim in the first scene:

> I know. . . . If you could hear that voice which seems to come from so much beyond herself! . . . Many a time he makes her sing music fit to damn angels! It is incomprehensible and dangerous. A woman, after all, is not a lute. . . . But he won't accept! He is not aware that it's her very soul which is departing with the song . . .

This passage with its echoes of Hoffmann is entirely Debussy's invention, although it may be traced to the epigraph to Poe's tale, a quote from the popular French poet Béranger:

> Son coeur est un luth suspendu
> Sitôt qu'on le touche, il résonne.
>
> His heart is a suspended lute
> Whenever one touches it, it resounds.

Moving away from Poe's tale, Debussy has made the Lady Madeline the center of a complex musical structure: she does not only represent, as in Poe, the obsessive, incestuous love that governs Roderick's life and finally drags him to death. She embodies music, the only art practiced by Debussy's Roderick, who in Poe is also a painter and a poet, a total allegory of the artist.

Beyond the song of Lady Madeline, it is the entire musical structure that is supposed to take charge of expressing the tortures endured and revealed in Roderick's creative acts. In choosing this subject for an opera, Debussy assumed the daunting task of revealing through music what Poe termed in his tale:

> . . . that morbid condition of an auditory nerve which rendered all music intolerable to the sufferer, with the exception of certain effects of stringed instruments.

Even in the fragments that remain from the score, even in the reconstructed versions, the true nature of the musical texture remains a subject of conjecture since we have next to no information about Debussy's intent for orchestration.

The most formidable problem in dealing with the lyric theater, with a narrative source of any kind versus a dramatic source, is that of time. How can a plot that takes several weeks to unfold in the tale be concentrated in a one-act structure? We must remember that Debussy's third libretto is in two contiguous scenes, with no possibility of time elapsing between them. The spectator would then have to believe that the arrival of the friend, Lady Madeline's death, her entombment and subsequent ghostly reappearance, precipitating Roderick's death and the collapse of the house can take place in the real time of the opera, an impossibility, of course.

Debussy seems to have been unconcerned by this problem. In fact, the vagueness of time and place, their dreamlike interiorization, in this largely symbolic plot, their "mise en abîme" in the central poem "The Haunted House," may have attracted him to the tale. The elasticity of time, its indeterminacy, constitute one of the paradoxes of short narrative forms in general, and of Poe's tale in particular. In one of the fragment of Roderick's opening monologue in scene 2, Debussy achieves both through words and in music, the complete fusion of place and time, transcending, in the face of death, any measurable dimension of these elements:

"Stay! Stay! . . . die here." Be still, I'll obey. It's cold, the fog is rising. . . . What's that over there? . . . Near the grey rushes? A bird which has lost its way? There it passes through the fog, waving like a funereal hand. Its wings beat like time itself breathing.

Such a passage may of course suggest a comparison, from a literary point, with similar moments in *Pelléas*, but, musically, it clearly points forward to such scenes as the death of Wozzeck. In its unfinished state, it is because of Debussy's attempts at finding solutions to problems never tackled before him that *The Fall of the House of Usher* should retain our interest, since it will probably never function on the stage.

Similar problems of transposition from the short narrative genre to the stage have captured the attention of several composers in the twentieth century. Without knowing it, Debussy may have opened a whole tradition of operas derived from short stories or novellas. Recent attempts at setting *The House of Usher* to music include those of Clarence Loomis (1941), Kenneth Klauss (1952), Morris Hutchins Ruger (1953), Gregory Sandow (1975), and Hendrick Hofmeyr (1988). Philip Glass, in his two-act opera, first performed by the American Repertory Theater in May 1988, tackles the same problems as Debussy faced, with very similar solutions, on the dramatic level at least.

Another American composer, Russell Currie, has composed a Poe trilogy. His *Dream within a Dream*, based on Poe's *Fall of the House of Usher* and his *Cask of Amontillado*, have been performed by the Bronx Opera and as a double bill by the Jersey Lyric Opera in 1988.

Yet it is mostly the adaptation of Henry James's stories to the opera stage which furnish the most successful and illustrious examples of the tradition inaugurated by Debussy in his unfinished opera. *The Turn of the Screw* and *The Aspern Papers* find their composers (Britten and Argento) faced with the same difficulties as Debussy with Poe: how to give a plurality of voices to enigmatic first person narratives; how to turn around the focus from the literary to the elements needed at the center of an opera—melodic motifs, songs, even arias; finally, how to give dramatic and musical substance to concepts of time and place, which seemed inseparable from the short story or novella genre.

In finding solutions to these problems, these composers were certainly, if unconsciously, following the road opened by Debussy.

Notes

1. Debussy, *Letters*, selected and edited by François Lesure and Roger Nichols (Cambridge: Harvard University Press, 1987), p.194.

2. Giulio, Gatti-Casazza, *Memories of the Opera* (New York, 1941), p. 157.

3. François Lesure and Richard Langham Smith, eds., *Debussy on Music* (New York: Alfred A. Knopf, 1977), p. 234.

4. Letter to Robert Godet, 6 Feb. 1911, in *Letters*, p.235.

5. *La Chute de la Maison Usher*, version by Juan Allende-Blin (Paris: Jobert, 1979), 41pp., 400 bars.

6. E.M.I. Angel, 1984, D.S-38168. The cast includes Christine Barbaux, soprano (Lady Madeline), François Leroux, baritone (The Doctor), Pierre-Yves Le Maigat, bass baritone (The Friend), Jean-Philippe Lafont, baritone (Roderick). All quotes in my text are from the translation of Debussy's original French, by Elizabeth Buzzard, which accompanies the record.

The record itself furnishes interesting examples of Poe's impact on French music of the beginning of the twentieth century, since in addition to Debussy's unfinished opus, it presents performances, by the same orchestra and chef, of Florent Schmitt's *Etude pour "Le Palais hanté" d'Edgar Poe* (Opus 49, 1904) and of André Caplet's Symphonic Study for harp and orchestra *The Masque of the Red Death* (1908).

7. A translation of Debussy's final version of the libretto appears in Edward Lockspeiser, *Music and Painting* (New York: Icon Editions, Harper and Row, 1973), pp. 173–82.

8. *Letters*, p. 192.

9. *Letters*, p. 212.

10. *Letters*, p. 223.

11. *Letters*, p. 252.

12. *Letters*, p. 316.

13. *Letters*, p. 203.

Verdi, America, and Adelina Patti

MARTIN CHUSID

For a number of years Verdi's stage compositions have provided between 15 and 20 percent of all operas staged in the United States.[1] And it is not only *Rigoletto, Trovatore, Traviata*, and *Aïda* that are performed regularly. Each year between a dozen and fifteen different operas by Verdi are staged in America. These include regularly *Don Carlo, Otello, Falstaff, Ballo in Maschera, Luisa Miller, Macbeth, Simon Boccanegra*, and *La Forza Del Destino*. And then there are the more than occasional performances of *I Verspri Siciliani, Ernani, Nabucco, I Lombardi, Attila, I Due Foscari*, and most recently *Stiffelio* and *Aroldo* as well as the composer's nonoperatic works, the *Requiem*, the *Quattro Pezzi Sacri*, and the *String Quartet*. One can even hear on popular music radio stations the great chorus from *Nabucco*, "Va pensiero," Italy's unofficial national anthem, the lament of the exiled Hebrews in their Babylonian captivity.

My remarks will focus on a family of musicians responsible for the earliest performances of an opera by Verdi in the United States, *I Lombardi Alla Prima Crociata*, Verdi's fourth stage work, and one of the most successful of Verdi's early operas. For sheer number of performances at the time, it appears to have been surpassed only by his very next opera, *Ernani*.[2] Interestingly enough, it was *Ernani* which was the second opera to be heard in the United States. This took place about six weeks after the premiere of *I Lombardi*, but performed by a different troupe.[3]

The year was 1847 and the date for *I Lombardi* was 3 March. There were three impresarios for the production and two of them sang as well: A. Sanquirico, who took the bass role of Pagano, and the *tenore di forza*, Salvatore Patti, who sang Arvino. Patti was born in 1800 in Catania, the beautiful city on the east coast of Sicily, in which Vincenzo Bellini was born, only a year later.[4] Father of a large and extraordinarily musical family, Salvatore had been called to New York by Sanquirico to help manage and perform in

207

an opera house on Chambers Street in Manhattan. Heading the family with Patti was the successful, but by this time far from young, soprano Caterina Chiesa Barilli. With them were eight children. Caterina had given birth to the four oldest with her first husband, a composer and singing maestro who had discovered her singing at a fountain in Rome, and trained her for the stage. She was quite successful, and no less a composer than Donizetti wrote for her the part of the heroine in his opera, *The Siege of Calais*, first performed in Naples in 1836.[5]

After her husband died she sang in an operatic troupe in Catania, where she married—who else?—the leading tenor, Salvatore Patti. The year was 1837. Together, the Pattis had four additional children, and the youngest was born in 1843. She was Adelina Patti, probably artistically and financially the most successful singer in the entire nineteenth century. Among Caterina's children with Barilli was a son, Ettore, a fine baritone, who some years later was to sing the very first *Rigoletto* in America (in New York, February 1855). When discussing her training, Adelina later in life credited Ettore with being her first and best voice teacher.

Another gifted Barilli child was Antonio, a *basso profondo*, who was the vocal director for the American premiere of *Nabucco*, an opera given by the Sanquirico-Patti troupe the next year (April 1848). This took place in the new Astor Place Opera House in New York's Greenwich Village. The fact that he was a vocal director needs a bit of background. Precisely what is a vocal director? It should be borne in mind that till the middle 1860s, Italian operatic performances did not have a single conductor. Instead it had two directors. The first and most important was the vocal director. He was a composer, or maestro, who taught the singers their roles, corrected the parts from the score sent by the publisher, and adjusted the vocal lines and even, at times, wrote new music for the singers, for their special voice requirements. He also set the tempos for the individual sections and pieces of music, and he directed all the rehearsals and the first three public performances. It was only after this was done that the instrumental director, the first violin leader of the orchestra, called a *violino principale*, took over.[6] This was the system used by the Barilli troupe in New York.

A third Barilli child was Nicolo, who became a lyric bass and took the part of Sam in the Boston permiere of *Un Ballo in Maschera* (March 1861) under the direction of Emanuele Muzio. Muzio was Verdi's only composition student and became the composer's closest friend.

The single daughter of Barilli and Caterina was the soprano

Clothilde, who sang the part of Giselda, the principal soprano role in *I Lombardi* at the American premiere. According to a letter from the American composer-pianist Louis Moreau Gottschalk, Clothilde sang with great success not only in New York, but also in San Francisco and South America, where she died. Gottschalk, as we shall see later, knew the Patti family very well.

The oldest of the Patti children—that is, the four children who were born after Caterina's marriage to Salvatore—was Amalia, a contralto who sang Fenena at the U.S. premiere of *Nabucco*. She also performed Maddalena when her half-brother Ettore was singing Rigoletto the first time in America. By that date, 1855, Amalia was all of seventeen years and for five years had been the wife of the impresario for the *Rigoletto* and other Verdi premieres in the United States, Maurice Strakosch. At the Performing Arts Library at Lincoln Center there is also a program which lists Amalia for the part of Ulrica in early performances in New York of *Un Ballo in Maschera*, also conducted by Muzio.

The second of the Patti children was Carlotta, who began her musical training as a pianist and studied with the German virtuoso, Henri (Heinrich) Herzr. However, after the phenomenal financial success of her younger sister Adelina as a child prodigy, the family decided to develop Carlotta's voice rather than her keyboard abilities. She too had remarkable musical talent, and a flexible vocal instrument that reportedly could reach G and G sharp above high C. Programs of her concerts, again at Lincoln Center, indicate that she sang the arias of the Queen of the Night in Mozart's *Magic Flute*. They go up to F above high C, and there are some authors who claim she transposed the music *up* in order to show off her high G. Among her display pieces was the difficult aria called the Bolero from the last act of Verdi's *I Vespri Sicilliani*. On the lyric stage she performed among other parts the coloratura roles of Lucia di Lammermoor and Amina in Bellini's *La Sonnambula*. But her stage career was inhibited because she was lame, one leg shorter than the other, and she turned to a concert career instead. As with her sister Adelina, her success was worldwide, and she sang for approximately twenty years before marrying the Chevalier Ernest de Monque, a cellist, and retired from concert life.

The only Patti son, Carlo, studied violin with Luigi Arditi, and became a violinist, conductor, and composer. During the Civil War, Carlo is said to have led Confederate army bands, and afterwards traveled widely in Caiifornia and Mexico before settling finally in Memphis, Tennessee, as leader of an orchestra.

The star of the family, however, was the youngest, Adelina.

Born in Spain in 1843, she came to the United States a year or two later. She began singing professionally at seven and continued her career for more than fifty years. Since she did not return to Europe until 1861, two years after her operatic debut in New York, it is clear that she was brought up, trained musically, and well launched upon her career here in America. She is, in fact, the first great American singer. As an infant she was taken to the opera house every night that her mother sang, absorbing musical theater through her pores. Later in life she said that as a small child upon returning home after a performance, she recreated the entire evening for herself under the covers in her bed, acting and singing all the roles, and even taking the part of the audience. Audiences were not as quiet as our audiences today. In the process, she helped develop her phenomenal memory, as well as her skill as a mimic and as an actress.

In the years during which *I Lombardi* and *Nabucco* received their American premieres, the chief operatic competition to the Sanquirico-Patti company came from a traveling troupe based in Cuba, Marty's Havana Italian Opera Company. The leaders of the orchestra were the same Luigi Arditi who would later teach Carlo Patti violin, and the great virtuoso double-bass player, Giovanni Bottesini, who many years later was to conduct the world premiere of *Aïda* in Cairo, in 1871, and for whom Verdi wrote the double-bass part opening the final scene, the murder scene, of *Otello*. The Havana-based group presented the first performances in the United States of *Ernani*, in New York, and of *I Due Foscari*, in Boston, during April and May of 1847; and in 1850, they presented *Attila*, the title role taken by Ignazio Marini who had sung that part under Verdi himself at the world premiere (Venice, 1846). The company also gave the American premiere of *Macbeth*, with the remarkable soprano Angelina Bosio singing Lady Macbeth. Both events took place at Niblo's Garden, at South Ferry on the tip of lower Manhattan, during April of 1850.[7]

During one of their New York visits—probably the first one in 1847—Caterina Barilli-Patti brought little Adelina to Arditi's hotel room to sing for the violinist and for Bottesini. In his volume *My Reminiscences* (New York, 1896), Arditi wrote "How am I to give you an adequate description of the effect which that child's miraculous notes produced upon our enchanted senses? Both Bottesini and I wept genuine tears of emotion. We were simply amazed at the well-nigh perfect manner in which she delivered some of the most difficult and vared arias without the slightest effort or self-consciousness." Adelina's vivacity, when quite a tiny girl, Arditi went on, was remarkable. Nothing escaped her notice. And if she observed curious mannerisms in anyone, years afterwards she would remember and imitate them perfectly.

A letter from Bottesini to his father in Italy dated 17 April, 1847—shortly after the Havana troupe has arrived in New York for the first time—reports the presence of old friends in the Sanquirico-Patti group: Clothilde Barilli, the tenor Sesto Benedetti, and Sanquirico himself. And then he indicates in no uncertain fashion how much American audiences still had to learn about opera. He writes of their performances, "our company must thank the virginity of American eardrums, because otherwise there would be a massacre. If one excepts *Ernani*, the other operas were ruined! Horrendous discords, but always applauded. What luck! I don't know what we'll do returning to Italy."[8]

In 1850, at age seven, Adelina Patti, or as she was called at the time "Little Lina," embarked on the first of her many triumphant concert tours of America, with her brother-in-law, Maurice Strakosch, as pianist. Included were the major cities of the Eastern, Mid-Atlantic, and Southern states. As an indication of how successful the tour was, the traveling virtuoso violinist Ole Bull heard Adelina sing. He saw the audiences filling her halls and not his own, and arranged with Adelina's father and Strakosch to cancel his own tour and join theirs. This arrangement lasted several years. In 1857 Adelina toured with Louis Gottchalk, whom we mentioned before, in both the American South and the West Indies, and on Thanksgiving Day of 1858, at the advanced age of sixteen, she made her operatic debut. This was at the Academy of Music in New York. The opera, in which she was coached by the conductor of the work, Emanuele Muzio, was *Lucia di Lammermoor*. Adelina sang fourteen different roles that season, including four by Verdi (Elvira in *Ernani*, Gilda in *Rigoletto*, Leonora in *Trovatore*, and Violetta in *Traviata*). The latter role she herself called her favorite on a number of occasions. During her long career she added three other Verdi roles: Giovanna D'Arco, Luisa Miller, and during the seventy's and eighty's, when her voice had deepened a bit, she sang a splendid Aïda, both here and in Europe. Her favorite Radames was the tenor Ernesto Nicolini. Despite his professional Italian name, he was a Frenchman who became her second husband. Although he was sixty at the time, Nicolini sang the minor part of Pistol in the American premiere of *Falstaff* at the Metropolitan Opera in the middle 1890s.

As mentioned earlier, Muzio was Verdi's only composition student. But relatively early in his career he had largely given up his own composing to become a conductor. Not surprisingly, the works of his master and close friend were central to his repertoire. Some weeks prior to conducting Adelina's operatic debut, Muzio directed the first of three Verdi premieres in America—namely, *I Vespri Siciliani* on 7 November 1859. While in the United States, Muzio also conducted the premiere performance of *Un Ballo In Maschera* in New York (February 1861) and some years later, *Aïda*, also in New York (November 1873). He remained in our country throughout the Civil War, and wrote a number of interest-ing letters to Verdi about the political situation. As an Italian whose nation had just freed itself from Austrian domination, it is not surprising to learn that Muzio opposed slavery and that he de-clared himself to be "a Union man." His enthusiasm for all things American extended to a wife, and he married a young lady in Louisville. As Giuseppina Strepponi later suggested, the woman was somewhat young for Muzio, who was by then in his early for-ties, and the marriage did not end happily.

Strepponi, in the late 1830s one of Italy's leading dramatic sop-ranos, was Verdi's second wife. She was an extraordinarily intelli-gent woman who contributed much more to Verdi's growth as a composer than most people realize. In 1877 she wrote about Patti to Giulio Ricordi of the famous Italian publishing family: "Open your ears well. Don't lose a note. You've never heard her equal, nor will you ever again."

But we should give the last comments on Patti to Verdi himself. In the same year, and probably about the very same performances to which Giuseppina had reacted, the composer wrote from Genoa to his close friend, Opprandino Arrivabeni:

> Here there is nothing new except for three performances by Patti re-ceived with an indescribable enthusiasm—deservedly, because she is, by nature, an artist so complete that perhaps there has never been her equal. Oh, oh, and Malibran? Very great, but not always equal. Some-times sublime and sometimes bizarre, the style of her singing was not very pure. Her stage movements, not always successful. Her voice, shrill in the high notes. Despite all, a very great, marvelous artist. But Patti is more complete. Marvelous voice, very pure style of singing, stupendous actress, with a charm and naturalness that no one else has.[9]

Earlier that year Verdi had already written to Giulio Ricordi—this was when Patti was coming to Italy for her Italian premiere; she had never been there before as a singer. Verdi writes:

> Patti was then what she is now: perfect organization, perfect equilib-rium between the singer and the actress, a born artist in every sense of

the word. When I first heard her in London, she was 18. I remained dumbfounded, not only by the marvelous execution, but by some actions on stage in which she revealed herself as a great actress. I remember the chaste modest behavior when, in *La Sonnambula*, she placed herself on the soldier's bed, and when, in *Don Giovanni*, she came forth contaminated from the room with the libertine. I remember a certain piece of stage business in Don Bartolo's aria in *Il Barbiere di Siviglia*, and most of all, in the recitative which precedes the quartet in *Rigoletto*, when her father indicates her beloved in the tavern saying, "And you still love him?" "I love him," she replies. There is no expression that can reproduce the sublime effect of these words spoken by her. If you see Patti, give her regards on behalf of me and my wife. I'm not sending the usual congratulations because I really think that for her, it would be the most useless thing about her debut in Milan. But ever since I heard her the first time in London, almost a child, I judged her a marvelous singer and actress, an exception in art.[10]

Notes

1. See the annual listing of projected operatic performances in the United States of the major and most minor companies; normally printed in the first Fall issue each year by *Opera News*.

2. This remark is based on the extremely large number of librettos printed for performances of *I Lombardi* during the 1840s and '50s, which have been acquired in microfilm copies by the American Institute for Verdi Studies and housed in the Verdi Archive at New York University.

3. Information on early performances of Verdi's operas taken from my article "Casts for Verdi Premieres in the U.S. (1847–1975)", *Verdi Newsletters 2* (December 1976) and 3 (June 1977). *Newsletters* 1 and 2 printed as *Rivs Newsletter*.

4. Biographical information in this article derived from the following: *Enciclopedia dello Spettacolo* (1954–1962); Schmidl's *Dizionario universale dei musicisti* (1928–29, 1938), *La Musica: Enciclopedia Storica* (1966) and *La Musica: Parte Seconda, Dizionario* (1968, 1971); *Ricordi Dizionario della Musica e Musicisti* (1959) and *Ricordi Enciclopedia della Musica* (1964); *The New Grove's Dictionary of Music and Musicians*, 6th edition (1980); Herman Klein's *The Reign of Patti* (1920).

5. See William Ashbrook's *Donizetti and his Operas* (1982), pp. 113, 563, and 639.

6. See my article "A letter by the composer about *Giovanna d'rrco* and some remarks on the division of musical direction in Verdi's day," *Performance Practice Review* (Spring 1990).

7. See my article "Verdi's earliest U.S. premieres," *Opera News* (7 January and 4 February 1978).

8. Ibid.

9. See Annibale Alberti (ed.), *Verdi Intimo: Carteggio di Giuseppe Verdi con il Conte Opprandino Arrivabene (1861, 1886)* (1931), pp. 205–6.

10. See G. Cesari and A. Luzio (ed.), *I Copialettere di Giuseppe Verdi* (1913), pp. 624–25.

Part Six
The Moderns

Kansas City Composer Meets Regency Dandy: Virgil Thomson's *Lord Byron*

ALICE LEVINE

> "Not another Faust opera please."
> —Thomson, letter to a
> librettist, 25 January 1972

"Byron is dead." The opening words of Virgil Thomson's opera *Lord Byron* are blunt enough for a telegram. Yet, as the very words that the grief-stricken young Tennyson inscribed on a rock upon hearing the news of Byron's death in the spring of 1824, they also express the significance that Byron held for a generation of poets and readers, and the momentousness of his passing.

The Romantic myth of the aristocratic poet-hero, "feeling as he writes"[1] and sacrificing himself to the cause of Greek independence, would remain alive and well through most of the nineteenth century. In the world of music, not only his poetry but Byron's life and personality inspired settings by numerous major and secondary composers and can be seen to have made a significant impact on the work of Berlioz, Schumann, and Liszt.[2] However, for many of us today, the Romantic Byron myth is something very remote, something that indeed is, or should be, dead. We find it surprising, therefore, to see Lord Byron turn up as the subject of a modern opera.

Still more surprising is the fact that that opera was composed by Virgil Thomson. Kansas City–born Thomson was by natural inclination and self-cultivation the thoroughly American composer. The Baptist hymnbook, American-plains simplicity of his lyric style suited perfectly the gnomic minimalism of Gertrude Stein in his two earlier operatic masterpieces, *Four Saints in Three Acts* (1928), about Saint Teresa of Avila, and *The Mother of Us All* (1947), about Susan B. Anthony. Of the modern European composers, Thomson admired Erik Satie, whose music, Thomson wrote, "has

217

eschewed the impressive, the heroic, the oratorical, everything that
is aimed at moving mass audiences" [3]—in other words, everything
that Romanticism had become. The central ethos of Thomson's
style is thus antithetical to the Romantic subject of Byron's life. As
he himself acknowledged, years before contemplating a project on
Byron:

> . . . the travels of Lord Byron, like the private lives of John Keats, or
> of Emily Dickinson, are as far removed from anything we have ever
> known as is the demise of Richard Wagner's Isolde, who, with nothing
> wrong organically about her, stands in the middle of a stage and falls
> dead merely because her lover has just died.[4]

All the same Thomson contemplated writing an opera about
Byron as far back as 1960. After searching for a librettist he met
the poet-playwright Jack Larson and worked closely with him on
the opera, which took seven years of work to complete.[5] *Lord
Byron* is a work for large forces, involving a big orchestra, sixteen
soloists, a chorus, and a ballet. In its original three-act version,
conceived for a premiere at the Metropolitan Opera, it lasted a little over three hours. However, after the Met canceled its plans to
produce the work, it was cut to two acts for a premiere by the
American Opera Center of the Juilliard School on 20 April 1972.[6]
Additional cuts (including the entire ballet) were made for publication of the piano-vocal score, and in that version the opera lasts a
little over an hour-and-a-half.[7]

The history of the opera's critical reception is remarkably contradictory. To begin with, there was the Met's cancelation of the
premiere, after having arranged a commission for the work. Thomson says the Met never gave a reason for the cancelation, but
Rudolf Bing later wrote "frankly, we did not like the results." [8]
Most of the reviews of the Juilliard premiere were negative: "a
very bland score," according to Harold Schonberg; "a singularly
empty work from the musical standpoint," according to Andrew
Porter, who concluded, "Perhaps the British would like it—but not
for long." [9] However, registering a minority opinion at the time of
the opera's premiere, Leighton Kerner expressed high regard for
the work:

> I can predict . . . that "Lord Byron" will prove to be a necessary work
> for any opera company that cares at all about the international music
> of this century and will be given display space somewhere above Mr.
> Thomson's earlier operas and somewhere below Stravinsky's "The

Rake's Progress." . . . Everything of Thomson seems to be in this score. The cleanly simple-sounding hymns out of churches bleached by the Kansas sun, the choral dissonances grown in the gardens of neo-classical Paris, the still miraculous ear for setting English words to music, the unfailing wit that sometimes separates to confront you with a sudden stab of sentiment—all these ingredients of such outwardly dissimilar works as "Four Saints in Three Acts," "The Seine at Night," "The Louisiana Story" music, and various of the short choral pieces come together in "Lord Byron" as needed by the particular moments in the drama and by the particular impulses of a mind of the finest taste, and the result is not a potpourri but a beautiful and complete creation.[10]

Indeed, later evaluations have been largely praiseworthy. After a radio broadcast in December 1976 Porter recanted his earlier review and wrote enthusiastically about this unusual work, regretting only that cuts had been made for the published score.[11] Richard Jackson's entry in *The New Grove Dictionary*, moreover, declares *Lord Byron* to be Thomson's "most ambitious project" and rates it extremely high in his *oeuvre*:

> . . . there is a seriousness of tone, a comparative richness of texture and a lyrical expansiveness seldom encountered in his earlier works. . . . What finally sets *Lord Byron* apart from Thomson's previous work, however, is its emotional content: the opera rises to moments of real passion. This suggests a new dimension for a composer who frequently demonstrates his ability to entertain but whose expressive voice is always carefully muted.[12]

Still, after a rather weak, semi-staged performance by the New York Opera Repertory Theatre at Alice Tully Hall on 7 December 1985, John Rockwell dubbed *Lord Byron*, all things considered, "Mr. Thomson's problem child of an opera." [13]

Judgment errors are famously common in reviews of new and innovative musical works. However, the ambivalence in the early reception history of *Lord Byron* is, I believe, traceable to the contradictory character of the opera itself: the apparent incompatibility between the composer's style and his subject. This is not to say that the subject was an inappropriate one for Thomson or that he did not succeed in penetrating it. On the contrary, in its idiosyncratic recreation of the life of Byron, the opera illuminates the man precisely by deconstructing the layers of Romantic myth that have enveloped him since the publication of Cantos I and II of *Childe Harold's Pilgrimage* in 1812. Moreover, this opera is so straight-

forward and the music, like mostly all of Thomson's, so lyrical
and easy on the ear, that the ways in which it is innovative, or
even radical, are not easily perceived.

To begin with, Thomson's conception of Byron differs considerably from the Romantic myth of this "wandering outlaw of his own
dark mind," [14] famous throughout Europe for his adventures in the
East, for his thinly disguised autobiographical outpourings (*Childe
Harold*, *Manfred*, and the Oriental tales), and for his death at age
thirty-six in Greece. For one thing, Thomson sets his biographical dramatization in London from 1812 to 1815. This is the period,
as the opera explains, covered by the memoirs Byron wrote
in Europe, which—presumably because of their scandalous
contents—were burned by his friends and loved ones shortly after
his death. The opera, a fantasy-reconstruction of the contents of
the memoirs, is comprised of "memory scenes" that focus, as the
memoirs supposedly did, on the "facts" of his courtship, marriage,
and separation, and also on his relationship with his half-sister,
Augusta Leigh (which coincided with these events though it very
likely was not detailed in the memoirs).[15] This period shows Byron
not as a brooding, wandering outcast, but as a lionized young lord
of Regency high life, basking in his celebrity as a poet and regularly gracing aristocratic ballrooms with his charismatic presence.
Thomson was aware that this "very very English" setting was not
the traditional representation of the poet:

> Certainly our view of Byron is far from the standard continental ones,
> all of which are derived more from his heroes than from him. After all,
> my opera deals with a poet still under thirty and, in spite of his (largely
> private) misbehaviors, surrounded by posh people. His wife was a rela-
> tion of the Melbournes and the Lovelaces and Augusta was lady-in-
> waiting to the Queen. He himself was a sixth earl (Lizzie Lutyens
> insists "only a baron"), had been to Harrow and Cambridge, and cer-
> tainly knew how to behave in graceful society, including a skiplike
> walk with cane that he had perfected for not appearing to limp.[16]

It is not clear what Thomson means by "largely private" misbehaviors, since Byron's affronts to the Lords and affairs with the
Ladies were the talk of the town. What is apparent, though, is that
the myth of Byron has here been exchanged for the Byron of the
gossip column, with as much attention given to aristocratic rank
and the "posh people" of Byron's world as to Byron himself.

Consistent with a gossip-column approach, the opera's memory
scenes focus on Byron's relationships with women. We see him at a
party bantering with vain and doting females, who vie with one

another to be immortalized in his lyrics; we see him propose to the more serious, moralistic, and restrained, but for all that no less eager, Annabella Milbanke; we see him at a drunken bachelor's party with Hobhouse and Moore, girding himself for the wedding day; and we see him playful and tender with his sister, and callously abusive to his wife. For the most part, Thomson and Larson were careful scholars, sketching their portraits of Byron and his coterie from the letters and the detailed three-volume biography by Leslie Marchand, published in 1957. Certainly, there is ample biographical evidence of Byron's harsh treatment of his wife; and if in the opera it is she, rather than Caroline Lamb, who pronounces Byron "mad, bad and dangerous to know," she surely had at least equal provocation to do so.

The several scenes between Byron and Augusta Leigh or Annabella Milbanke or both explore a range of sexual politics. In general, Thomson chooses to illustrate the charm, as well as the silliness, of these relationships, rather than to romanticize them as manifestations either of evil or of ideal genius. Amorality seems to be the order of the day, both in the almost child's-play relationship between Byron and Augusta and in Lady Byron's exceptional obtuseness about what is going on around her and, perhaps, within her. The most gracious of Thomson's bel canto writing is found in the love duet between brother and sister in act two, scene three; the music never plunges to the tragic depths of unlawful passion but, when it is not entirely playful, is sweet and touching. In the same scene, a trio between husband, sister, and wife implies—with scherzando innocence and a certain piquancy—a ménage-à-trois in which Lady Byron is complicitous, if not entirely consciously so. Thomson allows Lady Byron to catch the other two *in flagrante delicto* to precipitate a crisis in operatic style. After Mrs. Leigh rejects Byron's rather impractical proposal that she elope with him to the Continent, he takes his leave of the women and of England.

What is the explanation for the selfish and self-destructive behavior of one so gifted and adored? Scholars have liked to speculate on the extent to which Byron's club foot determined the development of his personality, and the opera enthusiastically endorses this approach. The libretto refers to "his foot" no fewer than seven times. Thus, with typical sisterly teasing, Augusta—the only person whom Byron allows to mention his deformity in his presence—analyzes the great poet's wicked wit as a feeble sort of defense mechanism: "Poor baby Byron's little limp to his walk makes him scarum men with his naughty talk" (2.3.601–5).[17] After another reference is made to his limp, Byron essentially confirms Augusta's analysis: "'Tis my nature in all things to strive to be first. Since I cannot be the world's best man, I shall be its worst."

Clearly Thomson did not set out to recreate the Romantic myth of Byron as the best man; he finds "the worst" sufficiently interesting. And although a view of Byron as *homme fatal* is certainly not un-Romantic, Thomson supplies something thoroughly American to his portrait:

> [Byron] had to die before 40 . . . and it was the only way of being successful in politics. His other messes all came from having to humanize himself. As a lord, a millionaire, a genius, and a beauty, life would have been impossible without constant misbehavior, cutting himself down to size so he could work. . . . With *Don Juan* the poetry career was probably ending; certainly the beauty was mostly gone; love he'd had; the political apotheosis (with House of Lords impossible from the sister scandal) was available. So he had to take it in Greece and succeed by dying before he messed it up. I'm delighted with this tragical view. He's like Marilyn Monroe or James Dean—romance and violence, drunkenness and early death.[18]

The opera offers us a view of Romantic fatalism as filtered through the lens of Hollywood; perhaps the fact that the librettist resided there is no mere coincidence. (One wonders how the opera would have turned out if Robert Lowell or Robert Penn Warren, whom Thomson had also approached for a libretto, had written it.)[19] In fact it was Gore Vidal who planted the idea for an opera about Byron in Thomson's mind when he mentioned his own interest in writing a play about Byron. As Thomson recalled, in an interview in the *Times* in 1972:

> [Vidal] really didn't have too great a determination to write the play, but he had a second-act curtain line, which he thought pretty infallible in the theater. It had to do with Byron's declaration of having had a child by his half-sister, Augusta Leigh. Of course, that seemed a good deal more sensational or scandalous 10 years ago than it would be now, although not too many people that we know have had children by their sisters.[20]

Thus, from the beginning, Thomson's interest in Byron as an operatic subject was apparently less concerned with myth than with scandal, or at least gossip. That Thomson saw his subject matter as potentially scandalous is confirmed by his conviction that the Met rejected his opera because its Board was reluctant to present a work highlighting incest and pregnancy. Thomson's belief may not be justified, since these themes are hardly strangers to the operatic stage, but it does reveal his view of his material. Rather than make his opera an extended portrayal of poetic *Weltschmerz*, he preferred to tell what inquiring minds want to know about the whims and foibles of the rich, young, and restless of the Regency.

Reinforcing this atypical conception of Byron, Larson and Thomson's treatment of their subject differs substantially from Romantic approaches. They have set out not to make Byron a character-type with whom the audience is invited to sympathize and identify, but to emphasize Byron's historical and social situation, and thereby to keep him at a distance, as it were, for purposes of observation. We are reminded at the outset that Byron is dead, and the memory scenes, in which Byron is the key performer, employ a typical Hollywood technique: the flashback.[21] While we are drawn into the scenes, we are recurrently made conscious of the artfulness and fantasy of the reconstruction before us. Further, the memory scenes are set in an elaborate frame, the opera's "present," which is comprised of mourning Londoners, a select group of dead poets' spirits, and the close friends and loved ones surviving Byron. The setting is Westminster Abbey, Poets' Corner, 1824; Byron's friends and relatives are now dedicated to obtaining a Westminster Abbey burial for him and, with that end in view, arguing over what should be done with the troublesome memoirs. Nearly all of act one is devoted to the frame; Byron himself, or rather the spirit of Byron, does not appear until the act's final few minutes.

An appreciation of the effect of this frame is crucial to understanding the statement the opera is making about Byron and to appreciating the opera's sophisticated artistry. In lieu of a prelude, a one-bar introduction—a seemingly military roll of the snare and field drums, accompanied by an ascending scale—calls us to attention for important news, and the opening chorus of lamenting Londoners, set to dissonances rare in Thomson's music, is a paradigm of Byron myth-making that bears quoting in full:

> Byron is dead. Weep to hear it said.
> Say the sun fell from noon.
> Say night missed the moon.
> But Byron dead. Oh! weep to hear it said!
> The cannons of Greece report his death;
> The laureate decrees his epitaph.
> Hear the cobblestone hush.
> Can Childe Harold's thrush be dead?
> Oh, weep to hear it said. (1.2– 24)

The larger-than-life image of the man, the tragic death in Greece, all London mourning, the identification of the poet with Childe Harold: these encapsulate the Romantic Byron myth. Byron is the "poet hero of Greek freedom," as Murray will describe him shortly in the opera and as the opera never lets us forget, in spite of the fact that Byron's work in Greece is not its immediate dramatic focus. For the lines of the mourning Londoners, Larson borrowed not only Tennyson's famous inscription, but the well-known remark of Jane Welsh to Carlyle: "My God, if they had said that the sun or the moon had gone out of the heavens, it could not have struck me with the idea of a more awful and dreary blank in the creation." [22] The mourning continues with a dignified, understated processional of a select group of poetic spirits buried in the Abbey: Spenser, Dryden, Johnson, Milton, Gray, and Thompson. They are solemn and view the situation from a transcendent perspective:

> Their loss, not him wail they who fill the world with cries.
> Death slew not him, but he made death his ladder to the skies.
>
> (1.77–86)

Thomson treats the mourners and the poets with respect. There is never any question that it is a great man and a great poet who has died, who is the subject of the opera.[23]

However, the tone shifts from elegiac, impersonal sentiments to the concerns of the men and women who were involved with Byron during his lifetime. John Cam Hobhouse, the lifelong friend of Byron, enters first, cordially greeting the poetical spirits, addressing each by name, and expressing his wish to see Byron installed in the Abbey among them. The other principals enter one by one, and the scene builds from conversational fragments, interrupted by greetings and salutations, to a complex ensemble. Aside from accomplishing the task of introducing the characters on stage to the audience, the repeated formal salutations set us squarely in polite society. Their recurrence is like a facetious leitmotiv, at times waxing to a remarkably lyrical effect for so prosaic a recitative, as when with lilting triplets yielding to decorous sixteenth notes, Hobhouse announces the Contessa: Lady Byron, Contessa Guiccioli, Contessa, the Honorable Mrs. Leigh (1.255–58). It is clear that Thomson enjoys dropping these names.

The main characters each identify themselves in terms of their relationship to Byron: Hobhouse is the self-appointed protector of Byron's posthumous reputation; publisher John Murray acknowledges the debt his firm owes to the poet; Thomas Moore feels a special affinity with his fellow poet; Augusta Leigh is all simplicity and affection; and Lady Byron, now softened and forgiving. Hobhouse and the women favor the destruction of the memoirs. This idea is opposed by Murray, who had bought the rights to them from Moore (though Murray would be willing to be bought out), and of Moore, who identifies with the poet's commitment to let the "truth" emerge, but whose concerns are also somewhat tainted by venal interests. The three bent on burning, moreover, are not entirely high-minded either: the Ladies Leigh and Byron are terrified of the disclosures and have heirs to consider, while Hobhouse has something of a jealous grudge against Moore. In short, as the libretto deftly reveals, a certain amount of cant is still the order of the day. Anyone familiar with the detailing of post-mortem events in Marchand's biography will hear echoes in the opera's numerous quotations and paraphrases—such as in Murray's report of Gifford's description of the memoirs' contents ("fit only for brothels"), Moore's defense of them ("This is not a pest-bag. 'Tis the life of a great poet"), and Hobhouse's dig at Moore ("Lord Byron makes a gift of himself to Mister Moore, and Mister Moore sells his Lordship to a bookstore!"). The score cleverly emphasizes one important issue at stake, when all repeat Murray's assertion that the memoirs are now: "Property, property!" (1.347). Clearly, though Byron the man and poet has died, Byron the commodity is first being prepared for mass production.

This scene not only establishes scandal as the perspective from which we are to view Byron, but makes an astute and crucial point about the man at the center of the scandal. When Teresa Guiccioli and her brother, Count Pietro Gamba, bring on stage the Thorwaldsen statue that, in the opera, has accompanied them and Byron's corpse to England, each of the principals questions the Contessa about the statue.[24] Augusta asks, "Is it beauteous?" Hobhouse, "Has it greatness?" Lady Byron, "And melancholy?" Moore, "Is it not jolly?" Murray, "Is it poetic?" Teresa responds to each question either affirmatively or ambiguously enough to be interpreted affirmatively, and Gamba offers the final description, "And heroic." Thus, they all insightfully conclude: "If it is ev'rything to ev'ryone, it must be very like Byron" (I. 278–90). Byron himself recognized how central to his personality was the quality he called *mobilité*: the ability to be true to oneself while being different things to different people—a sort of social negative capability (or, in the words of *Don Juan*, "for surely they're sincerest / Who are most strongly acted on by what is nearest" [XVI.823–24]). Thomson and Larson's awareness of this "Changeable

. . . yet somehow 'Idem semper'" quality to their subject undoubtedly underlies their approach. In the opera, we meet Byron
first through the eyes of those who never knew him personally (the
mourning chorus and the dead poets), then through those of his
friends and loved ones. Eventually, we are given the unspeaking
statue, as the frame gradually closes in to reveal the man, whom
we finally meet *in spiritu proprio* at the very end of act one. He enters, accoutered with beribboned mandolin (á la Don Giovanni?),
singing his satiric verses to London (*Don Juan* X.82 and XI.25).
Even the "real" Byron, thus, is depicted in costume, and what he
speaks is his poetry. The scene closes with all on stage focused in
frozen admiration: the friends and poets staring at the statue, and
Byron at the vaulted Abbey, which by the opera's end will shut its
doors to him. The tableau is as much about the act of watching as
about the objects being watched. The audience is thus kept aware
of the playful artifice that lets the elusive reality of Byron tease us
out of thought.

Indeed, rather than encouraging a suspension of disbelief that
would foster an identification of the audience with the opera's subject, the opera consistently reminds us that what we are seeing is
an artful reconstruction of an essentially unknowable reality. Even
while they lend authenticity to the character portraits, the numerous exact quotations and paraphrases from the poetry, letters, and
reported conversations tend to reinforce, rather than diffuse, this
artfulness. These quotations and paraphrases are often seamlessly
interwoven into the texture of the libretto. The brilliant conversational idiom of *Don Juan* renders its lines irresistible as a dramatic
vehicle for Byron. In addition to the satiric verses he speaks in act
one, the first memory scene (in act two) shows Byron flirtatiously
warning Lady Jane and Lady Charlotte, "Alas! the love of women!
It is known to be a lovely and a fearful thing! [etc.]." At times, the
lyrics are isolated as set pieces. The meeting of the five survivors in
act one, for instance, yields to a virtual competition of dedicatory
verses. The famous farewell to Moore ("My Boat Is on the Shore")
is given a flowing setting, with a Highland flavor supplied by its
dotted rhythm. The warmth and C-major openheartedness of this
setting is characteristic of Thomson's conception of the Moore/
Byron relationship and contrasts noticeably with the songs and
duets involving some of the other characters. In act two, scene
two, Byron immortalizes Lady Charlotte on the spot with a setting
of "These Locks Which Fondly Thus Entwine" (though that poem
was actually written in 1805 and addressed to another young

lady). And when he takes his leave of Annabella and Augusta in act three, scene one, he does so to a rather subdued, regretful setting of a stanza from "Fare Thee Well," the poem he addressed to his wife after receiving her request for a separation. Although these "songs" occur in a context appropriate to the occasional nature of the verse, our awareness of quotation, the unreality of verse pouring forth on the spot, and the songs' interruption of the events unfolding in the opera all create a mood akin to that of early musical comedy—though here the effect is self-consciously achieved and the result, enlightening. These musical "numbers," along with the fact that the lyrics here are not by Larson but by Byron, remind us how much it is through the art that we recreate this poet's life.

Consistent with its attempt to put the audience at a remove from the scene being played out on stage, the opera makes frequent use of well-known musical quotations. These further break the spell of realism and, at the same time, reinterpret the Romantic myth through a popular idiom. Most of these musical allusions occur in act two. When Moore opens the manuscript of the memoirs (in the first scene of that act) and argues in favor of publication based on Byron's love of the truth, he sings, to the familiar tune of "Believe Me, When All Those Endearing Young Charms": "Remember, the poet we knew with our heart / Is known only to others in books. . . ." This is a nice touch: while the unsung lyric "those endearing young charms" has a certain comic applicability to the present subject of the song, Byron; the audience may also remember that those words for the Irish melody were indeed written by Moore. In scene two, a "rough and rhythmic" instrumental canon of the drinking song "Ach, du lieber Augustin" introduces the Burlington House Waterloo victory celebration. A trio of "Auld Lang Syne," sung by Ladies Melbourne, Milbanke, and Leigh, opens scene four. This is a particularly artful "scene on two levels": on one part of the stage the three women discuss, not without qualms, Annabella's impending marriage; on the other is a drunken bachelor's party modeled after one actually held by Byron, Hobhouse, and Moore. The men's scene culminates in a mock marriage ceremony set to a witty rendition of "Three Blind Mice." A reprise of "Auld Lang Syne," this time by the sextet, set against the orchestral thumping out of "Ach, du lieber Augustin," brings the scene and act to a rousing, and ominous, finale. Thomson refrains from exploiting the uniquely operatic possibility of treating the two scenes simultaneously, but alternates between the two "levels," until the final sextet; clearly, he is more interested in the detailing of each tableau than in a rich and ingenious musical texture.

Invariably, the musical allusions have a humorous effect . The "pop" connotation of these tunes, and the combination of their familiarity and odd appropriateness to the moment, not to mention the cleverness of Thomson's musical treatment of them, place the listener in a playful relation to the subject at hand. The musical quotations, thus, have a de-Romanticizing function. They help debunk any notions of Romantic seriousness; they serve to "cut" Byron and his coterie "down to size": the purpose, according to Thomson, underlying Byron's own misbehaviors and, it seems, an important objective of the opera.

This cutting of Byron down to size, however, is not intended as a denial of his stature; it is, rather, a way of confronting us simultaneously with the immortality of a poet and the life of a man. The Abbey setting as a backdrop to these particular memory scenes symbolically achieves such a juxtaposition. Even though we are shown the frailties of Byron's supporters, of Byron himself, we are not at all meant to side with his detractors. After the memoirs are burned, Dean Ireland's moralistic refusal of Abbey burial in spite of Byron's heroic death in Greece becomes his own self-parody, as he explains, "Freeing countries is hardly our king and country's aim." This is a paraphrase of a sardonic remark Byron once made, which is all the more ironic spoken by Ireland, who is apparently unconscious of the irony. Ireland's socially proper exit is followed by the pure strains of the Abbey choir, and we may, perhaps, infer from the chorale an implicit critique of the Dean and his world:

> Blessed Spirit, brooding o'er us,
> Chase the darkness of our night
> 'Til the perfect day before us
> Breaks in everlasting light.

(3.2.565–73)

The dead poets, now with Shelley and Byron among them, have the final say, as they recite Byron's bitter lines of personal triumph, quoting from the fourth canto of *Childe Harold*:

> From mighty wrongs to petty perfidy,
> Had I not seen what human beings could do?
> From the loud roar of foaming calumny
> To the subtler venom of the reptile crew.

And if my voice break forth,
'Tis not that now I shrink from what is suffered
Let him speak who hath beheld decline upon my brow
Or seen my mind's convulsion leave it weak;
But on this stage a record will I seek.

Have I not had my brain seared, my heart riven,
Hope sapped, name blighted, life's life lied away?
And only not to desperation driv'n
Because not altogether of such clay
As rots into the souls of those whom I survey.

(stanzas 136, 134, 135)

At first glance, this text, bristling with personal resentment, seems to be an extremely odd choice for a finale intended to elegize Byron. The score performed at the Juilliard premiere did include the more traditionally quoted "epitaph" Byron wrote for himself in this same passage:

But there is that within me which shall tire
Torture and Time, and breathe when I expire;
Something unearthly, which they deem not of,
Like the remembered tone of a mute lyre,
Shall on their softened spirits sink, and move
In hearts all rocky now the late remorse of love.

(stanza 137)

However, even with these seemingly more transcendent lines in the finale, the opera has made us see how the entire passage—like so much of Byron's poetry—is not merely the brooding of a selfless poetic soul, or the expression either of some generalized *Weltschmerz* or high-minded moral outrage. Without drawing an explicit connection between these lines and the events of the marriage, separation, and scandal, to which they indeed refer, the opera, by having shown us the Byron it has, strongly suggests how these lines arose from and refer to the circumstances of Byron's life, circumstances not too lofty for the gossip columns.[25]

Lord Byron, thus, is not a Romantic opera. It employs neither the melodrama nor the chromatic harmonies that focused Romantic subjects in the works of Verdi or Wagner or, in the present century, of Schoenberg or Berg.[26] As Andrew Porter noted in his second, favorable review of the opera:

"Lord Byron" must inevitably disappoint anyone expecting a really romantic, heart-on-sleeve, conventionally "Byron" opera; it has nothing in common with Berlioz's "Le Corsaire" or "Harold en Italie," Verdi's "Il Corsaro" or "I Due Foscari," Schumann's or Tchaikovsky's "Manfred," or any of the other numerous nineteenth-century compositions that Byron's poetry inspired . Thomson and his librettist, Jack Larson, have not dramatized the poet as the poet dramatized himself. Their opera, an elegant and cultivated piece, affords pleasures kin to those of witty, lively, precise, shapely conversation on an interesting subject.[27]

Thomson and Larson were clearly engaged by their Romantic subject, and one never loses the sense of their respect for Lord Byron as a poet and a popular hero. However, they wrote an opera that preserves distance from and reflects coolly on Byron—the man and the phenomenon—offsetting the myth by the gossip, placing the music in quotation marks. Its irony—and its radicalism—lie precisely in its dialogic, open-ended conception ("A witty, lively . . . conversation"), in conjunction with its yoking of incompatible musical and literary images. It gives us Byron not by trying to get us to feel *with* him, but by making us conscious of the distance between him and us.[28] It does not attempt to deny, or to transcend, the Romantic myth of Byron—which, after all, is a part of even as it is more than Byron—but to situate itself outside the Romantic representations and view them through its own self-conscious perspectives.

Notes

1. From Byron's review of Wordsworth's *Poems* (two volumes, 1807) in *Monthly Literary Recreations*, July 1807, rpt. in *The Works of Lord Byron. . . . Letters and Journals*, ed. Rowland E. Prothero, six volumes (London: John Murray, 1898–1901), 1. 341.

2. For an extensive listing of musical settings of Byron's works, see *Musical Settings of British Romantic Literature*, ed. Bryan N. S. Gooch and David Thatcher, two volumes (New York and London: Garland Publishing, 1982). See also my essay, "Byron and the Romantic Composer," in *Lord Byron and His Contemporaries: Essays From the Sixth International Byron Seminar*, ed. Charles E. Robinson (Newark: University of Delaware Press, 1982), 178–203; both that essay and the present one are part of a book that I am writing about composers' interpretations of Byron's poetry.

3. As quoted by Richard Jackson in *The New Grove Dictionary of Music and Musicians* (London: Macmillan, 1980).

4. Ibid.

5. During this period, Thomson composed another work inspired by Byron:

Shipwreck and Love Scene, based on the Haidee episode from canto two of *Don Juan*; this work for orchestra and tenor solo, commissioned by the New York Philharmonic for its 125th anniversary celebration, was composed in the summer of 1967 and given its premiere on 11 April 1968.

6. The opera was given three performances at Juilliard, and a recording made from one of them is available at the New York Public Library at Lincoln Center.

7. The English/German piano-vocal score was published by Southern Music Publishing Co. (New York, 1975); other sources for the genesis and revisions of *Lord Byron* include John Gruen, "Virgil Sings of 'Lord Byron'" (*The New York Times*, Sunday, 9 April 1972) and Andrew Porter, "The Memory of Byron" (*The New Yorker*, 17 January 1977).

8. Gruen, "Virgil Sings of 'Lord Byron'"; Sir Rudolf Bing, *5000 Nights at the Opera* (New York: Doubleday & Co., 1972), 212.

9. Harold C. Schonberg, *The New York Times*, 22 April 1972; Andrew Porter, "Rake's Egress," *The New Yorker*, 24 April 1972.

10. Leighton Kerner, "A Kansas Sun, London Clouds," *The Village Voice*, 27 April 1972.

11. Porter, "The Memory of Byron."

12. Jackson, *The New Grove Dictionary*.

13. John Rockwell, *The New York Times*, 6 December 1985; Porter's favorable view of the work persisted (see *The New Yorker*, 24 February 1986).

14. *Childe Harold's Pilgrimage* canto III, line 20.

15. See Leslie A. Marchand, *Byron: A Biograpy* (New York: Alfred A. Knopf, 1957), 2.822.

16. Letter to Andrew Porter, 25 January 1977, *Selected Letters of Virgil Thomson*, ed. Tim Page and Vanessa Weeks Page (New York: Summit Books, 1988), 358.

17. All quotations from the opera are, unless otherwise noted, from the piano-vocal score by Southern Music Publishing Co. and are cited by act, scene, and measure.

18. Letter to Maurice Grosser, 15 May 1965 (*Selected Letters of Virgil Thomson*, 321–22).

19. John Gruen, "Virgil Sings of 'Lord Byron.'"

20. Ibid.

21. Romulus Linney's play *Childe Byron* (1980) also recreates the life of the poet through the flashback technique. I don't wish to press this comparison too far since Linney's play offers an entirely different sort of representation of the poet: a more intimate and psychological study of Byron and his relation to his daughter Ada. At the very least, however, in both content and in the flashback format, both works evoke a Byron as seen or known by others and stress the power of his impact upon others. And that a famous British rock star played the role of the poet in the London production of *Childe Byron* in 1981 further suggests a comparison with the opera's conception. Linney did, in fact, dedicate *Childe Byron* to Virgil Thomson.

22. D. A. Wilson, *Carlyle Till Marriage*, 328, as quoted in Marchand, *Byron: A Biography*, 3. 1248.

23. Thomson frequently expressed his admiration of artists and appreciation of their lives. In having as its subject an artist-hero, *Lord Byron* may be linked to Thomson's two Stein operas, whose protagonists are exceptional, dedicated, and heroic in a way analogous to this conception of the artist.

24. Pietro Gamba actually arrived on another ship, and Teresa did not visit En-

gland until 1832 (see Marcharld, *Byron: A Biography*; 3. 1242–43); the Thorwald-sen statue was not commissioned until years after Byron's death (Marchand, *Byron: A Portrait* [New York: Alfred A. Knopf, 1970], 477).

25. The presentation of Byron in this opera is, thus, consistent with recent studies which assert the profound relevance of a socially contextualized reading of Byron's poetry. What is tantamount to the coexistence of different meanings or voices for given lines and passages—one intended for an "uninitiated" public, one for "the knowing ones" in Byron's milieu—allow for revisionary interpretations of his works that reinforce their social immediacy and undercut, or at least complicate, their more universal truth claims. Such readings, again in a way similar to the opera, bring us closer to Byron even as they register the gulf between the world to which the poems refer and our world. See, for example, Jerome J. McGann, "Lord Byron's Twin Opposites of Truth" in *Towards a Literature of Knowledge* (Chicago: University of Chicago Press, 1989) and "Lord Byron and the Truth in Masquerade" in *Byron: A Critical Reappraisal; Essays from Hofstra University's Byron Bicentennial Conference*, ed. Alice Levine and Robert N. Keane (New York and London: Garland Publishing, forthcoming).

26. In the chapter from which the present essay is taken, I contrast Thomson's and Schoenberg's relation to romanticism through their Byron settings, *Lord Byron* and the *Ode to Napoleon Buonaparte*. Doing this in fact helps define polarities in musical modernism in terms of a shared cultural background and divergent responses to it.

27. Andrew Porter, "The Memory of Byron."

28. In this regard, I think John Rockwell evades an important point in his 1985 *Times* review, when he reasons that "Folk songs might seem an odd idiom for an opera about the elegantly English Lord Byron, yet . . . it's no odder than Verdi's nineteenth-century Italian for Shakespeare" ; for there is an essential incongruity in Thomson's opera between not just "odd" or different, but essentially contradictory or incompatible idioms, and the message that the opera tells is traceable to the audience's provoked awareness of that contradiction—an awareness that is not, I believe, provoked by Verdi's Shakespeare operas.

A Strange Case: Louis Gruenberg's Forgotten "Great American" Opera— *The Emperor Jones*

MARJORIE MACKAY SHAPIRO

At its 1933 Metropolitan Opera premiere, *The Emperor Jones*, based on the play of the same name by Eugene O'Neill, with music by Louis Gruenberg, was hailed as the long-awaited Great American Opera. The subject was American, the play's author was American, and the composer was American as well.

Reviewers were almost unanimous in their praise. The *New York Times* critic Olin Downes wrote, "for an American opera to appear which not only stands on its own feet, but represents a treatment of the form that could only come from a new country and a young people fully alive to the present day, is the thing which makes this success of Mr. Gruenberg so gratifying and important to the future."[1] Downes described the audience as one of the largest the Metropolitan has ever known and the opera as an instant and sweeping success. The protagonist and the star of the production, playing Brutus Jones, was Lawrence Tibbett, whose extraordinary performance landed him on the cover of *Time* magazine that same month. The role of *Emperor Jones* required not only a good singer but a superb actor as well, and the popular baritone was perfect for the role. In its front-cover review of the premiere, *Time* magazine said of the singer, "Twenty times last week, a strapping, coffee-colored man in a baby-blue wrapper went out in front of the curtain of Manhattan's Metropolitan Opera House in a shattering storm of applause. Tibbett sang [his aria] with sweat gleaming all over his brown body. Down people's spines it sent shivers that they did not get later on, even when the drums reached their greatest crescendo and the chorus, shouting and wailing in conflicting keys and rhythms, closed in on him [Jones]. For Tibbett the moment was a career's fine crown."[2]

The Emperor Jones was given fourteen performances in two seasons, published by Cos Cob Press, received the David Bispham medal, and, according to those present at the performances, enjoyed tumultuous praise from the public. Gatti-Casazza, the Met's director, recounts in his memoirs: "Almost all critics agreed 'Emperor Jones' was one of the most effective American works we had presented. The public, by its attendance and by its enthusiasm at the various performances, gave ample endorsement of this opinion."[3] Downes describes the opening night audience: "To this music drama the audience listened, absorbed, deeply moved, from the first tones of the orchestra, from the first savage cries of the concealed chorus, to the final closing. . . . Then came the explosion of applause which follows long minutes of accumulating excitement, and a procession back and forth on the stage, for uncounted recalls. . . ."[4] Clearly, the production had captured the imagination of the packed audience.

The story of *The Emperor Jones* is as follow: An American ex–Pullman porter, Brutus Jones, after having committed several crimes, including murder, escapes to a West Indian island, where eventually, through more lies and crimes, he becomes emperor. With cunning and an appeal to their superstition, he exploits the natives until they rebel and he is forced to flee into the jungle. There he has a series of hallucinations while trying to escape his pursuers. Just as they are about to capture him, he kills himself with his last "silver bullet" which he had persuaded the natives was the only way he could be killed.

The significance of the play is not in the rather thin narrative, but in the character of Jones, which is conveyed through a gradual breaking down of his conscious ego and the revelation of his personal and collective unconscious. Jones's hopeless flight through the forest from the natives represents a flight from himself, gradually revealing his true nature. The hollow masked evil behind which Jones has hidden, the last layer of his civilized outward self, is peeled away and he is returned to the dark, primitive world of the unconscious, naked and helpless. That Jungian fundamental theory, the existence and power of the collective unconscious and its effect upon human behavior, which informs the play, was dear to O'Neill's heart. He writes:

As far as I can remember, of all the books written by Freud, Jung, etc., I have read only four, and Jung is the only one of the lot who interests me. Some of his suggestions I find extraordinarily illuminating in the light of my own experience with hidden human motives.[5]

A number of factors coalesced in the twenties and early thirties to make *The Emperor Jones* the instant success it was. First was the presence of the Italian opera impresario, Giulio Gatti-Casazza, at the Metropolitan Opera from 1908 to 1935. Gatti-Casazza brought with him not only a philosophy of opera performance in its original language, but also a strong commitment to establishing an American operatic tradition. He wrote "My hope when I came to America was to be able to discover some good American operas, which I could produce and maintain in the repertoire. . . . It seemed to me that one of the inescapable obligations of the great American lyric theatre was to foster and promote the development of American opera. . . ." [6]

The complex nature of opera created even greater obstacles to achieving an American identity than did other musical forms. It required the united skills of composer, librettist, director, designer, choreographer, performers, and impresarios to create a finished product. Costs were often prohibitive for most American theaters. Also, as Patrick J. Smith points out, "In the past most great opera composers served an apprenticeship in the field, learning from their failures and from the direct experience of working under theatrical conditions." [7] The opera-producing theaters in major American cities preferred to put on museum works from the European repertory (much like today), and few American operas were programmed. He continues, "no wonder that little memorable work was created." [8]

During the 1920s and even earlier, the search for the Great American Opera was endlessly discussed in modern music circles as part of what Aaron Copland called the "affirm America movement." [9] Operas on American subjects were tried, such as Indian settings; for example, Victor Herbert's *Natoma* (1912) and the West coast composer Mary Carr Moore's *The Flaming Arrow* (1922). Some, like *Natoma*, even made the Metropolitan opera roster during the Gatti-Casazza period. They fell from notice because they could attract neither the interest of American opera companies, nor support of American audiences, nor indeed, the support of some of our own American composers.

In the midst of this "affirm America" movement was *Jones*'s composer, Louis Gruenberg, who already had established an international reputation, and had been an important spokesman for American composers throughout the twenties, in both his music and his writings. Gruenberg was a frequent contributor to a variety of periodicals both here and abroad. In the first volume of New York's *Modern Music* magazine in 1924, he wrote:

> In an effort to appraise music today in Paris, London, Berlin and Vienna, it becomes my firm conviction that the American composer can only achieve individual expression by developing his own resources . . . these resources are vital . . . for we have at least three rich veins indigenous to America alone: Jazz, Negro spirituals and Indian themes. It seems to me that it is the indefinable and at the same time unmistakable atmosphere in America that must be youthfully interpreted in a new idiom, not merely exploited in a characteristic melody. A new technique should be invented which will combine a knowledge of tradition and the modern experiment.[10]

Through many of his earlier works, Gruenberg gained a reputation as an important innovator in the use of jazz and the "Negro" spiritual. These pieces include *Four indiscretions for string quartet* (op. 20), *The Daniel Jazz* for voice and eight instruments (op. 21), *Jazzberries* for piano (op. 25), and *Jazzettes* for violin and piano (op. 22). It is not within the scope of this paper to discuss them specifically, but they were important in establishing Gruenberg's reputation as the voice of hope for indigenous American music and the American composer. (He also had become well known in opera circles for his work as accompanist for Enrico Caruso, often playing for the famous tenor on concert tours.)[11]

During and after World War I European society became obsessed with things American, especially its culture. This was particularly true in Germany where *Der Jazz* became very popular in the Weimar Republic. Gruenberg, who was living there at this time, became one of America's musical spokesmen. For example, he contributed articles to the 22 April 1925 special issue on jazz of the magazine, *Anbruch*. Susan C. Cook describes Gruenberg's status in Germany: "Generally recognized as a jazz authority, Gruenberg contributed another essay, 'Vom Jazz und anderen Dingen,' . . . in which he described his own turn to jazz and gave predictions for its future use." [12] In his book, *Das neue Jazzbuch*, Alfred Baresel has a chapter on improvisation. In it he discusses *Kunstjazz*, the use of jazz in art music, and gives as an example, Gruenberg's *Jazzberries*. Perhaps Gatti-Casazza's choice of Gruenberg's *Emperor Jones* in 1933 was influenced by Europe's obsession with American jazz. For Gruenberg, the American jazz idiom was a crucial element in his career, which culminated in his opera, *The Emperor Jones*.

In addition to being considered an important innovator in the use of jazz, and a "published" composer, Gruenberg was also a leader in the New York music community, including the League of

Composers and the International Composers' Guild. His leadership role in modern music circles, his international reputation, and his writings about music in journals both here and abroad all contributed to establishing Gruenberg as a prime candidate for authorship of a successful "great American" opera.

Another factor contributing to the opera's success was the source of Gruenberg's libretto. O'Neill's *The Emperor Jones* was in 1933 an enormously popular play. Gruenberg's biographer writes, "The significance of the *Emperor Jones* as a play cannot be overstated. . . . first performed in 1920, it had a continuous run of 204 performances." [13] "By common consent, O'Neill was considered America's greatest playwright and an artist of international renown." [14] He joined a band of iconoclasts: H. L. Mencken, Sinclair Lewis, and Sherwood Anderson, who were all slowly lifting the lid off the reality and ugliness of American life and exposing it to public view. While O'Neill's works ranged over the same themes, his underlying melancholy was even more poignant than that of his peers.

After reading the play Gruenberg corresponded with the author, with whom he agreed upon a copyright and royalty arrangement.[15] O'Neill refused to have anything to do with preparation of the libretto, but after he read Gruenberg's version, he heartily approved of the final product. In a letter to Gruenberg dated 11 April 1931 O'Neill wrote:

> I read it [the libretto] last night with the greatest interest and have no suggestions to offer. You have made a damn good job of it and it should prove extraordinarily interesting with the music I know you will write. I certainly look forward to hearing and seeing the production.
>
> All good wishes to you; may your composition be all you hope for it![16]

Once all the arrangements were made Gruenberg sequestered himself in a cottage in Maine and wrote what today may be considered his most significant success as a composer, as *Emperor Jones* had been Eugene O'Neill's first significant success as a playwright ten years earlier.[17] Thus, the presence of Gatti-Casazza at the Metropolitan Opera, the burning wish for the Great American opera and an American operatic identity, the established international reputation of Louis Gruenberg as an American voice, and the great popularity of Eugene O'Neill's play all came together in the performances of *The Emperor Jones* in 1933 and resulted in its resounding early success.

The one hour and fifteen minute opera has four main sections:

I. Orchestral prologue with chanting chorus
II. Act I—at the Emperor's palace
III. Orchestral interlude—again with chanting chorus
IV. Act II—in the forest—Jones' flight

The music is largely made up of dramatic speech songs, a parlando style similar to Schoenberg's *Sprechstimme*. Gruenberg had conducted the first American production of Schoenberg's *Pierrot Lunaire* in 1923 and was quite familiar with its *Sprechstimme* technique.[18] The opera also uses spoken dialogue and recitative, except for one expanded lyrical moment in the opera, a critical point in his downfall, when the protagonist sings a brief song based on the famous "Negro" spiritual, "It's Me, O Lord, Standin' in de Need of Prayer."

The opening of the prologue is a dramatic Copland-like fanfare, providing motivic material used throughout the opera. Gruenberg's dynamic marking of *Vivo e feroce* sets the tone for both drama and music. Its syncopated nervous energy is one of the recognizable criteria he lists as an "American" sound, as revealed in a speech to The American Opera Society on 6 November 1934.[19] (Others were: speed, restlessness, mystery, ballyhoo, display, and uplifting quality). Gruenberg, in his continuous search for the "American" sound, turned to "Negro" spirituals as early as 1925.[20] The opening measures of the prologue reveal two patterns characteristic of these spirituals. The first is their use of repeated rhythmic syncopated patterns, and the second is repetition of tonal patterns. The music also avoids leading tones, giving it a pentatonic quality. The interval of the fourth (five of them in the first three beats) is used extensively throughout the opera, a useful way of avoiding tonal structure.

An unusual feature of the opera is Gruenberg's use of the chorus. At the beginning, they act as a kind of Greek chorus singing from the orchestra pit in muted tones. They state their case against Jones swearing vengeance upon him:

> Enuff! Enuff! He mus' die!
> He mus, he mus! Dis stranger!
> Dis slave driver! De Emperor!
> He steal our money, He steal our women.
> He makes us bump our heads on de ground!
> To him lik' a God! Huh!

(see appendix: Ex. C, pp. 3 & 4)

As the story progresses, the chorus' voice strengthens even more, becoming Jones's greatest tormentor. In act 2 the chorus dispenses with speech altogether. By the end of the opera they chant completely without word-articulation. Olin Downes describes the chorus' actions rather vividly:

> As the opera proceeds, at certain special moments the chorus reiterates threats and prophecies, with the effect of an immense crescendo. As this motive of retribution develops and gains in power, the bodies of the blacks emerge from the orchestra, looming higher and higher over the rim of the stage, until at last the witch-doctor jumps over the footlights, pointing to Jones, dancing his fiendish dance, and all the Negroes, swinging and swaying, close in upon his black majesty. Whipping out his pistol with the last bullet of silver, Jones kills himself. . . . The savage triumphal songs of four tribes intermingle, grow fainter, echo from the distance. The stage is empty and silent as the curtain falls.[21]

Nowhere in O'Neill's work is his theatrical skill more evident than in Jones's flight through the jungle to the drumbeat, which begins at a normal pulse rhythm and grows faster and faster, louder and louder. Gruenberg uses this pulsating drumbeat (just as O'Neill did in the play) in the score's powerful ending, coupled with the placement of ten-inch, twelve-inch, and fifteen-inch tom-toms stationed in a semi-circle around the opera house and beating relentlessly. This must have had an incredible theatrical impact at the old Metropolitan Opera House!

Gruenberg adapted O'Neill's text almost verbatim, thus maintaining the integrity of the drama. One exception was his insertion of the spiritual mentioned earlier, "It's Me, O Lord, Standin' in de Need of Prayer" that is sung toward the end of Act 2. The composer places the song at a high point of the drama when the terrified Jones has seen the last of the three "formless fears" of his seedy past and has entered a deeper level of his "racial or collective unconscious." The subjective transformation of objective reality which Jones's psyche experiences is almost complete and it is about to destroy him. Jones "suddenly throws himself on his knees and raises his clasped hands to the sky in a voice of agonized prayer." [22] He confesses himself a "po' sinner" and cries for the Lord to answer his prayers and save him. Before he actually begins the spiritual, Jones expresses repentance in O'Neill's words:

> Lawd, I done wrong! And down heah
> what dese fool bush niggers raises

> me up to the seat o'de mighty, I
> steals all I could grab. Lawd, I
> done wrong! I knows it! I'se sorry!
> Forgive me, Lawd! Forgive dis po' sinner!

His pleas are accompanied by an ostinato syncopated figure of descending fifths, and Jones chants them in a very low register, beginning very softly, gradually ascending to higher pitches with increased volume. In the score, most of the accompaniment for his pleas are simply the omnipresent tom-toms.

The major change Gruenberg makes from the traditional spiritual is the lower octave register to which Jones moves on the words "its not my brother . . . ," and where he remains for the rest of the song. This is in keeping with the dynamics Gruenberg calls for in the song, from triple forte to ending on triple *piano*.

The final musical number of the opera is the war-dance. Just before this moment Jones sees that the natives are closing in on him. Anguished pleading is heard: "Lawd, save me. Lawd Jesus. Heah my prayer." What immediately follows is defiance in these words: "De silver bullet. You won't git me. I'se Emperor yit!!" Gruenberg's directions:

> (*"He fires at his own head and falls down heavily."*)
> *Jones*: (*gasping*) "Jesus" (*Dies*).[23]

The soldiers scatter at first when the shot rings out, then gradually return, see that he is truly dead, and go into the frenzied war-dance.

Gruenberg made another important change in the opera's ending. The play has no last-minute defiance followed by suicide; its natives kill Jones as he whimpers in fear. Perhaps in Gruenberg's mind, a man obsessed by fear could overcome it, thus controlling the events around him through his own actions. It is this writer's opinion that the reason for the change was most likely a theatrical rather than a philosophical one. (The music critic Edward Downes concurred with this view in a recent conversation.) It is easier for an audience to accept one's defense of his dignity to the end than one's destruction by a frenzied mob. Even O'Neill approved of the changed ending.

In every opera there are two separate critical elements that bond to establish the character of the work. The libretto provides the drama projected by its words; the score provides esthetic content in the beauty of the music. When the blend is right the opera knows success. And so it was for *The Emperor Jones*. The intellectual content sprang from the genius of Eugene O'Neill, and the esthetic content from the genius of Louis Gruenberg. In January 1933 the blend was right and early success of the opera was the result. But something occurred that made it impossible for the two elements to sustain each other synergistically. In the years since the opera's premiere, style and culture have changed. Perhaps the psychological premise of the denouement and the expressionistic Jungian philosophy, of crucial importance to the opera's story, no longer seem relevant to today's opera going public, as it did in the 1920s and early 1930s.

In a thoughtful 1979 review of a rare revival Andrew Porter considered the opera puzzling and questioned whether either the play or the opera was performable in today's world given its offensive language like "bush niggers" and "blarsted niggers" used liberally throughout the work. Yet in this same review he observed that "*The Emperor Jones* has a place in [American] operatic history." [24] (Regrettably, he does not say what he thought that place to be, leaving us to speculate.) Yet, Porter's comments raise an important issue of racial characterizations and African-American music in opera that is not within the scope of this paper, but remains to be addressed in future discussions of American opera.

What did not change is the strange beauty of the music. Andrew Porter says of Gruenberg's score: "*something* is holding one's attention—propelling, shaping, and articulating the drama, and making it vivid in a way that a plain spoken performance would not be." [25] While *The Emperor Jones* did not turn out to be the "Great American" opera hoped for by the 1920's modernists, it did provide many opera lovers with an extraordinary theatrical experience. Let us hope this forgotten opera will not remain so.

Notes

1. Olin Downes, *New York Times*, 8 January 1933.
2. "O'Neill into Opera," *Time* magazine, 16 January 1933, 20.
3. Giulio Gatti-Casazza, *Memories of the Opera*, ed. and trans, H. Taubman (New York: Vienna, 1973), 244. Maestro Gatti-Casazza commissioned more works by American composers than any other director, either before or after his twenty-five year tenure. *The Emperor Jones* was his fourteenth American production.
4. Downes, *New York Times*, 8 January, 1933.
5. Letter from Eugene O'Neill to Barrett Clark concerning *Mourning Becomes Electra*, quoted in Clark's *Eugene O'Neill: The Man and His Plays* (New York, 1948), 136.

6. Gatti-Casazza, *Memories*, 236-237. The author describes the American operas he produced before *The Emperor Jones*: (a) *Mona* by Horatio Parker—"a cold and arrid thing" [1912] (238). (b) *Madeleine* by Victor Herbert—"was a mild success, being a little too light for grand opera" [1914] (239). (c) *Canterbury Pilgrims* by Henry DeKoven—"to tell the truth, the work did not have great originality" [1914] (239). (d) *The King's Henchman* and *Peter Ibbetson* by Deems Taylor were "the two most successful American operas given at the Metropolitan prior to the 1932 season" (242). The above operas represented a rather conservative style in American music. Gruenberg's style was thought by the famous impresario to be "atonal music perhaps, but perfectly clear" (244).

7. Patrick J. Smith, "Toward an American Opera," New World Records (NW 241, 1978), liner notes.

8. Ibid.

9. Aaron Copland and Vivian Perlis, *Copland, 1900 Through 1942* (New York, 1984), 94. While Copland is actually referring to the movement in Paris, its influence was felt in New York as well.

10. Louis Gruenberg, "For an American Gesture," *Modern Music* 1 (June 1924): 27–28.

11. Robert Nisbett, *Louis Gruenberg: His Life and Work*, Ph.d. diss, Ohio State University, 1979, p. 23. "A considerable part of Gruenberg's livelihood came from work as an accompanist. His most notable tour was with Enrico Caruso. This took place in 1920."

12. Susan C. Cook, *Opera for a New Republic, The Zeitopern of Krenek, Weill and Hindemith* (Ann Arbor, Mich.: UMI Research Press, 1988), 66.

13. Nisbett, *Gruenberg*, 222.

14. Theodore Eustace Kalem, "Eugene O'Neill," in *Encyclopedia Britannica*, vol. xvi, 966.

15. Nisbett, *Gruenberg*, 42. "In late April (1930), Gruenberg received a contract from O'Neill's agent, but it contained two conditions which he could not accept. They were: 1) the contract is void if the opera should not be performed within two years in America and 2) the contract is valid only for ten years. Gruenberg wanted this changed to: 1) the performance can be anywhere including Europe and within three years and 2) the contract is binding forever. O'Neill accepted these changes and in June a contract was signed.

16. Ibid., 43.

17. George Sturm, "Look Back in Anger: The Strange Case of Louis Gruenberg," *MadAminA!* (1981): 13. Sturm tell this story: At the cottage in Maine, Gruenberg, in order to prepare himself for writing Jones' "hallucination" music, ran around naked, yelling and screaming. Unfortunately for him, a Salvation Army band took the cottage next door. He not only had to put his clothes back on, but they drove him quite mad with their cornet practice.

18. Gruenberg had twenty-two rehearsals for the concert. In a recent interview with Claire Reis' daughter (3 April 1990) she stated that Gruenberg, ever the perfectionist, had insisted on all those rehearsals, much to the dismay of her mother and the Guild.

19. Louis Gruenberg, private papers, New York Public Library, Lincoln Center. Gruenberg lists six criteria as recognizable American characteristics: "Speed, restlessness, mystery, ballyhoo, display and uplifting quality."

20. In 1926, Universal Edition published *Negro Spirituals* transcribed by Gruenberg.

21. Downes, *New York Times*, 2 October 1932.

22. Louis Gruenberg, *The Emperor Jones*, piano-vocal score (New York: Cos Cob Press, Inc., 1932), 123.

23. Ibid., 172.

24. Andrew Porter, *The New Yorker*, 5 April 1979, 116.

25. Ibid.

The Spectacle of Samuel Barber's
Antony and Cleopatra

JON SOLOMON

It cannot be attributed entirely to coincidence that two of the most memorable artistic disappointments of the last thirty years— Joseph L. Mankiewicz's film *Cleopatra* (1963) and Samuel Barber's opera *Antony and Cleopatra* (1966)—both portrayed the same heroine. They were written and appeared within three years of each other, and for both their creators the history of the artistic tradition surrounding Cleopatra, the Hellenistic Queen of Egypt, signified enormous and lavish spectacle. The actual historicity of Cleopatra aside, simply the name "Cleopatra" has for several centuries evoked romance, political and military struggle, grandeur, feminine beauty, and orientalism in Western arts ever since Shakespeare revived Plutarch's *Life of Antony* and adapted it for the stage in 1607. Since that time there have been over seventy-five operas, a half-dozen feature films, and countless novels and romances about the Egyptian monarch, her entangling alliances with first Julius Caesar and then his successor, Marcus Antonius, and her subsequent suicide. Over this period the story of Cleopatra with her Roman love-triangle has come to represent the pinnacle of tragic romance, large-scale politics, and artistic magnificence.

Recognizing the powerful attraction Cleopatra has for the viewing public and for artists even two thousand and twenty years after her death allows us to appreciate the thrilled anticipation felt nearly thirty years ago in the early sixties by film- and operagoers when they learned that Cleopatra would be both the subject of the greatest cinematic spectacle ever filmed and also serve as the seductive, oriental protagonist inaugurating the greatest modern opera house in the world—the Metropolitan Opera House in Lincoln Center.

The resulting artistic products, Mankiewicz's *Cleopatra* (1963) and Barber's *Antony and Cleopatra* (1966), greatly disappointed both audiences and critics and, in this respect, were at the time considered rather colossal, dismal failures. It is well worth the effort to look back upon this period to understand why these two mammoth artistic productions should have been mounted within a few years of each other and why both fell under their own weight. There were two significant linkages, both of which will be reviewed here, the one being the cultural climate of the period which not only allowed but expected the story of Cleopatra to be produced in such a grand, expensive, epic fashion, the other being the artistic imput of Franco Zeffirelli. Let us approach both by first reviewing the persona of Cleopatra and how her historical demise turned out two millenia later to be the epic ideal (and demise) of the sixties.

Fatal attraction to Cleopatra was first felt by Westeners just over two thousand years ago when Julius Caesar, then struggling in a great civil war against Pompey the Great, sailed to Egypt in 48 B.C. to secure his grain supply from the rich Nile valley. Ever the efficient Roman proconsul, Caesar established the Macedonian Cleopatra as queen, made her brother Ptolemy (XIV) her consort, and then sailed back to Italy. Within the year, however, she produced a son which she claimed was Caesar's, and in 46 she came to Rome at Caesar's invitation. She left after he was assassinated on the Ides of March, 44 B.C., but she then became involved with Caesars's lieutenant Marcus Antonius (Mark Antony) in Tarsus in 41. She bore him twins, became his most valuable political ally, lost the naval battle of Actium with him in 31, and followed his suicide with her own on 10 August, 30 B.C.

Even during her lifetime her political ambition and her sexual promiscuity were unfairly characterized and then exaggerated by Octavian, who was about to emerge as the first Augustus of the Roman Empire. Shortly after her death, the talented Roman lyric poet Horace wrote his famous "Cleopatra Ode," [1] wherein she is hated as a political monster although nonetheless apparently respected for her noble suicide. In fact, this kind of dichotomy was to be used in characterizing Cleopatra for years to come.

More than a century and one-half later it is found still in Plutarch, a Greek, who summarized ancient knowledge about Cleopatra and secured its survival in his *Life of Antony*. From this biography (and other sources) we know that Cleopatra was actually not Egyptian, i.e. "Oriental," but the descendant of Alexander the Great's Macedonian general Ptolemy. Unlike her Macedonian predecessors, however, she took care to learn the Egyptian language of her subjects and indulge them their religious practices. She spoke several other languages besides, and in general she is depicted as a bright, ambitious woman who loved only the two Roman generals and did her best in a Roman world to secure a lofty position for her Egypt. Although her love for Caesar earned her some Roman respect, Octavian, Antony's rival, misrepresented her badly. Our Cleopatra, then, continues to be the result of these two strains—the able and noble historical Cleopatra and the lascivious, manipulative, and manipulated product of Roman propaganda.

Shakespeare's *Antony and Cleopatra* was derived directly from North's (first) English translation of Plutarch's *Lives* published in 1579. Cleopatra then appears as a tragic opera figure already in 1653 (Canazzi), and an opera entitled or at least treating the character Cleopatra appears on average more than once each decade from that time on.[2] Theda Bara portrayed her as a "vamp" in the silent film era, Cecil B. DeMille had Claudette Colbert play the role of Cleopatra (taking a bath in mule's milk) for his cinematic production of 1934, and we can pause just after the conclusion of World War II.[3]

Because of the great contemporary political struggles then occurring in the forties, public and artistic interest in ancient subjects had generally waned. Caesar's struggles against Pompey seemed trivial, and any attempts at glorifying the ancient Romans echoed too loudly the Italian propaganda of Mussolini. In the case of opera, the long-standing (and original) association between opera and the ancient world was at a low ebb. Even the romances of Caesar, Cleopatra, and Antony had a twenty-six year hiatus from 1940—its longest since Canazzi's 1653 version. Shortly after the conclusion of the war, however, Cecil B. DeMille again turned the film industry on its ear by reaping huge profits for Paramount Studios with the biblical spectacle *Samson and Delilah* (1949) and, later, *The Ten Commandments* (1956). MGM countered with its epic *Quo Vadis?* (1951) and then its remake of *Ben-Hur* (1959). Warner Brothers with *Helen of Troy* (1955), Universal with Stanley Kubrick's *Spartacus* (1960), and so on. As the decade of the fifties progressed and these Hollywooden spectacles became greater, larger, more expensive, and even more lucrative, Twentieth-Century Fox planned to "out-spectacular" all the other studios with its grand producton of *Cleopatra*. Besides the lavish production, the film was to star the "hot" cinematic duo involved in the most celebrated "movie-star romance" of the decade; this duo was, of course, Elizabeth Taylor and Richard Burton.

Perhaps some readers remember the spectacle, the "hype" that surrounded the production of this movie. I was twelve years old at the time, but I still remember picking up several issues of *Life*

Magazine and seeing Liz and Dick on the cover week after week. I learned my first Italian word at that early age—the word "paparazzi." The spectacular advertisements in the newspaper consisted of a full-page drawing of Cleopatra strewn along a richly laden couch, Antony at her side, and not even the name of the film accompanying the ad; the name was not necessary! The expense of the film was extraordinary—some $32 million, still a large amount for a film produced in 1991, but this was thirty years ago. Elizabeth Taylor's hairdresser alone cost $800 a week. As the costs mounted, Fox's stock dropped from $55 to $15 a share, and its president was fired.[4]

And then the film was released. It was the longest major motion picture ever released at well over four hours, and critics complained of boredom, of beautiful sets and costumes filled with meaningless dialogue and unrealistic characters. An embarrassed Elizabeth Taylor pleaded with Fox in vain to overdub her voice, and Richard Burton to his death, so far as I have been able to discern, never viewed the film. Fox haphazardly tried to improve the film by cutting its extraordinary running time, but critics subsequently nicknamed this clumsily prepared version "the Amputee."

Thirty years later the film does not appear to be so horrible to us, and through television release and video sales the film is now turning a profit. But the lessons should have been learned at the time. The historical Cleopatra is a very complex character who incorporates the "good" Cleopatra apparent in Plutarch and the "bad" one of Octavian's propaganda. Not to highlight her most wonderful authentic characteristics—her charm and wit, her carefully played polical ambition—is to invite ridicule and disbelief. And yet, her unbridled passion must be intense and believable. In this particular performance, Taylor's passion, thinned by her surgically weakened voice, seemed too calculated; her final tragedy, therefore, seemed equally meaningless.

Perhaps of greater significance was that the era of the Hollywood epic had during the filming of the most spectacular Hollywood epic ever filmed come to an end. Audiences no longer craved size, grandeur, and lavish spectacle. They no longer wanted the thrills of spectacle which had been much enhanced by the advent of cinemascope in 1954. The boom of the fifties and the post-war era was nearing its end, and *Cleopatra* appeared just a year or two too late.

One other item of immediate importance for our purposes here is that during the year of the cinematic *Cleopatra*'s release, Franco Zeffirelli was working in Italy with none other than Richard Burton and Elizabeth Taylor. He was serving as the director (and co-writer) of *The Taming of the Shrew*, another Shakespearian work. Zeffirelli's career had blossomed since his famous productions of Rossini's *Il Turco in Italia* (La Scala, 1954) and *Lucia di Lamermoor* (Covent Garden, 1959), the former of which was remembered as a highpoint in Maria Callas's career, the latter as the occasion for the first international acclaim for Joan Sutherland. His 1964 *Falstaff* was considered one of the best ever at the (old) Met, and now he was commissioned to design and stage the production of Barber's *Antony and Cleopatra* for opening night at the new Met in September of 1966. He was also asked to collaborate on the libretto, for which the Shakespearian poetry was to be adapted directly.

The near-contemporaneity of the productions and the presence of Burton, Talyor, and Zeffirelli suggest that there are more connections between the two *Cleopatra*s than were or could be remembered at the time. Zeffirelli was not one to think that the disappointment and critical failure of Fox's *Cleopatra* would in any way interfere with the success of his production. In fact, one might have guessed that he would achieve success despite the fiasco on the silver screen, or that he would achieve success in an opera using Leontyne Price and Shakespearian dialogue where a Hollywood script delivered by Elizabeth Taylor on the silver screen could not. Whatever his line of reasoning may have been, the greatest irony of his own production was that he opted to use even more spectacle and less restraint than the cinematic version of the story.

He found it easy to justify his plans. After all, this was the gala opening of the greatest modern opera house in the world, the lighting controls of which were affectionately referred to as "Cape Canavaral," with a stage twice as deep as that of the old Met, and the largest seating capacity of any opera house in the world. Since there was so much stage machinery to employ—even the chandeliers above the audience moved, as we all now know—he would employ as much as he could. The sphinx would rotate, the pyramids would split open to reveal dramatis personae, the battle of Actium could be portrayed in the distance, and there was plenty of room for horses, a camel, goats, and a few hundred extras. In brief, it was to be colossal, an epic masterpiece filled with what Zeffirelli described as "baroque exuberance."[5]

After the economic and artistic failure of the cinematic *Cleopatra* in 1963, it is remarkable that a Cleopatra romance was chosen for the gala opera at all. The genesis of *Antony and Cleopatra* began in 1964 when Rudolph Bing sat next to Samuel Barber on an ocean liner crossing the Atlantic and requested from him an opera which he could put on as part of the opening season of the new building in the fall of 1966. Barber was asked since he had received the 1958 Pulitzer Prize in music for his opera *Vanessa*, and he accepted the task. Barber talked first to Tennessee Williams about a libretto, but their negotiations came to an impasse. Barber next talked to James Baldwin, but Baldwin was at that time preoccupied with the civil rights movement.

While still contemplating what subject and librettist to use, Barber was called at his home ("Capricorn") in Mount Kisco, New York, by Met conductor Thomas Schippers. Schippers wanted a new, American opera for the opening night. and he asked Barber to write it even though he was already somewhat panicked at the prospect of staging two years hence an opera for which he had not even found the proper libretto. Disappointed by Williams and Baldwin, and apparently pressed for a decision, Barber turned to his "favorite play," Shakespeare's *Antony and Cleopatra*, even though his musical settings heretofore had been to more modern poetry.[6]

There are several possible explanations for Barber's choosing this tragedy. He may have thought that Shakespearean tradition and poetry would eliminate some of the problems encountered in the film, and he made it clear later that he certainly did not envision the opera as a lavish spectacle. Barber may have also believed that the operatic genre had nothing to do with the cinematic, which would have generally been true except for the notoriety of the particular subject matter at hand—Cleopatra. Like Zeffirelli, Barber may have thought naively that his Cleopatra (with Shakespeare's assistance) would not suffer as had Fox's.

Once the decision had been made to write a "Shakespearean opera," Zeffirelli was the immediate and obvious choice to stage it. What Barber did not realize at the time and only later discovered and admitted publicly was that Zeffirelli was to be involved in the creation of the libretto as well, and that Zeffirelli would prove to be utterly overbearing in his treatment of the subject.

The anticipation and preparation were extraordinary. Barber wrote the Cleopatra part specifically for Leontyne Price, an honor which she greatly appreciated on behalf of herself and all black people—still called "Negroes" at the time[7]—in America. She greatly reduced her performance schedule for an entire year so that she could study and prepare her role for the opening night. Barber traveled to Tuscany in the summer of 1964 to discuss the libretto with Zeffirelli. Because Shakespeare had already fleshed out the characters and written the poetry, all that was needed was to cut and rearrange. Their work consumed only fifteen days, although at the time they were still planning on presenting the opera in two acts. Later it was broadened to three (with nineteen scenes)

Zeffirelli arrived in New York in late July of 1956, having just completed his work with "Liz and Dick" on *The Taming of the Shrew*. His conception of *Antony and Cleopatra* was grand, to say the least. In an interview with *The New York Times* one month later (28 August), Zeffirelli said

> From the beginning I was concerned with shaping the whole opera. The form and concept of the libretto and the production itself developed simultaneously. The conception came to me as one idea, and I simply elaborated it. We inherited a love story in which there are no real love scenes. We emphasized the disturbing elements in the relationship between Antony and Cleopatra from the outset, concentrating all the emotions of love into the second act scene which is their last moment of happiness. It is a spectacular opera, so I wanted a big choral scene for the opening.
>
> The sets are a fusion of metal and geometry. Just as a stone thrown into a lake produces circles on the surface, everything here comes from the central idea and form of the pyramid. The basic materials were metal, plastic and wood. I am using the eighteenth-century practice of changing sets in view of the audience. The only curtain will be at the end of each act. Lights and sliding things will do the work. I am using the enormous space of the new house more than its elaborate machinery. The barge scene will stretch from the footlights all the way back to Amsterdam Avenue—that's 146 feet deep!
>
> The costumes are a pastiche of Elizabethan, Roman, Egyptian, and modern. The production will have a baroque exuberance. What I saw as a whole event two years ago in Tuscany has not changed. I have learned that I like my original ideas better than later ones. You must trust your mind, good or bad.[8]

Interestingly, in the same article of 28 August 1966,[9] an interview with Leontyne Price informed us that part of her preparation was to read Plutarch. She also explained that she visited Zeffirelli in Rome that June and met Elizabeth Taylor at the filming of *The Taming of the Shrew*. "She said she thought her movie, *Cleopatra*, was the worst thing she'd ever seen and said Richard Burton had refused to see it even once." Like Zeffirelli and Barber, Price clearly thought their operatic tale of Cleopatra was immune to the diseases that plagued the cinematic version.

That there should be a multi-page magazine article on the opera, its director, composer, and vocal celebrity a month before its premiere indicates the kind of anticipation that was felt in New York, and equally instructive is Zeffirelli's use of such terms as "enormous" and "baroque exuberance" and his contention that his original ideas were the right ones, "good or bad." Clearly the disaster of Fox's *Cleopatra* had served as no warning to them. As I suggested, it even seems to have goaded them on to greater heights of excess.

Opening night was predictably gala. Ten thousand onlookers lined up behind police barricades to catch a glimpse of the celebrity parade, which walked with the protection (from twenty-five Vietnam protestors) of one hundred policemen up the 163-foot red carpet into the packed lobby. Orchestra seats were selling for as much as $250. In attendance were Vanderbilts, Whitneys, the First Lady Mrs. Lyndon Johnson, Secretary of Defense Robert Mc-Namara, United Nations delegate Arthur J. Goldberg, Governor John D. Rockefeller, Mayor John Lindsay, and the first Lady's guest, President and Mrs. Ferdinand E. Marcos of the Phillipines. (We can assume that Mrs. Marcos had purchased a new pair of shoes for the occasion.)

The opening of the new Met occasioned a foot-wide photograph on the front page of the *New York Times* the next day (17 September 1966).[10] Charlotte Curtis's headline article accurately described the situation with her opening sentence: "The premiere of Samuel Barber's *Antony and Cleopatra* was only one of the diversions at the super-gala opening of the new $45.7 million Metropolitan Opera House in Lincoln Center last night." The reviews of the opera reveal just how much the production overwhelmed the music. Harold Schonberg described it as

> the grand, grand opening of the grand, grand Metropolitan Opera. It was quite a spectacle, situated on the cosmic scale somewhere above the primeval atom that caused the original Big Bang, and somewhere below the creation of the Milky Way. . . . It was a big, complicated package: big, grand, impressive, and vulgar. . . . The emphasis, quite understandably from the point of view of the Metropolitan Opera, was to show the public what nearly $50 million worth of opera house could do.

After describing the stage works as "a big Erector set," Schonberg finally in the eighth paragraph gets around to describing the opera itself. Barber's score, he said, "was big in sound but stingy with with arresting melodic ideas. It abounds in declamation and pageantry rather than in an exploration of the subject—love between man and woman." "The singing," he adds later, "was good." In conclusion he writes, "Now that the opening night hysteria is out of the way, the Metropolitan can go back to its proper business, that of producing opera as honestly, tastefully and imaginatively as possible."[11] Ironically, Schonberg interpreted Zeffirelli's eighteenth-century/Renaissance hybrid as the last remnant of German Expressionism.

The criticism of Zeffirelli's production of *Antony and Cleopatra* was widespread. *The London Times* described the production as "narcissistically childish, in poor taste, and simply ugly." [12] In fact, the critics' and audience's memory of the evening deteriorated as the weeks, months, and years moved on. Originally, Schonberg providing a good example, critics thought the opera was tolerable, the production intolerable. By 1983, a *New York Times* article described the evening as a "near fiasco." [13] Another in 1975 called it "haircurlingly awful . . . a landmark of vulgarity and staging excesses." [14]

Such criticism spilled over onto Barber's opera. Barber was mortified. He returned to Italy and stayed in seclusion for several years. In a rare interview in 1971, Barber remarked

> As far as I am concerned, the production had absolutely nothing to do with what I had imagined. . . . The Met overproduced it. The opera didn't call for it. . . . Zeffirelli wanted horses and goats and 200 soldiers, which he got, and he wanted elephants which he fortunately didn't get. The point is, I had very little control—practically none. I was not supported by the management. On the other hand, management suppported every idea of Zeffirelli's. Then, of course, there were all those mishaps of a first night in a new house. I was simply the major victim of all that.[15]

Finally, apparently at the urging of Menotti, his boyhood friend, he revised the opera for a Julliard revival in 1975. Henehan wisely pointed out in the *Times* review that in previous centuries a number of operas that are now much admired were revised, rewritten, and ultimately published in a variety of versions and forms.[16] The opera was revived again at the Spoleto festival in 1983, and some of its music is used separately for concert suites/arias.[17] The Lyric opera of Chicago revived it in 1990—somewhat successfully.

Not since those years in the sixties has there been such anticipation on the part of critics and audiences for the premiere of an opera or film, and not since has there been such a grave disappointment or fiasco of production. The expansion years of the previous decade had developed in opera and film to the extent where Fox could plan a huge cinematic spectacle and New York a lavish, brand new opera house. There have been other, previous operatic premieres greatly anticipated, of course, and many of them were quite successful. With both the operatic *Antony and Cleopatra* and the cinematic *Cleopatra*, however, the anticipation of the producers as well and the carte blanche they gave themselves created expectations so excessive that they overwhelmed not only the audience and critics but the subject matter itself. Simply put, Cleopatra was a fascinating, alluring ancient monarch whose grand, amorous entanglements Shakespeare molded into the quintessential tragic romance.

Audiences in the 1960s were no longer allured by historical romance and felt the grandeur to be excessive. The principal parts in the history of these spectacles were played by Elizabeth Taylor, Richard Burton, Franco Zeffirelli, Leontyne Price, and Samuel Barber, all of whom spent time in Italy in various combinations in 1964/5. Perhaps it was the distance from America, or their luxurious lifestyles. In any event, they made serious miscalculations as to what the critics and public would find accceptable or artistically excessive. *Antony and Cleopatra* was not acceptable. Cleopatra had had her day of mid-twentieth-century popularity.

Notes

1. Horace, *Odes* 1.37.

2. Charles H. Parsons, ed., *The Mellen Opera Reference Index*, vol. 9 (Lewiston, N.Y.: E. Mellen Press, 1989), 31–32.

3. For other films including Cleopatra as a central figure, see Jon Solomon, *The Ancient World in the Cinema* (South Brunswick, N.J., and New York: A. S. Barnes and Company, 1978), 41–52.

4. See Walter Wanger and Joe Hyams, *My Life with Cleopatra* (New York: Bantam Books, 1963).

5. Robert Sussman Stewart, "The Vision of Franco Zeffirelli," *New York Times Magazine*, 4 September 1966, 11–18.

6. Howard Klein, "The Birth of an Opera," *New York Times Magazine*, 28 August 1966, 32 and 107.

7. E.g., Emily Coleman, "Leontyne Makes a Date with History," *New York Times*, 11 Semptember 1966, D21.

8. Klein, "Birth of an Opera," 107.

9. Ibid., 110.

10. Charlotte Curtis, "New Metropolitan Opera House Opens in a Crescendo of Splendor," *New York Times*, 17 September 1966, 1.

11. Harold C. Schonberg, "On Stage, It Was Antony and Cleopatra," *New York Times*, 17 September 1966, 16.

12. "Everything Fine at the Met but the Opera," *London Times*, 19 September 1966, 6.

13. Bernard Holland, "Opera: Spoleto Revives 'Cleopatra' by Barber," *New York Times*, 30 May 1983, 11.

14. Donal Henehan, "Juilliard Rehabilitates Barber 'Antony and Cleopatra,'" *New York Times*, 7 February 1975, 13.

15. John Gruen, "And Where Has Samuel Barber Been . . . " *New York Times*, 3 October 1971, 2, 15, 21, 30.

16. Henehan, "Juilliard," 13.

17. Holland, "Opera," 11.

Part Seven
Opera and Contemporary Culture

Adam in Wonderland: Krzysztof Penderecki and the American Bicentennial

JOANN KRIEG

As any student of American culture knows, America loves a celebration, and, most of all, America loves to celebrate itself, for the country retains a kind of "Wonderland" attitude toward its history. At every opportunity the states, either collectively or singly, will bring up the cannon, beat the drums, and shoot off rockets in noisy commemoration of some individual, institution, or event. Usually these celebrations are homegrown, that is, specific to the history and accomplishments of the United Status and heralded by its citizens. On occasion, however, other nations have played a part, the most notable example of these having occurred when France celebrated the idea of Liberty by raising its symbolic representation on American soil. More recently an American celebration may have been the occasion for an artist of another nation to celebrate here the idea of Freedom then denied his own countrymen. The question of who got the better of the deal is somewhat like the question, "Who owns the Brooklyn Bridge?" the answer in each case being, it depends on who's selling and who's buying.

When the official history of the Bicentennial of the United States is compiled, it will be necessary to extend the chronology to include an event which, by its delayed appearance, had to have been the last hurrah of that observance. The event, the premiere performance on 29 November 1978 of Krzysztof Penderecki's opera *Paradise Lost*, was, inevitably, an anticlimax. Coupled with the less than enthusiastic critical response to the work, its lateness has caused it to remain a sort of footnote to the national commemoration. For students of American culture, however, and of opera in America, the array of historical and political factors involved make neglect of the opera, whatever its musical evaluation, a serious omission.

Right from the start there were dissenting voices raised when the Chicago Lyric Opera Company announced the commissioning of a

work by a Polish composer for the observance of the U.S.
Bicentennial. No one seemed to recall that in 1876 Richard Wagner had received $5,000 to compose a piece of music for the open-
ing ceremonies of the centennial observance in Philadelphia. True,
his "Centennial March" remains one of Wagner's lesser accomplishments (though his claim that while writing it he received the
inspiration for the Flower Maidens' song in *Parsifal* redeems it
somewhat), but nonetheless it was a precedent.[1] When queried on
the appropriateness of the choice of a foreign composer for the
national event, Penderecki fell back on the more familiar example
of Egypt's commission to Verdi for an opera to hail the opening
of the Suez canal in 1869, a commission which resulted in the creation of *Aïda*. Something prophetic lurked in this response, for both
operas were actually produced two years later than the events they
were to mark.

The Lyric Opera later claimed that the intent of its commission
was to offer a special contribution to the Bicentennial celebration
by providing "an original addition to the permanent opera repertoire, not one which might disappear after the American
anniversary festivities had subsided. . . ."[2] In considering a subject matter that would retain its appeal over time and command international interest, the field was narrowed to either the history of
the United States or, as the program notes described the premise
of the opera actually produced, "the universal condition of man."
But the announcement of subject, John Milton's seventeenth-
century epic poem *Paradise Lost*, met with a stony silence. The
very title seemed an affront to a nation which, even before its inception, considered itself a second Eden, a Paradise regained. Yet
here was this representative of a nation ruled by what many Americans of the time considered the source of all contemporary political evil, communism, offering as a "tribute" to our two hundred
years of nationhood a work titled *Paradise Lost*!

Even had it borne a different title Penderecki's choice would
have been unsettling. Many felt he might have chosen an American literary classic on which to base his score, as had Benjamin
Britten in the well received *Billy Budd* and, again, in *The Turn of
the Screw*. Britten was considered for the commission by Chicago
Opera, as was Gian Carlo Menotti, Hans Werner Henze, and
Luigi Dallapiccola, but all were rejected in favor of Penderecki
who on the basis of such compositions as "Threnody in Memory of
the Victims of Hiroshima" (1961) and his opera, *The Devils of
Loudun*, had established a reputation as the foremost creator of
modern music.[3] Clearly the Lyric was in search of the spectacular,

something boldly experimental, something no less bold than Milton's stated intent for his poem, "to justify the ways of God to man."

But Milton's *Paradise Lost* seemed a sterile, intellectual text on which to base an opera. (Bear in mind that this was before Americans had even considered the possibility of an opera based on something so prosaic as a President's visit to a foreign country.) The opera company applauded itself for offering "a daring reappraisal of one of the immortal achievements of Western civilization," a literary classic which it claimed has been, in our time, "left to a silent reverence, a Sphinx among our arts and letters, respected but unknown." Setting aside the patronizing tone of this self-congratulation, it must be said that Milton's poem harked back to a Puritan past which Americans in the 1970s were less than eager to reembrace. The turbulent decades of the 1960s and 1970s need not be reviewed here, except to point out that in that period the civil rights movement led to the free speech movement and eventually to the anti–Vietnam War movement, and that all of these led in turn to the strategies of President Richard Nixon and Attorney General John Mitchell to prevent what they saw as impending revolt. With the benefit of hindsight, Penderecki's choice for an operatic subject matter can seem less irrelevant, but by July of 1976, with the Vietnam War ended and the Watergate hearings over, Americans were in no mood to consider the subject of sin, collective or private: 1976 was to be a time of all-out celebration, and everyone wanted in on it.

It was this determination, to have a truly nationwide celebration, that allowed the Chicago Lyric the freedom to commission an opera which, though intended for the American Bicentennial, was a joint production with Teatro alla Scala in Milan. The U.S. Congress had chosen to decentralize the observance of the Bicentennial rather than follow the practice of one hundred years earlier when all activities were held at the Philadelphia site. The 1976 observance was intended to spread the wealth, with state and local events encouraged. This brought about a full range of plans, everything from the painting of municipal fire hydrants in red, white, and blue, to the production of some very fine pieces of history based on solid research. In between these extremes lay the various city and state events, notably New York City's Operation Sail which brought the "tall ships," sailing vessels from fifty-five nations, into New York's harbor on 4 July and Chicago's commission to a Polish composer for an opera to be presented in the fall of the Bicentennial year.

General Manager of the Chicago Lyric Opera at the time was the late Carol Fox, one of the Company's founders, who had taken over the managerial reins in 1956, two years into its operation. Though by many accounts a difficult person, Fox had in her favor the good will and generosity of some Chicago benefactors, among them the company's executive vice-president, James C. Hemphill. It was Hemphill who provided funds to carry out the company's plans to commission a Bicentennial opera that would become a part of its standard repertory. Since its initiation the Lyric had premiered only one other work, Vittorio Giannini's *The Harvest* (1961), which was quickly forgotten. For the city of Chicago, the 1976 offering would be the first world premiere of an opera by a European composer since the 1921 debut of Prokofiev's *Love for Three Oranges*.[4] It was with great excitement, then, that the company and Hemphill announced the commission in May of 1973, and, a short time later, the appointment of Samuel Wanamaker as stage director of the proposed work. By the time the opera made its belated debut, however, Wanamaker had departed the scene (as had his successor Virginio Puecher who had directed several productions for the company but who could not work with Penderecki), and Hemphill had died.

Indeed, the work seemed clouded in difficulties, almost as if the ill feelings with which its announcement was met cast a shadow over its production. In fairness, the objections of American composers should be taken into account. *Composer* magazine attempted to do just that by asking for the reactions of number of contemporary American composers. Some used words such as "sad" and "incomprehensible" describe their feelings, while others either saw no harm in it—provided other commissions went to American musicians—or indicated a belief that in view of the recent Watergate scandal America should not even plan a celebration. Predictably, there was a reference to the commission as "the worst Polish joke in American music." Only one composer raised the question of opera's appropriateness in twentieth-century America by speculating that "a *relevant* American composer" who would be willing to undertake the commission probably could not be found.[5]

Publicly Penderecki took no notice of the controversy, claiming that it was "a private commission by a man in Chicago who likes opera and has given money for productions." If, in fact, Penderecki saw the commission in this way, as a private rather than a public event, Hemphill's death midway in the composition process may have encouraged the composer to adopt a more general and unrestricted approach to the work. More likely, however, it was the influence of the text upon which it was based, a text which above all else emphasizes freedom as *the* most inalienable, to use the wording of the Declaration of Independence, of human rights.

Penderecki was drawn to Milton's poem because it was large in form and grand of theme, attributes he hoped to claim for his own. He professed an inclination toward such themes as the Creation and Last Judgment, and toward the composition of a requiem. Milton's poem, he acknowledged, offered an opportunity to fulfill in one great work many of his musical intentions.[6] Language was no barrier, as the maestro grandly pointed out that he had composed for texts in many languages, including Greek, Latin, German, and Russian. He did, however, indicate his reluctance to touch Milton's text, claiming (with some justification) "it is like touching the Bible."[7]

Samuel Wanamaker suggested Christopher Fry as librettist, a poet and playwright whose religious temperament seemed well suited to the task. Known chiefly for his verse play, *The Lady's not for Burning* (1949), Fry had also done the screenplay for the 1966 Dino De Laurentis film, *The Bible*. He'd had a relatively easy time in writing the filmscript, for it confined itself to the first five books, avoided commentary, and concentrated on the Biblical text. Ten years later when confronted by Milton's text, which is all commentary, his task proved far more difficult. Evidently as daunted by the poet as was Penderecki, Fry presented the composer with a libretto made up of lengthy, Miltonic speeches unworkable as opera.

Penderecki later blamed the unworkable libretto for the long delay in delivering a score, but at least as culpable was his own changed perspective.[8] Originally he intended to create a *sacre rappresentazione* of about ninety minutes length. The choice of form, which was a forerunner of the oratorio, was an attempt to follow the dictates of Milton's time when it was the medium for sacred drama with music. (It was, in fact, one of the theatrical forms Milton considered when he began work on "Adam Unparadiz'd," the work which evolved into *Paradise Lost*.) What Penderecki gained theatrically from this was the possibility of offering dance, spoken words, and whatever other effects he wished to add to the musical drama. Further, it meant that his production could be presented, with some alteration, in a theater, opera house, church, or concert hall. In the course of composition, however, a new vision of the work began to take shape in the composer's mind. Influenced perhaps by the scale of the Miltonic theme, the sweep of which lies behind much of American literature, including Whitman's

"Passage to India," or perhaps by the breadth and scope of the nation whose mythical history his subject encompassed, the work grew proportionately. "I began to realize we were involved in an enormous undertaking," Penderecki later said, "a piece of perhaps three and a half hours playing time. I could not rush it." It may have been at this point in composition, with only a third of the opera completed, that he broke off work on it and undertook conducting engagements in various countries, leaving the Chicago company in suspense.

In its final form, presented two years late, the opera consisted of approximately twelve hundred verses set in two acts requiring (as its composer had predicted) three and a half hours to perform. The chorus required 130 singers, plus a children's choir, ballet dancers, and hosts of angels and devils. The scenery was built in Europe and shipped to Chicago where ten moving vans were used to transport Heaven and Hell to the opera house. The production was mounted first in Chicago, later at La Scala, and was performed once at the Vatican for the Pope and College of Cardinals. It employed an elaborate doubling device that included a dancing Adam and Eve, whose skin-toned leotards served as metaphor for nakedness, along with a singing Adam and Eve dressed in flowing choral robes, an arrangement for six male voices of ancient Samaritan texts to represent the voice of God, and a speaking part for God and the poet Milton, both played by the late actor Arnold Moss.[9] It should be mentioned that for the performance at the Vatican the dancing progenitors in the leotards were eliminated.

Reviews of the Chicago premiere were polite but unimpressed, this despite Chicago Opera's attempts to bring attention to the opera's overdue appearance with an on-air seminar devoted to the work and a live radio broadcast of the premiere performance. Less polite were the comments of those who declared the work boring, citing long stretches of music with no movement. (Lovers of Wagner's operas, however, can attest that this formula need not add up to boredom.) Official neglect of the work extended to the heavily Polish Archdiocese of Chicago which totally ignored the opera in spite of its religious theme and, more importantly, ignored the composer's personal friendship and shared nationality with the newly installed Pope, John Paul II. In Milan a reviewer referred to the work as "clever, sumptious, and entertaining," adding that the music was "distinguished but not stimulating." It has been reported that Chicago Lyric was three years recovering from the cost of the production, although the figure involved has not been made public.

In political terms what did it mean that Krzysztof Penderecki was given a commission for the U.S. Bicentennial? Perhaps a great deal, though there is no documentation[10] to support the speculation. In 1973 when the commission was announced the world had not yet seen its first Polish Pope, nor had it heard of a Polish Solidarity movement. Yet on the national radio broadcast of the premiere of *Paradise Lost*, conductor Bruno Bartoletti, speaking through an interpreter, observed that because the commission was "for the Bicentennial of the United States, it was necessary to choose an artist who had a strong belief in the ideals and concepts on which the United States is built, as well as one who shared the religious context of those ideals."

These avowals of Penderecki's democratic sentiments were more easily made in 1978, following his shift away from purely experimental and, according to his own insistence, "unpolitical" works, toward more traditional composition, most of it religious. That is, the avowals were more easily made in 1978 than they would have been in 1973 at the time of the commission. Then the composer had a relationship of rare privilege with the Polish Communist government. He and his wife, a biophysicist, had been allowed to leave the country seemingly at will, so that Penderecki had frequently conducted in the West and was for a number of years on the music faculty at Yale University. The national pride in this musical genius that allowed such freedom of movement seems to have been matched by Chicago Opera's desire to "cash in" on the prestige of a distinguished Communist composer offered up in the interest of an American celebration.

In the end everyone got what he or she wanted: Penderecki the commission and the publicity, and Carol Fox and the Lyric Opera its production and some attention, though certainly not what it had hoped for. But the whole affair remains one of those bizarre kinds of events often associated with large scale celebrations. In retrospect, however, one wonders if Milton's grand justification of the ways of God, based as it is on the poet's deeply held political and theological conviction of human freedom as a divine gift, was perhaps Penderecki's political statement to his own government, much as Auguste Bartholdi's statue *Liberty Englightening the World* was intended as a symbol of the republic which Bartholdi hoped to see established in France.[10] By the time Bartholdi's monument was erected in New York's harbor in 1886, fifteen years after its inception, his republican hopes had been realized. As subsequent history has revealed, Penderecki, had he been able to delay as long—and if this was, indeed, his intent—would have had the same satisfaction.

Notes

1. Wagner's "Centennial March" had its actual premiere in his Bayreuth Theatre on 2 July 1876. On *Parsifal*, see Ernest Newman. *The Life of Richard Wagner* (New York: Knopf, 1946), vol. 4, pp. 474–75.

2 Gregory Speck, "The Making of *Paradise Lost*," program, Lyric Opera of Chicago, November 1978.

3. Mary Lou Humphrey, "*Paradise Lost*: Penderecki's Operatic Enigma," *Music Journal* 37 (January 1979): 11–13.

4. Hans W. Heinsheimer, "Paradise Regained," *Opera News* 43 (November 1978): 48–55.

5. "Five Questions: Fifty Five Answers," *Composer* 7 (1976–77): 16–25.

6. Krzysztof Penderecki, in a radio seminar broadcast the day of the premiere on WFMT, Chicago Public Radio. No print record of this seminar exists, but it is included in an audio tape made of the performance.

7. Heinsheimer, "Paradise Regained," 5.

8. Penderecki, in radio seminar.

9. In the preparation of this paper I was much indebted to Mr. Moss who not only told me about the experience of being part of the opera production, but provided me with an audio tape of the premiere performance so that I might hear the opera, which remains unrecorded. A copy of this tape is now in the Hofstra University music library.

10. Marvin Trachtenberg, *The Statue of Liberty* (New York: Penguin Books, 1986), pp. 29–30.

Modern Pop Currency in Contemporary American Opera: A Case Study of Elvis in Vancouver's Production of *Carmen*, 1986

CHRISTOPHER NEWTON

On opening night . . . when in what was admittedly a sacrilegious attack on this operatic warhorse, the toreador Escamillo grabbed his crotch, gave a few pelvic thrusts and then had his shirt ripped off by adoring fans, there were strong hisses from the balcony. A medley of boos and bravos greeted the end of the second act. Then the arguments began.[1]

I couldn't tell a sandbag from a person. You had a midget. You had a man on stilts. You had a three ring circus and you should have billed it as such.[2]

Carmen is one of the comparatively few operas that are both a treasure for musicians and a sure success with the public . . .[3]

These three quotes tell us a great deal about *Carmen*, and the first two reveal much about the Vancouver Opera's production in 1986. The criticisms quoted explain almost as much about Lucien Pintilie's revision as they do about the audience itself. Punk rockers in attendance demanded their money back at intermission because they claimed the opera was not traditional. Music and opera devotees went to forums and could not see the irony of their vehement complaints of being bored at the show, given the uproar surrounding it. Still other regular subscribers boasted that Vancouver was now on an operatic level with the Met.[4] The professional critics were just as divided and unguarded in their comments. The two major Toronto papers divided into separate camps much as the Vancouver audience did: traditionalist against innovator. Stephen Godfrey in his *Globe and Mail* review[5] ended with the idea that the character Carmen would have loved the joke played on the audience. William Littler, in the *Toronto Star*[6], suggested that as in the Beatles' song, "Roll Over Beethoven," Bizet was rocking unhappily in his grave.

Passion over an avant-garde opera production may be fairly regular in New York, Paris, or Frankfurt, but in the rainy outpost of Vancouver, it is unusual. The causes of this rare passion are important for behind the turmoil of this West Coast production lie indications of the future of opera in American regional presentations. Certainly innovative work occasionally appears for West Coast audiences (amid the more standard musical reviews and touring shows), but the irregularity of a sustained opera offering has left the opera-going public without a consistent picture of modern opera developments elsewhere. Much interesting work that does come to Vancouver is met with good natured appreciation, but rarely with true audience engagement. Critics of the Canadian psyche have described the national character as being the losing combination of French ineptitude for discipline and organization and Scottish Presbyterian savoir-faire. Add the British Columbia Tumbleweed and apparent is a landscape considered by many to be largely inhospitable to a traditional art form. *Carmen* was to be an exception for the proud Vancouverites showing the rest of the world that they could play on the world stage. The translation of opera from the European tradition to the new and vital West Coast presentation initially encouraged high hopes, but ultimately left many involved with unfulfilled expectations. The quotes already mentioned suggest that some in the audience were expecting something as mummified as the King Tut tour. On the other side, stage director Lucien Pintilie walked out a week before opening because he could not get his way with the conductor. What remains is the evidence of a production that illustrates the pitfalls of translating an opera for an audience that resists translation. Pintilie wanted a space where he could satisfy his international aesthetic notions, and Vancouver audiences largely wanted a stamp of cultural approval. What they both got was more of a reflection of their clashing attitudes than they bargained for. The crotch-tugging Escamillo is only one representative example. In the end, the Carmen of Expo '86 was very true to the spirit of Bizet's original, but ground-breaking in its execution. In what ways was this production true to the spirit of Bizet's original? Before describing the innovations and liberties that the creative artists included in this production, it may be wise to review Bizet's original conception of *Carmen*.

The howls of critics and audience members proclaiming Pintilie's desecration of the grand traditional chestnut of *Carmen* could probably have been silenced by a little bit of homework. In 1875, when Bizet completed *Carmen*, his venue was the Opera Comique and not grand opera at all. The distinction is important because in Paris at the end of the nineteenth century there were many forms of musical entertainment—Théâtre Lyrique, Bouffe-Parisienne, Opera Comique, Grand Opera—each with its own set of real and implied restrictions. Though the Opera Comique form was in a period of fluctuation when Bizet submitted his final work, there were significant restrictions on what could be offered to the middle-class family audience. And within his own time, Bizet shocked his audience with *Carmen*. Mina Curtiss recounts a delightful exchange that highlights the rigidity that producers anticipated from *Carmen's* audience back then.

Ludovic Halevy, acting as a promoter of Bizet's adaptation, suggested a compromise acceptable to the family audience,

> that Carmen would be "softened, toned down, that a pure opera-comique character had been introduced, a very innocent, chaste young girl." There were gypsies, he admitted, but "comic" gypsies. As for the inevitable death scene, it would be "sneaked in at the end of a very lively, very brilliant act, played in bright sunlight on a holiday with triumphal processions, ballets, and joyous fanfares." After a long struggle, de Louven capitulated, but as Halevy left his office he said: "please try not to have her die. Death on stage at the Opera-Comique! Such a thing has never been seen!—Never!"[7]

It is true that *Carmen* was innovative for the Opera Comique (using elements of both bourgeois tragedy and operetta), nevertheless Bizet received much of his inspiration for music and dramatic action from the one hundred and fifty year old Opera Comique tradition.

Bizet's approach to his works was highly experimental. It is valuable to recall that his major work before the *Carmen* project was *L'Arlesienne*, a straight drama at Carvalho's Vaudeville. Bizet wrote an accompaniment to Daudet's play in a collaboration to revitalize the melodrama with serious content and sophisticated music. The play was met with jeers and the music with indifference. A review of *L'Arlesienne* highlights the rigidity of the critics' adherence to form. Francisque Sarcey wrote, "Music is rarely welcome in drama . . . it is used solely as a stopgap. . . . Very pretty the music may be; useless it certainly is."[8] The audience agreed and by the third act on the premiere the house was three-quarters empty. Daudet was permanently discouraged, but Bizet moved on to search for another audience for the marriage of drama and music. Unlike *L'Arlesienne*, which tried to bring music to the drama, the story of Carmen brought serious drama to family music theatre. The popular reception was even worse for *Carmen* than for *L'Arlesienne*. In hindsight, the rejection of *Carmen* by its first critics is amusing. Nevertheless, it is important to realize that Bizet's unrecognized treasure was nurtured by the historical growth of a hybrid form from numerous genres. Grand opera has since tried to patent *Carmen* for itself, but the history behind Bizet's creation reveals the ridiculous and impossible nature of such a notion. *Carmen's* background is like that of a multiple personality: conception in the bawd of the medieval fair, birth in the scrubbed and sentimental pastoral, adolescence during the French Revolution, maturation in a time of tame parody and tidy mediocrity, and finally old age and synthesis, grasping at all forms younger and more vital. Nietzsche[9] suggested *Carmen* as the better model (over Wagner) for the direction of music drama. Pintilie, one hundred years later, recognized the highly flexible *Carmen* with its smorgasbord of historical baggage as a great vehicle for international presentation. One reason why Vancouver's production was so startling to its viewers was the integration of the previously overlooked Opera Comique roots.

One cannot give too much credit to Pintilie's innovations, of course, for *Carmen* has been brilliantly translated into such reincarnations as the black musical *Carmen Jones*, the Rita Hayworth film, and the contemporary Peter Brook *Tragedy of Carmen*. The important difference with Pintilie's production was that the modern treatment of the *Carmen* material was still within the framework of a traditional proscenium opera presentation. This raises important questions: Can opera's traditional format withstand innovations and cultural translations (that is to say, can one work "within the system"?) and also, will an audience that expects one form suggested by the theater and tradition accept another suggested by the director or writer? The evidence of Pintilie's Vancouver *Carmen* indicates a qualified "yes" to both questions. Although this production was met with boos and a few scathing reviews, it also had some energetic supporters. *Carmen* sold out all of its performances and generated a fierce and prominent debate.

Describing the performance approach of Pintilie's translation suffers as all descriptions of performance do. Pintilie's heavy emphasis on the visual bonanza is especially difficult to recapture with the written word. However, I would like to discuss developments that led to Pintilie's *Carmen* that are clearer in print than in spectacle. First, we need to examine the evolution of the genre critically. Pintilie's task of translation was not simply a matter of finding contemporary equivalents to the broad tradition of Opera Comique, it also necessitated finding a way to use those equivalents in a contemporary genre. I believe that this process must be understood before a description of the performance itself can be relevant.

When Bizet decided on Mérimée's *Carmen* as a source for his opera he was indeed justifying Gauthier's definition[10] of Opera Comique as a bastard form. The Carmen of the novel has strong elements of the tragic genre with the inevitability of the hero and heroine's end. Bizet, writing for a middle-class audience, concentrated, however, on the moral element.[11] By the end of the opera *Carmen*, everyone in the audience recognizes that obsession has driven Don Jose beyond tolerable limits. We do feel sorry for him, but as in most melodramas we also feel superior to him. The change from a tragic to a melodramatic genre is important because it reveals a process that the translator of older works must accommodate.

Melodrama has evolved, too. Certainly the plot machinery of melodrama is still very popular and useful. The most modern works of stage playwrights like Shepard and Mamet are still based on the melodrama format, but there is a difference in the seriousness with which artists and spectators take melodrama's notion that moral virtue triumphs over immorality. Audiences are increasingly unreceptive to the notion that any society can be idealized, even in fiction. A skeptical society treats traditional forms with increasing irony and satire. Northrop Frye[12] suggests at this cynical point another transformation in the genre occurs—a transformation from melodrama into ironic comedy. The aesthetic shift from Grand Opera to Opera Comique startled the Vancouver audience; the additional ironic examination of *Carmen's* melodramatic baggage encouraged argument.

But ironic comedy is not by any means a direct and didactic formula for social reform. There is a code or currency. Frye[13] suggests that with the ironic manipulation of the melodrama arrive the corresponding arts of advertising and propaganda, which encourage the attitude that nothing can be taken at face value. Advertising and propaganda in practice suggest a licence of exaggeration: we know that a deodorant will not insure financial success and sexual glory but we do like imagining such a scenario. In artistic concepts, irony encourages similar exaggeration with a compatible payoff.

The sword is double-edged, however, and it allows modern directors to slash both ways. On the one hand, ironic exaggeration can suck an audience into a kaleidoscope of commentary on substance. On the other hand, in cutting back against flights of fancy, the irony can easily unseat pleasant nostalgia by setting up jarring and unexpected comparisons. The destruction of predictable associations often goes so far as to undermine the spirit of the performance itself. When Escamillo, dressed as Elvis Presley, has his hat shot off by a rambunctious carnival reveler, he exclaims, "An inch lower and that would have been the end of the opera!" This gag draws attention to the fragility of ironic comedy burdened by the weight of exaggeration and licence. The opera has directed the gun at itself and demands that the audience maintain an ironic attitude, lest the hostage be liquidated. Frye[14] describes the director's admonishing attitude thus, "One notes a recurring tendency . . . to ridicule and scold an audience assumed to be hankering after sentiment, solemnity, and the triumph of fidelity and approved moral standards." In practice, ironic comedy appears self-conscious, chaotic, and decadent. These were, in fact, the major criticisms of the Vancouver production. But the ultimate desire of the ironic genre is not to distance the audience from the performance, but rather to encourage the audience to share in the irony. And as suggested by Escamillo's ironic wisecrack, character is the most important link between ironic comedy and the audience.

Carmen and Don Jose are most important as agents of the dramatic action since their relationship is the substance of the story. There is another archetypical figure that serves additional functions. In *Carmen* the toreador creates an environment for the drama; his exotic (for the French) profession serves as a focal point for the "Latin" in the opera. He also acts in his professional capacity as an agent suggesting that there is entertainment present; like the ancient chorus, he is the modern equivalent of the link between spectator and performance. The buffoon and entertainer type, as Frye describes[15], has affinities with both the parasite and, more importantly, with the master of revels. If the dramatic success of this character is vital in ironic comedy, then it becomes doubly crucial in an ironic treatment of a play translated to a foreign audience.

Escamillo, the entertainer in Bizet's *Carmen*, had the singularly important function of focusing the audience's sense of the exotic Spanish spirit. Though he does play a role in the inevitable demise of Carmen and Jose, he is most important to the opera as local color. Carmen would have moved on after a romance with the toreador, but she will always be faithful to the free spirit suggested by a figure like Escamillo. In Pintilie's *Carmen*, the shift from melodrama to ironic comedy necessitates a rethinking of Escamillo's presentation.

As the most important human agent in conveying the environment on stage, the recasting of Escamillo is critical in translating the opera to a modern audience. Certainly a bullfighter is exotic for a Vancouver audience, but a mere bullfighter would be so remote that his associative impact could have generated only the most banal images in most of the audience. One of comic irony's strengths is to add comment on top of commentary. Given an American audience (for the moment generalizing a shared Canadian and U.S. aesthetic), the most likely type to fit into the modern slot of singer-entertainer is the rock star. But more than a modern equivalency is required because the genre has evolved from simple exotic spectacle to an ironic treatment of the spectacle. Required is an equivalency that reveals the pomposity, the naivete, the disintegration, and the ripped seams. Elvis Presley as an archetype is wonderful for ironic comedy because his image contains both the elevated myth of a superstar and the ridicule of a man who ended pathetically, bloated and dead on a toilet. Pintilie's choice of an Elvis persona for Escamillo threw the notion of revered kitsch back at the audience. The Elvis element crystallized both a modern exotic setting and a contemporary dramatic form.

But the effect of putting the image of Elvis on the opera stage did not end with recasting an old *Carmen* into a new one. In the literal sense, Tom Pox as the Elvis Escamillo addressed the audience directly. His very first entrance was designed to undermine completely the spirit of spectacle and grand anticipation. Pintilie staged the cast facing out to the audience in great expectation as if the toreador would come gloriously through the auditorium. Instead, with orchestra going full tilt, Escamillo appeared upstage, facing the backs of the people anticipating his arrival. "Shit!" he exclaimed. The opera came to a grinding halt, and Fox exclaimed to the audience, "Who set this thing up? Shit! I'll never sing in Vancouver again!" He then charged the conductor to start again and the action lurched forward to the next ironic commentary. This bit of focal misdirection served a number of functions. It sarcastically suggested that it was the Vancouver audience that needed the hollow pomp and spectacle as the entire stage peered out looking for Escamillo's arrival in the house. More importantly, it initiated the audience to the agent of Elvis who was going to lead the spectators through the irony of *Carmen* much as a lounge singer leads a group of hotel barflies through a medley of tired old standards. There were a few other occasions when Fox addressed the audience directly, but this effect was used economically. The character juggled his presentation on three levels: the story of *Carmen*, the framing Central American carnival (which I shall discuss in a few minutes), and the Expo audience. Certainly with the widespread news on opening night that Pintilie had walked out on the production, the comment about not ever playing in Vancouver again carried the irony far beyond the footlights. But most of Escamillo's ironic message was conveyed by his relationship to his onstage audience.

Ultimately Escamillo's characterization was not achieved by direct address since Pintilie had to work with the sizable architectural dimensions of a large proscenium opera house. The carnival revelers indicated what Pintilie expected from the paying audience. Elvis Escamillo's hot pursuit by autograph seekers was a colorful commentary on the reverence with which grand opera is treated. The undressing and stroking of his chest by adoring fans during his first aria drove home this point by mocking those grim, prim audience members who just want to hear the music. Through the relationship between Escamillo and the revelers, Pintilie suggests that the uncritical worship of idols, operatic or popular, is a ridiculous pursuit. The inflationary ironic commentary pursued the issue to the contemporaneous controversy over the presentation of the Expo *Carmen*. In the production, exaggerated news cameras trained in on Escamillo and he preened for them, all the while shoving autograph-seekers back. This was a timely commentary on the visiting prima donna Kiri Te Kanawa's suggestion that singers walk out on Pintilie's production. It also served as a reminder that in ironic comedy the performance is always undergoing modification because of outside pressures. For all of the clever and perceptive criticisms of opera form, the audience, and the larger society, Pintilie does not offer anything significantly new except to suggest a fresh spirit of theatricality based on the local and familiar. The originality lies in the ironic treatment that links the old with the new. He reminds us that opera has a highly flexible dimension through his resurrection of Opera Comique elements. Pintilie's *Carmen* also attempts to reassure that a true work of art, "a super opera of mythical dimension"[16], will always find a contemporary currency even in regional presentations. With the recast of figures like Escamillo to Elvis, Pintilie advances the idea that opera needs to respond to the demands of a new ironic genre.

But Pintilie's *Carmen* was not devised as a lesson on Opera Comique roots or genre shifts. The important task for *Carmen* was to entertain and engage the Vancouver audience. What follows is a shorthand description of the visual tactics Pintilie used to relate the audience's world with that of the opera.

Flexibility of Mode

Pintilie chose *Carmen* for modernization and translation to a regional audience because the subject had the strength to take it. Other operas, he admitted, would not be suitable for his kind of treatment, but Bizet's work has, in his words[17], a strong "backbone." In CBC press releases he described *Carmen* as "more than an opera, it is a phenomenon. . . . " Perhaps the greatest part of the phenomenon is that it can withstand as much manipulation as it has and still play so effectively. The multiple personality already described in *Carmen's* Opera Comique heritage has insured that the opera will always offer something for every age. Much credit for *Carmen's* enduring success lies in the relatively simple plot, eminently hummable music, and universal exoticism.

Effects Currency

Once the new environment had been translated to an American context, with Pintilie's correlative Latin America to Bizet's Spain, the traditional dramatic effects had to be revised. The need for the translation is built into Opera Comique's heavy reliance on popular themes and fashions to maintain the audience's interest. Fashion changes quickly, but the process is reasonably predictable. Translating the elements of the dramatic spectacle is much like plugging new parts into an old machine: the interior running theory is the same, but the exterior suggests new efficiency and sparkle. Pintilie loaded up the *Carmen* machine with fresh visual flash and witty parody of popular styles. Bizet, of course, envisioned a similar kind of smorgasbord (with borrowed elements of the fair and operetta). Pintilie was criticized for lacking restraint. The production was described by William Littler as "spilling over the footlights"[18]. This very literally happened when, during the cigarette factory scene, dry ice filled the auditorium and started a chorus of coughing fits in the audience. One disdainful viewer in the front rows exclaimed, "Now they're trying to smoke us out!" Opera has traditionally been selected for extravagant treatment to disguise its simplicity of theme, but generally, its opulence adheres to a single style or genre. Even the innovative *Carmen Jones* remained more or less in a single environment. Pintilie, on the other hand, might be accused of going to the pawn shop to purchase his dramatic effects for the dramatic machinery of *Carmen*. The effects collected fall into three categories: effects of expansion, effects of dilution, and genre cameos.

Effects of Expansion

A certain unease with the presentation was apparent from the very beginning of the performance, and it derived from the director and designer's shared commitment to expanding the dramatic framework. Pintilie used a carnival to surround the "improvised" performance of *Carmen*. The carnival was a brilliant idea to relate the opera to the larger activity of Expo '86, but for the aesthetic demands of the performance it appeared that all efforts were underscored by a split-focus. Escamillo uttering "Shit!" after making a false entrance before his first number certainly interrupts what lyrical flow *Carmen* has. Almost all activity on stage had an expansive element that pushed the focus out of the theater. The chorus of undisciplined revelers surrounded the central action and frequently drew as much attention as the central characters. The result was that much of the core of *Carmen* (the music and the sentimental passion) was given as suggestion, not commitment. Here one might consider an analogy; ironic expansion is like the lounge singer's art of hinting at songs that are never completed as promised because the artist engages in a dialogue with the audience on some current affair. The larger context of festival was given deference. Pintilie, in his translation to the regional audience, inclined toward restructuring the imbalance between the superiority of the super opera *Carmen* on the one hand, and novice spectators on the other. According to this approach, expanding the effects to the familiar raises the stature of the audience so that it can feel secure enough to appreciate opera. Indeed, the idea is to consider the opera outside the theater. The fact that in this case the effects of expansion insulted much of the Vancouver audience highlights the difficulty in translating opera from one context to another.

Dilution Effects

If the effects of expansion of *Carmen* was an effort to present a more familiar context for the audience, then the effects of dilution that Pintilie used were designed to attack the perceived lofty stature of opera. An approach "that can free us from any preconceived stale appreciation of the world," as Pintilie described it in press releases[19], also requires a format that does not take itself too seriously. Using the persona of Elvis in opera is certain to undermine preconceived notions. Diluting traditional opera effects and adding new flavor with dramatic irony is an insurance policy against the charge that the form is no longer useful.

Perhaps the most extreme example of diluting the traditional opera form occurred with the most sentimental character in the cast, Micaela. Usually this character functions as a counterpoint to Carmen—the embodiment of innocent stay-at-home virtues against unrestrained individual passions. True, the good girl/bad girl set-up is a little hard for modern audiences to swallow, but Pintilie uses a very heavy hand in making Micaela a carnival party girl. Having Martha Collins improvise the character as a blind, pregnant ballerina was difficult for the traditionalists to accommodate. In the Vancouver production, the singer playing the character was alternately in the laps of men while participating in the carnival ("off stage") and running, blindly, on toe from men in her scenes as Micaela ("on stage"). The contrast is, of course, deliberate and it effectively devalues the traditional relationship of Carmen and Micaela. The result is to draw attention to the absurdity of traditional opera's polar stereotypes, and to suggest through ironic comedy that our preconceived notions of good and bad characters may be ill founded. Destroying a saccharine character with parody is not difficult or original, but for the purpose of translating the opera it becomes especially useful. Seeing "behind" Micaela enhances the familiarity of a very traditional character and it enlists the audience in redefining the dynamics on stage.

Pintilie also diluted two of the opera's most famous musical numbers with a peek behind the works. Both Carmen's flower song and Escamillo's toreador number were interrupted by false starts. The effect was created by each singer belting out the first few bars only to be interrupted by the adoring carnival crowd. The singing stopped, the ruckus died down, and with a very obvious nod to the conductor the music restarted. The music and singing were, in these cases, performed within the context of the dramatic world as special treats. This suggests that the music exists as a self-conscious set piece to please the audience. The onstage audience serves to highlight the degree of devotion opera lovers feel toward the music, whether the drama is served or not. This was ultimately a very honest way to suggest the presentation of music, for the audience does go to opera predominantly to hear the music. Acknowledgment that the musical chestnuts take on an elevated level beyond the dramatic spectacle encourages the audience to evaluate both elements on separate levels.

Finally, in one of the more subtle choices by Pintilie, *Carmen* sustained a running leitmotif of strength and weakness suggested by the amount of hair on the heads of the focal characters. Toward the beginning of the opera it seemed coincidental that Micaela had long black hair that was fondled by balding soldiers. Don Jose's baldness compared to Carmen's fountain of hair also appeared to be an arbitrary contrast. But in Act Three when Carmen appears in the smuggler's camp with a greased crewcut and challenges Don Jose's staring with, "What are you looking at?!", an artistic comment is being made. Pintilie's commentary on his own comment takes place when Escamillo makes his final exit, whipping off his cowboy hat and revealing a displaced toupee. This running gag may have been an "in-joke" as much as anything serious, but it does parallel the consistent effort to violate the self-importance of the characters on stage. The emphasis on baldness and wigs both expanded and diluted the opera by humbling it so that the spectators could feel simultaneously superior to and insightful of the action on stage.

Genre Cameos

The carnival framework suggests masks (some crowd figures wore these) and wigs as aids to the sanctioned activity of disguise. In a larger sense, Pintilie presented *Carmen* as an Opera Comique with an acknowledged series of disguises. The leveling of the formidable grand opera tradition by exaggerated expansion and dilution should not be seen as a parasitic process that nourishes itself and gives nothing in return. Much of Pintilie's translation involves substitutions of Opera Comique spectacle with his own parade of genre cameos. Carnival disguises were not limited to creations by the hairdressers. Pintilie mixed and matched styles much as his predecessors, Daudin and Bizet, had. The disturbing issue for the traditionalists in the audience was not the mixing of styles, but rather that they were twentieth-century styles in a nineteenth century piece.

From the very beginning of *Carmen* it was obvious that Pintilie was willing to be reckless. The overture runs the lengthy gamut of Opera Comique with an assortment of carnival characters who juggle and walk and a tight rope walker in modern military gear, complete with ammo belts. In a strong signal to the audience that this production dismantles all elements of grand opera, the overture ends with the tightrope walker being shot off his precarious perch. From the beginning, ironic commentary is more important than consistency with tradition.

Some elements of the Opera Comique were maintained religiously. The traditional elements, however, were used by Pintilie as a springboard to develop irony. Carmen began her seduction song by breaking a plate on stage and using the pieces as castanets just as Galli-Marie had done in 1875. In 1986, our contemporary Carmen resorted to the plate pieces only after she appeared not to find her "castanets" in Don Jose's trousers. She also makes her entrance in the final scene in her traditional white dress, but it was rather a tarnished vision of nineteenth century feminine beauty since the audience had already experienced Carmen in a crewcut (act 3). Pintilie had done his homework on the Opera Comique tradition. His goal was not accurate historical representation, but rather, the manipulation of expectations.

The cigarette song provides a vicious example of traditional elements used as a setting for irony. The scene of the cigarette ladies leaving work (act 1 scene 4) was very wittily staged in a 1940s pin-up style that looked alternately like the last scene of *Casablanca* and a Chesterfield cigarette ad. The factory door was belching smoke (dry ice that eventually filled the house), and the chorus of women came out singing and smoking. If the image of smoking opera singers was not enough to make the audience a little uncomfortable, the waiting men outside were cast as derelict alcoholics trying to bum some smokes. As the women sashayed on stage, they formed a commercially seductive tableau on a revolving platform just out of reach of the pleading men. This entire image is in keeping with the spirit of Bizet's original idea of women exploiting their allure, but the emphasis on the sale of tobacco made the scene appear more than somewhat crass. The final ironic punctuation at the end of this scenario was the discovery that some of the cigarette women were being played by male chorus members in drag. The number ended with the voluptuous image being destroyed by wig pulling and dress ripping. With this ironic genre cameo, Pintilie hints at social criticism while still allowing the audience to indulge in a currency of nostalgia.

The wealth of genres Pintilie uses included the most contemporary. With contemporary images and issues the greatest ironic treatment of the opera is explored. Here also is where the greatest argument from the audience appears[19] as current issues rise in striking contrast against the backdrop of a traditional form. The Central American setting provided the contrast of Latin festival and cruel war. Pintilie mixed the two elements to support a consistent theme that entertainment comes with a price. The guerrilla genre drew upon current issues in the media with images of camouflage fatigues, modern weapons, and instruments of torture. Perhaps one of the most frightening pictures was the use of a black hood over Zuniga's head. Another small effect crystallized the inseparable relation of festival and terror in the modern world; when Carmen calls for a feast from Don Jose's cherished coins, someone shouts the warning, "grenade!" Everyone falls to the ground. A blast occurs and through the smoke appears a dwarf bearing fruit for the party. With this choice, Pintilie seems to suggest that a grenade might well be an orange and vice versa. This is more than a mere hint at violence since Zuniga and Don Jose die by firing squad.

The last scene in the opera is brief. After Don Jose repeatedly stabs Carmen, he becomes paralyzed by a red light. A carnival reveler quickly ties a crimson blindfold onto the kneeling Jose. Shots ring out as the stage fades to black. The traditional triumphant trumpets of the toreador are heard, but they are muted by the shots. Death is "sneaked" in, with echos of both de Louven's original pleas to Bizet and, in our more modern consciousness, of television accounts of recent executions by Central American death squads. But these are not the only echos at the opera's end. Elvis Escamillo is not able to claim Carmen as his prize. Instead, his toreador theme, interrupted by gunshots, brings back reverberations of the earlier shooting incident that led to the line, "A little bit lower and that would have been the end of the opera!"

The sensational aspects of Pintilie's production are alluring because they seem to come from beyond the pale, when in fact, they follow a chartable course through opera history. The contribution of Opera Comique to *Carmen* and to the evolution of ironic comedy consists of simple elements that were overlooked by a few critics, as well as by some of the audience members. The refashioning of Escamillo follows naturally when one considers the above conditions and the opera's need for relevance to a North American regional audience. It is not necessary to maintain the text's purity to continue the allure of the opera. When it comes to presenting engaging opera, effective cultural translation is more important than historical accuracy. Indeed, exaggerated effects of dilution and expansion will keep Bizet's flexible opera in the repertoire as regional operas in North America continue to draw on old sources and play to new audiences. As modern audiences become increasingly distanced by time and geography from the original context of Bizet's creation, the need for a familiar bridge between audience and production arises. In opera capitals such as New York, the dominance of the grand opera form will always be felt. Regional audiences, however, without a prevailing grand opera tradition, will embrace with increasing frequency forms drawn from a large collection of cultural currencies. Elvis will, in time, be replaced by a more contemporary and equally startling persona. The resulting controversy will once again affect the future direction of opera.

Notes

1. Stephen Godfrey, Toronto *Globe and Mail*, 6 May 1986, section D5.
2. Stephen Godfrey, Toronto *Globe and Mail*, 14 May 1986.
3. Winton Dean, *Bizet* (London: Dent and Sons, 1948), p. 204.
4. Godfrey, 14 May 1986.
5. Godfrey, 6 May 1986.
6. William Littler, Toronto *Star*, 10 May 1986, section F3.
7. Mina Curtiss, *Bizet and His World* (New York: Knopf, 1958), p. 351.
8. Ibid., p. 338.
9. Dean, *Bizet*, p. 205.
10. Martin Cooper, *Opera Comique* (New York: Chanticleer Press, 1949), p. 66.
11. Northrop Frye, *Anatomy of Criticism* (Princeton: Princeton University Press, 1973), p. 38.
12. Ibid., p. 47.
13. Ibid.
14. Ibid., p. 48.
15. Ibid., p. 175.
16. Vancouver Opera news release, 3 April 1986.
17. Canadian Broadcasting Corporation *CBC Television* press release, "New Look Carmen," 17 May 1986.
18. Littler, 10 May 1986.
19. *CBC Television*, 17 May 1986.

Toward a Popular Opera

SHEILA SABREY-SAPERSTEIN

The brochure of the Lyric Opera of Chicago's 1990 season reads: "Of course you understand opera . . . because at Lyric performances, the text is translated above the stage in easy-to-read Projected English Titles."[1] The only Lyric production not using titles that year was Gluck's *Alceste* because of the insistence of its leading lady, and while favorable to the Robert Wilson/Jessye Norman production, the *Chicago Tribune* reviewer, John von Rhein, felt that clarity was lacking partially due to the absence of titles.

The information found in the Lyric flyer can be found in most opera company flyers today. Titles are a *fait accompli* in major as well as minor opera houses across the country and, it should be noted, they are often used for operas sung in English. Titles are presented as the solution to the problem of audience understanding and, therefore, audience development. Opera producers and directors point out that titles involve the audience to a greater degree because the story is clear and the action makes sense. Greater communication between the stage and the audience reinforces the position that opera is drama.

Opposition lingers, however, most notably at the Met where James Levine's famous "Over my dead body" remark still reverberates. The Met's adamant stand against the use of titles reinforces its position as America's truly elitist European opera house.

The fact remains that though the purist position has its points, understanding opera is a bigger point and there has been a general increase in audience attendance at non-English performances due directly to the presence of titles in the opera house. The unanimous and immediate acceptance of titles by the opera-going public can be taken as evidence that the content of an opera is important to them. The audience has made it clear: it wants to understand the plot in addition to enjoying the music and the spectacle.

Actually the popular "battle" between the "purists" and the "popular opera" *aficionados* originated with the argument fondly

debated in nineteenth-century music circles: which is more important in the operatic form, the words or the music? This is the logi-
cal extension of the eternal and unanswerable chicken or egg
question: which comes first in the creation of an opera? Does the
composer compose the music and then give it to the librettist or
vice versa? Richard Strauss' last opera, *Capriccio* (1942), dramatized this subject as the poet and the musician argue in act I, scene 1:

> *Olivier*: "Prima la parole—dopo la musica!"
> *Flamand*: "Prima la musica—dopo le parole!"

Historically, the pendulum has swung from one side to the
other. In earlier times the vocal and orchestral aspects of opera
appealed more to the audience. The earliest composers of opera,
the *camerata*, had emphasized recitative in their classical revivals
but when composers of stature left writing cantatas to compose
operas, the literary aspects became secondary to the music. In Italy
operas were performed in large theaters and the words became
secondary to music and spectacle. The Italian art of virtuoso singing, which emphasized vocal pyrotechnics over text, simply added
fuel to the fire.

Another school of thought argued that the opera libretto in itself
was essentially a weak form. Strong music can dominate a libretto,
can elevate it, and can survive without words, but very few librettos survive without the music; those which come practically intact
from the stage are the exception. In the United States radio broadcasts from the Metropolitan Opera of New York, beginning in
1931, introduced opera to a mass audience, and contributed to the
stature of the libretto as a second class citizen. Listeners were so
accustomed to the Metropolitan broadcasts and recordings in the
original languages, which they tuned out, that an English translation came as a rude shock.

In spite of all this, the defenders of the downtrodden libretto are
legion. George Bernard Shaw, a champion of the written word,
quotes Christoph Gluck's message on librettos to his colleagues:

> "Gentlemen, let us compose our operas more rationally. An opera is
> not a stage concert, as most of you seem to think. Let us give up our
> habit of sacrificing our common sense to the vanity of our singers, and
> let us compose and orchestrate our airs, our duets, our recitatives, and
> our sinfonias in such a way that they shall always be appropriate to the
> dramatic situation given to us by the librettist." And having given this
> excellent advice, he proceeded to show how it could be followed.[2]

Herbert Graf, an Opera-in-English champion, wrote in *Opera for the People* that, in essence, there would be no opera without the libretto:

> The basic requirement for any opera is the *book*—the libretto. Its first task is to make the musical treatment possible, and there is, therefore, a fundamental difference between a legitimate drama and an operatic book. In a libretto the main purpose is to indicate, not the dramatic action itself, but its underlying feeling.[3]

Graf made the libretto the basis on which the artistic unity is established.

In *Opera As Drama* Joseph Kerman defines opera as a separate art form including both musical and poetic values:

> The postulate is that opera is an art form with its own integrity and its own particular limiting and liberating conventions. The critical procedure involves a sharpening of musical awareness and an expansion of our range of imaginative response to drama.[4]

Perhaps it is this twentieth-century viewpoint from which opera can be studied to its greatest advantage—i.e., a return to the original premise of the Italian Camerata's drama through the means of music, emphasizing neither the music nor the libretto at the expense of the other.

My doctoral dissertation, "Opera-in-English: The Popularization of Foreign Opera in America" was written during the introduction and emergence of titles in the opera house. Titles, together with televised opera and performances of regional Opera-in-English companies, were examples of how opera can become a more popular art form in the United States. The thesis was that opera will never become popular in the United States until it is understood on the spot and without a great deal of background information.

One of the first attempts to attract the non-elitist audience came in an increased use of English translations. In 1980 Maria Rich of the Central Opera Service summarized this phenomenon in a letter to the present writer:

> Opera-in-English . . . seems to come up on many occasions and leads to inexhaustible and always inconclusive discussions. Regional companies perform opera almost exclusively in English, feeling they can better attract new audiences by presenting works in the vernacular. Those presenting primarily or exclusively American singers also favor

English texts. However, even in these two cases, there are a number of exceptions.[5]

Ms. Rich went on to cite five major companies that sometimes offered their season in two series; one in the original language, the second in English with an alternate cast in the major roles: Houston Grand Opera, Michigan Opera Theater, Greater Miami Opera, Seattle Opera, and the New York City Opera. Since that report these companies have come to rely more on titles and the number of Opera-in-English offerings has declined.

Opera-in-English as sung in viable translations seems in no danger of dying as a result of the titles' explosion. Prior to the advent of titles, two of the four international American companies had continuous Opera-in-English programs: the New York City Opera and the San Francisco Opera. City Opera, as America's national opera company, continues its tradition of Opera-in-English performances in its main season, and today titles are often used for further clarity. San Francisco uses captions for its main season productions, and its Opera Center satellite programs are performed in English.

Two regional companies, Seattle and Houston, have received international recognition for productions in English. Houston premiered *Nixon in China*, composed by John Adams and staged by Peter Sellars, and Seattle's *Ring* was produced for years in concomitant English and German versions. Today, Seattle titles all its productions, and its touring program is performed in English. Houston's new Wortham Center has two theaters: a larger space for titled original language productions and the more intimate theater for performances in English.

Then there are the smaller Opera-in-English companies which have produced opera in the vernacular so loyally for so long. These are the companies that begin the popularization of opera at the grass roots level, in the community, attracting a popular audience and providing performance opportunities for the American-trained singer-actor. Many of these companies have the same philosophy as the companies of old Europe: opera in the vernacular is more accessible and approachable to a greater number of people; therefore, if you want opera to become a popular art form, and you want to build an audience, do it in the native language of the country where it is being performed.

One of the most successful Opera-in-English companies is the Chicago Opera Theater. Alan Stone explained to me in an interview how and why he created his company:

When I started, Lyric was the big international company that did everything in its original language and I had no dream or ambition or ideal to emulate the Lyric. I wanted to do something else so we were more like a folk's opera. We wanted to build an audience and I remembered my European experiences when everything was in the vernacular and I thought, let's do Opera-in-English. This is our country and our language and the audience should feel part of the experience. Opera-in-English has helped in the growth of opera. It has helped economically by bringing in a broader audience.[6]

Stone pointed out that many Opera-in-English companies like his are second to an international company in a large city. There can be a complementary relationship as each can make its own artistic statement, but he added:

When there is no other company, little companies do a mixture because there are still certain people who like to hear opera in a language that they don't understand; it has an allure for them. It's exotic, has some mysticism for them. They don't want to understand it, they want to make up their own story to a certain degree. They don't want to be too confused. They want to listen to the singing and not have to figure out the words; it's too much. Many of these people don't want anything to do with Opera-in-English, but then again, opera in the original language wouldn't have gotten far in places like Fargo, North Dakota.[7]

Second companies exist in Chicago, Cleveland, Dallas, Milwaukee, Toronto, Philadelphia, and Boston. In most instances, the Opera-in-English company and the international company have quite different artistic missions; through the complementary efforts of each, the community is treated to a full spectrum of the riches that opera and musical theater have to offer, from the traditional to the new, from opera in the grand style to smaller-scale, intimate stagings.

Opera-in-English companies believe that titles are a great help and a wonderful educational tool. Titles have helped popularize opera in the bigger international houses when there really was no other way to do it, but they are no substitutes for the immediacy and total understanding of an Opera-in-English performance. The contemporary audience does equate the words with the music, for it grew up with the familiar story lines of the American musical theater as well as televised and filmed operas. Opera-in-English provides the best introduction to opera for a new audience; and these Opera-in-English companies are doing exactly that across the country.

All of my research and interviews point to one fact: foreign opera today is understandable throughout the country, whether it be through titles or translations. The future of opera in America lies in broadening this understanding through education. What is still needed is the integration of the art form into community life. Companies should expand their educational programs for adults as well as children in order to establish a deeper appreciation of and an identity with the art form. Perhaps the day will come when children are sent off to the Saturday opera matinee rather than to the movies. The conclusion of Opera America's *Profile: 1986* expresses this idea best:

> The essence of the operatic experience is communion: a live performance unites an audience through the sharing of heightened emotional experiences. With the belief that art exists for the common good, opera companies today realize that they reach their greatest communicative power when they are fully accessible to all parts of our society. They also recognize that they must function not in isolation from community life, but integrated into the cultural, social, economic and intellectual fabric of the cities.
>
> An opera company enriches a community far beyond the impact of the performances it presents on the stage. The presence of an opera company means performance opportunities for singers, orchestral musicians, dancers, pianists, and other artists, both on the main stage and in dozens of outreach performances. It means hope and professional guidance for outstanding young singers who are emerging from small towns throughout the country, many of whom will advance to become our nation's foremost artists. It means access to the educational experiences that are uniquely provided by opera, an art form which unites all other arts and provides a pathway to exploration of the great humanistic and artistic traditions. Given the youthful age of most of our institutions, the vast potential for opera companies to contribute to the human community is only beginning to be tapped.
>
> As these institutions bring vitality to local communities, collectively they revitalize our national cultural life. Ardis Krainik's testimony encapsulated perfectly the position of the opera company in our society today: "From sea to shining sea, we of the arts *are* pursuing and achieving that excellence to which we aspire. We are an indispensable ingredient of that quality of life which Americans are so proud of. We inform, we entertain, we inspire, we exalt! We are glamorous and glorious!"[8]

Outstanding drama combined with sublime music should not be the privilege of a few. Opera audiences in America of the 1800s did not necessarily understand the language of their opera, but they kept returning because it was expected in their social circles. Current audiences may still be relatively indifferent to the language because social elitism continues to exist, and because there are other elements in a major operatic production which do communicate and gratify, i.e., the visual elements of elaborate scenery and costumes. America's potentially broader audience does not very often sit in the Metropolitan or the Lyric. Radio and television have done much to reach this "outer" audience, but the place of opera in American culture is still an uncomfortable one. This leads to three recommended areas: 1. Opera must be understood (in the vernacular for smaller regional houses; in titles for larger houses). 2. Opera must entertain and therefore be relevant and relatable. For example: Wilson's *Alceste*, Sellars's *Nixon in China*, Yuri Ljubimov's *Lulu*. 3. Opera must be done well. The visual and aural should unite in the goal of opera achieving its rightful place as the ultimate union of drama and music. This includes the necessity of top notch training for singers, composers, musicians, directors, and designers.

The opera elitist is in the minority today and opera is more popular in America than ever before. Opera-in-English *is* the popularization of foreign opera in America, whether with titles or effective English translations.

Notes

1. *Lyric Opera of Chicago* (1990 season brochure/flyer), 1.
2. Ulrich Weisstein, *The Essence of Opera* (New York: W.W. Norton and Co., Inc., 1964), 259.
3. Herbert Graf, *Opera for the People* (Minneapolis: University of Minnesota Press, 1951), 21.
4. Joseph Kerman, *Opera As Drama* (New York: Alfred A. Knopf, 1956), 6–7.
5. Maria Rich, letter to the writer, 22 April 1980.
6. Alan Stone, personal interview, 11 August 1987.
7. Alan Stone, personal interview, 11 August 1987.
8. *Profile: 1986* (Opera America booklet, 1986), 1.

Part Eight
American Musical Theater

More Singing! Less Talking!: The Operatic American Musical

MONICA T. ALBALA

American musical theater has developed in response to the demands of the American public to create a entertaining hybrid form of opera. Examination of the American musical reveals that it is an adaptation of American opera as a story told mainly in song, accompanied by connecting dialogue—and cyclic in its emulation of operetta. These roots are most evident in recent musicals of the past decade which do not rely on dialogue as a bridge between songs in order to compete and survive on the Broadway stage with imported musicals which emulate opera. The response of the American musical, in jeopardy, is to become more innovative in its evolution as a form of opera.

Julian Mates states that "critical discussions about whether *Porgy and Bess, The Most Happy Fella, Lost in the Stars, Amahl and the Night Visitors, Song of Norway*, and *Sweeney Todd* are really operas or musicals are constantly surfacing, and the very critical confusion is an indication of the closeness of American opera to the American musical."[1] This is also an indication of the embracing of the operatic musical by American audiences and critics as part of the picture of opera in the "Golden West." The more like opera musical theater is, the more opera is a part of American culture. A recurring theme is the adaptation of elements of operetta and opera in creating the phenomenon of the American musical which would not have occurred without these influences.

The musical and musical comedy are chiefly derived from operetta or Light Opera. David Ewen defines operetta as "a romantic play containing songs, musical numbers, and dances" and that it "differs from a musical comedy in that the musical score is of a more ambitious character."[2] Gerald Bordman observes that "At heart, operetta trafficked in a roseate, earnest romanticism, frequently transporting both its characters and its audiences to far-off, exotic lands and far-off, fondly remembered times." He notes that "by contrast, musical comedy professed to take a jaundiced, cynical look at everday and, more frequently than not, very contemporary foibles."[3] These are the distinctions between operetta and musical comedy which tend to blur as one form meshes with the other. Often the two seem identical in structure. The loftiness of theme in operetta can relate more closely to grand opera, apparent even in "concept musicals" which apply morals of good and evil, such as Stephen Sondheim's *Sweeney Todd* and *Into The Woods*.

Andrew H. Drummond declares that "the history of opera in America is a history of borrowings, mainly from European sources, but with an increasing awareness of the native material that can be treated."[4] American operetta is largely derivative of English comic opera in the tradition of Gilbert and Sullivan as well as English ballad opera which employed common folk music and farce themes. American opera has been influenced by French, Italian, German, and Viennese opera, as well as English opera.

The greater appeal of some opera forms to the general public in America became part of the opera culture and also influenced future musical theatre. Richard Kislan states: "The popular French comic opera known as the *opéra bouffe* arrived in the United States first, when soon after the Civil War Jacques Offenbach's *La Grande Duchesse de Gerolstein* opened in New York to a favorable reception. Unlike the native American forms, the comic opera offered (1) a story with music that was more popular in tone than the music of serious opera, (2) spoken dialogue, (3) light subject matter, (4) comic interludes, and (5) a happy ending."[5] The popularity of French comic opera set the climate for Gilbert and Sullivan's more literal and witty works to be presented, altering the direction of American musical theater. Gerald Bordman declares that their operetta "*H.M.S. Pinafore*, along with two light opera companies it helped establish, determined the course and shape of the popular lyric stage in England and America for the final quarter of the nineteenth century. . . . Without *Pinafore*, conceivably, there might have been no Victor Herbert, no George M. Cohan, no Jerome Kern, no George Gershwin, no Richard Rodgers."[6] The number of composers who have ventured into musicals and been influenced by Gilbert and Sullivan is endless.

Gerald Mast notes that "musicals exist in a historical and cultural paradigm that includes other familar forms: opera, operetta, vaudeville, variety, burlesque, music hall, minstrel show, medicine show, the circus. . . . The musical vaguely seems an aesthetic middle ground among them—born from an unlikely marriage of nineteenth-century opera and variety entertainments."[7] That American musicals provide a middle ground in opera tradition is a key to its popularity among all classes of people. Although musicals exist somewhere between operetta and opera, the art form is not static, it is flexible and creative at the designs of its composers and its audiences. Musicals in American society also solidify the place of opera's tradition in American music.

The place of American musicals in American opera is also assured by the growing trend among many opera companies in adding musicals and musical comedies to their repertoires. Stanley Green states: "Not only does this help break down artificial artistic barriers, it also creates new audiences for such notable examples as the Kern-Hammerstein *Show Boat*, the Gershwin-Heywood *Porgy and Bess*, the Rodgers-Hammerstein *Carousel* and *South Pacific*, the Lerner and Loewe *Brigadoon*, the Weill-Hughes-Rice *Street Scene*, the Weill-Anderson *Lost in the Stars*, the Bernstein-Sondheim-Laurents *West Side Story*, the Bernstein-Wilbur *Candide*, the Sondheim-Wheeler *Sweeney Todd*, and—almost inevitably—the Sondheim-Lapine *Sunday in the Park With George*."[8] In turn, Gilbert and Sullivan's operetta, *The Pirates of Penzance*, played on the Broadway stage in 1981, introducing audiences of musical comedy to its roots.

Since 1979 several prominent musicals have experimented with formats, styles, and themes bordering on opera. This is a testament to the close relationship musicals share with opera in the past, present, and future. The status of the American musical has been in jeopardy due to the large preponderance of English musicals which are overshadowing American musicals on Broadway. The future of American musical theater may lie in returning to opera tradition. According to Richard Traubner, Andrew Lloyd Webber's *Evita* "was a rock opera, an oratorio-like form that eliminated dialogue entirely (and which was in some cases born in the recording studio)."[9] Gerald Mast observes that "while American musicals have refused to keep in their place throughout this century, bumping against opera on the one side and burlesque on the other, the new rock operas settle the conflict by adopting European opera forms while preserving modern pop-rock sounds. *Les Miserables*, part English and part French in its creation, is even through-sung."[10] The success of these musicals has provided a climate of experimentation as well as a testing ground for the survival of the American musical as a form of opera and art form. Innovation is the order of the decade since 1979. Dialogue is being diminished in the interest of the songs which advance the action of the story. It is fairly easy to follow the storyline as well as the songs on most recordings of musicals. Several American musicals have followed this model since Stephen Sondheim's *Sweeney Todd* (1979).

As Glenn Litton states, "Sondheim had written a very demanding score, one that frequently called for solo and ensemble voices of operatic dimensions."[11] Allan Wallach comments that Sondheim "certainly uses many of the techniques of opera—leitmotifs, for example, and duets that build stunningly into trios and quartets—but he has retained the humor and accessibility we associate with the musical stage."[12] The tale of Sweeney Todd, the deranged avenging barber, is told almost completely in song. The opening song, "The Ballad of Sweeney Todd" is remininscent of Bertolt Brecht. Alan Jay Lerner says of the work: "Musically, it mixed opera and song in a fashion reminiscent of Kurt Weill's *Street Scene*, but without those moments when melody took flight."[13]

Gerald Mast cites Sondheim, Harold Prince, the director, and Hugh Wheeler, author of the book, as taking "their style from a tradition of musical and literary depiction of London low life—from Defoe's *Moll Flanders* and Gay's *The Beggar's Opera* through Dickens, Mr. Hyde, and Jack the Ripper to Brecht's *Threepenny Opera*."[14] *Sweeney Todd* presents a macabre and ironic tragedy worthy of opera to match sardonic songs like "My Friends," Todd's lovesong to his barber knives and "A Little Priest," a humorous and ironic discussion of meat pies made from Todd's victims. *Sweeney Todd* was performed in 1984 by the New York City Opera. As an ensemble work, it contains twenty-five songs with pointed connecting dialogue. As an operatic musical it provides high drama, social commentary, and memorable songs. It also marks a trend in modern musicals in being closely aligned with opera roots.

Barnum (1980), a musical biography of P. T. Barnum, the circus impresario, with music by Cy Coleman and lyrics by Michael Stewart, offered "a total circus concept with the entire cast constantly in motion tumbling, clowning, marching, twirling, and flying through the air," according to Stanley Green.[15] The ballad, "The Colors of My Life" presents an intuitive solo by Barnum. The musical focuses on the career of Barnum the showman and the conflict with his wife for a more ordinary life. Other songs like "Come Follow the Band" and "Join the Circus" reflect the nineteenth-century operetta theme.

A Day in Hollywood / A Night in the Ukraine (1980), billed as "A Musical Double Feature," presented a one-act musical revue on 1930s movies and a mock Marx Brothers one-act comic operetta taken from the 1888 Chekhov play *The Bear*. Songs like "Samovar The Lawyer" about and sung by the Groucho Marx–like character and "Natasha" sung by "Samovar" about the virtures of the Margaret Dumont–like rich widow are reminiscent of Gilbert and Sullivan's *The Mikado*. Lazarus and Vosburgh wrote the farce.

Nine (1982), based on Frederico Fellini's 1963 acclaimed semiautobiographical film *8½*, about the midlife crisis of a Italian film director who tries to find direction for his next film and sort out the various women in his life, used an operatic score by composer and lyricist Maury Yeston. Prominent songs include the "Overture dell Donne," "My Husband Makes Movies," "Only With You," "Nine," "Be Italian," "Simple," and "Be On Your Own." A full orchestra provided accompaniment worthy of an operetta.

La Cage Aux Folles (1983), an old-fashioned musical farce with an operetta score by Jerry Herman, was based on the 1976 French film and play of the same name by Jean Poiret about a homosexual couple, Georges, the owner of a St. Tropez drag club, and Albin, his flamboyant star ("Zaza"). They have to impress their son's future in-law, the local morals politician, and the machinations that ensue result in their pretending to be "straight." The Herman songs have a continental and operetta flavor of romance and humor. Some of the songs with opera overtones are the declarative "I Am What I Am," "With You On My Arm," "Song On The Sand," "Look Over There," and "The Best of Times."

Sunday In The Park With George (1984), Stephen Sondheim and James Lapine's modernist musical, loosely based on the life of the impressionist artist Georges Seurat and the making of his famous painting *A Sunday Afternoon on the Island of La Grande Jatte*, is innovative and traditional in providing dramatic songs which advance the characterization of the actors in the manner of narrative opera. It is not a musical comedy or typical operetta. Some of the operatic songs are "Sunday in The Park With George," "Color And Light," "The Day Off," "We Do Not Belong Together," and "Sunday." There is also a great deal of choral and scattered solo singing among the company, as found in opera. The score features conflict between characters in the songs in dialogue fashion, like opera. Gerald Mast describes Sondheim's work as "a Wagnerian *Gesamtkunstwerk*, a total theatrical universe of sound, color, light, drama, performance, music, and myth."[16]

Big River (1985), Roger Miller's musical based on Mark Twain's book *Huckleberry Finn*, is worthy of mention since it employs indigenous American country and jazz music in a score of seventeen songs to tell its story and characterize the cast. There are declarative songs such as "I, Huckleberry, Me," "Worlds Apart," and "Leavin's Not The Only Way To Go," which show conflict and highlight individual characters as in opera.

The Mystery Of Edwin Drood (1985), Rupert Holmes's "Solve-It-Yourself Broadway Musical," a play within a play, English Music Hall version of Charles Dickens's unfinished novel whose conclusion is voted on by the audience, is an operetta. This "Musicale with dramatic interludes," as it is referred to by the character Mr. William Cartright, has notably operatic songs. "Moonfall," "The Wages of Sin," "Perfect Strangers," "No Good Can Come From Bad," and "The Garden Path To Hell" are some notable songs. There is little incidental dialogue.

Into the Woods (1987), Stephen Sondheim and James Lapine's musical with operatic overtones and drama, combines famous fairy tale characters including Cinderella, Rapunzel, Red Riding Hood, Jack of "Jack and the Beanstalk," and two princes in a quest involving morality and responsibility. Prominent songs are "Into the Woods," "I Guess This Is Goodbye," "Agony," "It Takes Two," "Lament," "Moments in the Woods," and "No One Is Alone."

Romance Romance (1988) is Barry Harman and Keith Herrmann's double bill of two one-act musicals. The first is *The Little Comedy*, a late 1890s operetta based on Viennese author Arthur Schitzler's story of the same time period; the second, *Summer Share*, is a contemporary twentieth century musical comedy adaptation based on French playwright Jules Renard's 1899 play, *Household Bread*, which explores starting a romance and sustaining it after marriage. *The Little Comedy* featured several operetta-inspired songs including the title song, "It's Not Too Late," "Oh, What a Performance!," "Women of Vienna," and "A Rustic Country Inn."

Grand Hotel (1989), Tommy Tune's musical based on Vicky Baum's big 1930 novel (and the source of the Greta Garbo movie), featured songs by Robert Wright, George Forrest, and Maury Yeston, understated since the dancing was emphasized. There is one ballad, "Bonjour Amour," by Yeston, cited by Frank Rich of *The New York Times* that "may give Andrew Lloyd Webber his first opportunity to accuse another songwriter of being derivative."[17]

City of Angels (1989), Larry Gelbart's musical comedy with songs by Cy Coleman and David Zippel is a 1940s jazz musical within a movie told almost completely in songlike operetta. There the resemblance to opera ends with the jazz songs highlighting and developing the characters.

Musicals are definitely featuring more singing and less talking as scores contain over a dozen songs; some have over twenty. Cast albums are much easier to follow then ever and dialogue is taking second place to the songs. The American musical is surviving on the merits of the music.

Notes

1. Julian Mates, *American Musical Stage: Two Hundred Years of Musical Theatre (Contribution in Drama and Theatre Studies, Number 18)* (Westport, Conn.: Greenwood Press, 1985), p. 65.

2. David Ewen, *Encyclopedia of the Opera: New Enlarged Edition* (New York: Hill and Wang, 1963), p. 368–369.

3. Gerald Bordman, *American Musical Comedy: From Adonis to Dreamgirls* (New York: Oxford University Press, 1982), P. 4.

4. Andrew H. Drummond, *American Opera Librettos* (Metuchen, N.J.: Scarecrow Press, 1973), p. 1.

5. Richard Kislan, *The Musical: A Look at the American Musical Theater* (Englewood Cliffs, N.J.: Prentice-Hall, 1980), p. 94.

6. Gerald Bordman, *American Operetta: From H.M.S. Pinafore To Sweeney Todd* (New York: Oxford University Press, 1981) p. 16.

7. Gerald Mast, *Can't Help Singin': The American Musical On Stage and Screen* (Woodstock, N.Y.: The Overlook Press, 1987) p.4.

8. Stanley Green, *Broadway Musicals: Show By Show, Second Edition.* (Milwaukee, Wisc.: Hal Leonard Books, 1987), Foreward, p. xix.

9. Richard Traubner, *Operetta : A Theatrical History* (Garden City, N.Y.: Doubleday & Company, 1983), p.421.

10. Mast, *Can't Help Singin'*, p. 349.

11. Cecil Smith and Glenn Litton, *Musical Comedy In America* (New York: Theatre Arts Books, 1981), p. 338.

12. Allan Wallach, "Songs That Can't Hide Behind Scenery," *Newsday*, 15 July 1979, Part II, p. 3.

13. Alan Jay Lerner, *The Musical Theatre: A Celebration* (New York: McGraw-Hill Book Company, 1986), p. 230.

14. Mast, *Can't Help Singin'*, p. 350.

15. Green, *Broadway Musicals*, p. 256.

16. Mast, *Can't Help Singin'*, p. 333.

17. Frank Rich, "Tune's Swirling Vision of a 'Grand Hotel'," *The New York Times*, 13 November 1989, sec. C, p. 13.

Operatic Conventions and the American Musical

JOSEPH P. SWAIN

Someone looking at the history of the American musical theater might note some curious parallels with the history of European opera. The mature Broadway tradition found its founding father in Jerome Kern, had its boy genius who died young in George Gershwin, its long-lived and expert practitioner of inherited forms in Richard Rodgers, and its reformer in Stephen Sondheim. But the dependence of the Broadway musical tradition on the techniques and prevailing style of nineteenth-century European opera remains clear. Like any artistic tradition Broadway has known a set of conventions, time-honored ways of constructing and placing their musical numbers in a show, and the similarity of these conventions to those of European opera is indeed striking. Simplified though they may be, standard operatic techniques show up throughout the best musical plays of the American theater.

Perhaps the most fundamental of all operatic conventions in the West is the distinction between the textures of recitative and aria. Indeed, one can imagine the history of opera as nothing more than a record of the changing relationship between these two ways of writing dramatic music. Of course, during most of the period of the mature American musical play, from 1927 onward, the terms "aria" and "recitative" only aroused suspicion. Instead one spoke of the "verse" and "refrain" of a song. The verse begins the musical number, and while it cannot be said that it would easily be mistaken for operatic recitative, the verse often presents a musical passage marked by aperiodic phrasing, ambiguous harmonic direction, and a weakened sense of meter that are hardly associated with songs. All these produce the introductory texture that mimics the function, if not always the sound, of recitative, the function of preparing the musical and emotional ground for the stability of the refrain to follow, and also the transition from spoken dialogue to song. The refrain, on the other hand, has an unmistakable meter and is often composed in four phrases of the form A A B A, a kind of miniature da capo. Like an aria, the refrain expresses a rather static sentiment for the character who sings it in well-articulated phrases and directed harmonic progressions.

The contrast in sound and function usually arises from a number of musical elements. Although Frank Loesser's "My Time of Day," no. 17 from *Guys and Dolls*, would never be taken for a *secco* recitative, its sense of meter is so obscured as to make it not far removed from the nineteenth-century *scena*. Changes of time signature and irregular subdivisions of the beat work together to weaken the sense of downbeat while chromaticism in both the main melody and underlying harmony obscures the sense of key as well, so that it is difficult for the ear to assign any important rhythmic status to a tonic note. The function of this unusual number is clarified when, at the end, it leads directly into the following number, "I've Never Been in Love Before." Here are the stable harmony and clear meter typical of a Broadway song. "My Time of Day" acts just like an *accompagnato* that prepares its following aria.

Set pieces for more than one character singing simultaneously also seem to have a European ancestry. Operatic ensembles more involved than a duet are rare in the American theater during the thirties and forties but from the fifties onward their numbers steadily increase to the point where, in Sondheim's work particularly, they can outnumber the solo pieces. One ensemble that resembles very closely its European ancestors is the superb quintet from *West Side Story*. The piece is a summary of the emotional states and dramatic roles of the five principal players at a crucial point in the play, and so its dramatic function corresponds exactly with what is expected of an ensemble of any opera. But more remarkable still is the similarity of its construction: its classical, almost Mozartean design allows each character a solo to explain himself in the first half of the composition, and only then, after all sentiments have been clearly expressed, does the piece give way to contrapuntal invention to achieve its purely musical climax.

Finales, of course, hold sway throughout the Broadway tradition, and if they often fail to measure up to their forbears in musical sophistication and dramatic content, their essential character and function of bringing down the curtain remains unchanged. Broadway overtures, too, are simplified versions of their European counterparts of the nineteenth century: the practice of writing into the opera overture one or more of the most important themes of the opera is matched on Broadway by the medley overture, a loosely constructed sequence of the best song tunes. Significantly, some of the more serious works of the tradition, such as *Carousel* and *The Most Happy Fella*, dispensed with this practice in favor of a more abstract composition, one musically related to the play that followed. Like a famous opera reformer from Germany, these composers refused the traditional term of "overture" and preferred the term "prologue."

The most signal link of the Broadway tradition with European romantic opera is its dependence on the reprise for incisive dramatic effect. The reprise has been cynically described as the repetition of a sure-fire song after intermission as an easy way to win applause and keep the audience involved, and in the case of many second-rate shows such a characterization is not far wrong. In the work of those composers more sensitive to dramatic meaning, however, the reprise becomes Broadway's answer to the leitmotif, and just as many of Wagner's and Verdi's greatest dramatic statements depend upon a carefully developed leitmotif scheme, so do Broadway's more limited achievements. And these reprises make their effects in precisely the same way: not through changes in the music or lyrics, although such changes may contribute, but through changes in the dramatic situation against which the familiar song is sung. The reprise juxtaposes for the audience both the original context and the new, and thereby gives rise to a host of possible ironies and dramatic meanings. When Billy Bigelow sings "If I Loved You" in the second act of *Carousel*, when Maria helps Tony through "Somewhere" at the end of *West Side Story*, the musical and lyrical alterations are quite minor. The power of these moments derives from the accumulated meanings of these pieces. So the stamp of European opera can be seen in a number of tried and true Broadway conventions: verse and refrain, overture, finale, reprise, and the occasional ensemble. How might this relationship be explained?

Direct influence would be the first idea that comes to mind. Broadway composers studied the European repertoire and simply applied their lessons. "Study" in any formal sense is probably too strong a term, for most had little training in serious music, but there is no doubt that many of these composers knew at least the standards of that repertoire. There were also the examples of Gilbert and Sullivan and the more serious operettas of Victor Herbert and Sigmund Romberg to offer more direct experiences of operatic conventions. Yet, the answer of direct influence leaves something to be desired. For one thing it fails to account for an important distinction in the American musical, that it is more often a spoken play with musical numbers, closer perhaps to German *Singspiele*, than a continuous music drama. Why should a recitative-like texture be necessary at all? And for another thing, why should composers of the American theater deliberately try to imitate their illustrious European forbears when for many years the idea of presenting "opera" to the ticket buying public was anathema to Broadway producers? After everyone had seen how the achievements of a *Porgy and Bess* or *The Most Happy Fella* could be smothered in critical controversies over whether the works were musicals or operas, why should composers allow themselves the risk of seeming too "operatic"?

Such questions can hardly dismiss direct influence of European opera out of hand, but explaining the striking similarities in musical procedure and form will require appealing to a more fundamental need of Broadway composers. The best ones were interested in the same artistic goal as opera composers: writing music drama. Are the requirements of music drama such that, given a common culture and musical language, certain solutions are likely to arise and prove themselves over time? Is there an aesthetic explanation?

The refrain of a Broadway song and an aria of an opera both take advantage of western music's primary dramatic power: to sustain and imitate on a deep level a character's emotional state. The basic characteristics that the aria shares with the song are most apt for this purpose: the steady meter and clearly formed structure seem to correspond with a consistent emotion. Does it not make sense that any dramatic tradition that uses music in a dramatic way would have such a convention? Would this convention not require some device that prepared such a heightened expression? In lyric opera the preparation is largely one of information, and the recitative gives it over in the most economical way while still remaining music. In the musical theater, however, there needs to be a transition, some easing of the intrusion of the song into the world of normal speech, and so the verse, the beginning of the song that is not very songful, takes on some of the character of recitative even as it is turned to a different purpose.

The conventions of ensemble, finale, and overture would probably be the strongest cases for the direct influence of European opera, and yet one is still prompted to ask if there isn't something inherently useful about an instrumental beginning, if matching the musical climax to the end of an act isn't somehow inevitable. And if an ensemble is called for by the dramatic situation, surely there is no clearer way to compose it than to let each character have a moment for himself. The only puzzling aspect of the ensemble question is why more European ones are not written as lucidly as the quintet from *West Side Story*.

As for the reprise, it could be the strongest case for an essential aesthetic of music drama. The leitmotif seems like a very specific influence of Wagner because he made up a word for it and theorized about it, and of course his works make the most extensive use of it, but the idea of bringing back music of significance at a point where it can illuminate the drama in a way no new music could goes back to Monteverdi's *Orfeo* and is found to be important in a good many operas after that. There can be little doubt about its basic dramatic value.

Perhaps the real influences of Europe on the American theater are not any particular way of doing things, but more fundamental gifts of the nineteenth-century musical language, which has been the bread and butter of Broadway until the 1970s, and a more general notion of music drama itself. Given those two things, it is understandable that certain techniques, certain solutions to common problems in the creation and staging of a musical drama would prove themselves nearly indispensable. They grow naturally out of the demands of music drama, and are dispensed with as a last resort when they can for some reason not meet those demands in a particular situation. Richard Rodgers and Oscar Hammerstein II tried hard to begin *Oklahoma!* with a chorus, a convention of both musical plays of that time and a great many Italian operas, and reluctantly refused it only when they came to believe that it could not be reconciled to the dramatic situation at hand. The art of music drama is the rule for understanding both the origin of conventions and why they may be abandoned.

This means that the common labels of "opera," "operetta," "musical," and so forth distinguish not so much the substance of what is going on as the sophistication with which it is carried out. All refer to music drama, but the composer of opera will aim to project his drama with the most expansive structures in the most complex musical idioms, while the theater composer works with materials that are inherently simpler. Sophistication promises greater power of expression but also greater expectations from audiences, which perhaps explains how some of the best American musicals have now won the respect of many opera singers and producers at the expense of some of the less felicitous creations of the Old World.

Sources

Bordman, Gerald. *American Musical Theatre*. New York: Oxford University Press, 1977.

Engel, Lehman. *The American Musical Theatre: A Consideration*. New York: Macmillan, 1967.

Kerman, Joseph. *Opera As Drama*. New York: Vintage Books, 1956. Rev. ed. London: Faber, 1989.

Swain, Joseph P. *The Broadway Musical: A Critical and Musical Survey*. New York: Oxford University Press, 1990.

Bibliography

Arditi, Luigi. *My Reminiscences*. New York: Dodd, Mead, & Co., 1896.

Armstrong, W. G. *A Record of the Opera in Philadelphia*. Philadelphia: Porter & Coats, 1884.

Belasco, David. *The Theatre through its Stage Door*. New York: Benjamin Blom, 1919.

Bonner, Eugene. *The Club in the Opera House*. Princeton: Princeton University Press 1949.

Bordman, Gerald. *American Musical Theatre: A Chronicle*. New York: Oxford University Press, 1978.

———. *American Operetta: From "H. M. S. Pinafore" to "Sweeney Todd"*. New York: Oxford University Press, 1981.

Brockett, Oscar. *History of the Theatre*. Boston: Allyn and Bacon, 1982.

Camner, James. *How to Enjoy Opera*. Garden City, N.Y.: Doubleday, 1981.

Carner, Mosco. *Puccini: A Critical Biography*. New York: Alfred A. Knopf, 1959.

Cone, John Frederick. *Oscar Hammerstein's Manhattan Opera Company*. Norman: University of Oklahoma Press, 1966.

Cooper, Martin. *Opera Comique*. New York: Chantlcleer Press, 1949.

Cowell, Joseph. *Thirty Years Passed Among the Players in England and America*. New York: Harper, 1844.

Davis, Ronald. *A History of Music in American Life*. Malbar, Fla.: Robert Krieger Press, 1982.

———. *A History of Opera in the American West*. Englewood Cliffs, N.J.: Prentice-Hall, 1965.

DiGaetani, John L. *An Invitation to the Opera*. New York: Anchor/Doubleday, 1991.

———. *Penetrating Wagner's Ring: An Anthology*. New York: Da Capo, 1991.

———. *Puccini the Thinker*. New York: Peter Lang Press, 1983.

Drummond, Andrew H. *American Opera Librettos*. Metuchen, N.J.: Scarecrow Press, 1973.

Dunlap, William. *History of the American Theatre*. New York: Burt Franklin, 1965.

Eaton, Quaintance. *Opera Production I and II: A Handbook*. Minneapolis: University of Minnesota Press, 1974.

Engel, Lehman. *The American Musical Theatre: A Consideration*. New York: Macmillan, 1967.

Ewen, David. *Music Comes to America*. New York: Allen, Towne, & Heath, 1947.

FitzLyon, April. *Lorenzo da Ponte*. New York: Riverrun, 1955.

Gallegly, Joseph S. *Footlights on the Border: The Galveston and Houston Stage Before 1900*. The Hague: Mouton, 1962.

Gatti-Casazza, Giulio. *Memories of the Opera*. New York: Vienna House, 1973.

Green, Stanley. *Broadway Musicals: Show by Show*. Milwaukee, Wisc.: Hal Leonard Books, 1987.

Grimsted, David. *Melodrama Unveiled: American Theater and Culture 1800–1850*. Chicago: University of Chicago Press, 1968.

Grout, Donald Jay. *A Short History of Opera*. New York: Columbia University Press, 1979.

Henderson, William J. *The Story of Music*. New York: Longmans, Green, 1912.

Hipsher, Edward Ellsworth. *American Opera and Its Composers*. New York: Da Capo Press, 1989.

Hodges, Sheila. *Lorenzo da Ponte: The Life and Times of Mozart's Librettist*. London: Granada Press, 1985.

Howard, John Tasker. *Our American Music*. New York: Thomas Y. Crowell, 1946.

Ireland, Joseph N. *Records of the New York Stage from 1750 to 1860*. New York: Benjamin Blom, 1966.

Jackson, Stanley. *Caruso*. New York: Stein and Day, 1972.

———. *Monsieur Butterfly: The Story of Giacomo Puccini*. New York: Stein & Day, 1974.

Kellogg, Clara Louise. *Memoirs of an American Prima Donna*. New York: Putnam, 1913.

Kislan, Richard. *The Musical: A Look at the American Musical Theater*. Englewood Cliffs, N.J.: Prentice- Hall, 1980.

Kolodin, Irving. *The Metropolitan Opera*. New York: Alfred A. Knopf, 1966.

Lahee, Henry C. *Grand Opera in America*. Boston: L. C. Page, 1902.

Lawrence, Vera Brodsky. *Strong on Music: The New York Music Scene in the Days of George Templeton Strong*. New York: Oxford Univeristy Press, 1988.

Lerner, Alan Jay. *The Musical Theatre: A Celebration*. New York: McGraw-Hill, 1986.

Ludlow, Noah M. *Dramatic Life as I Found It*. 1880. Reprint. New York: Benjamin Blom, 1966.

Marker, Lise-Lone. *David Belasco: Naturalism in the American Theatre*. Princeton: Princeton University Press, 1975.

Martin, George. *The Companion to Twentieth Century Opera*. New York: Dodd, Mead, 1984.

Mast, Gerald. *Can't Help Singing: The American Musical on Stage and Screen*. Woodstock, N.Y.: Overlook Press, 1987.

Mates, Julian. *The American Musical Stage Before 1800*. New Brunswick, N.J.: Rutgers University Press, 1962.

———. *America's Musical Stage: 200 Years of Musical Theatre*. Westport, Conn.: Greenwood Press, 1985.

Mattfeld, Julius. *A Hundred Years of Grand Opera in New York*. New York: The New York Public Library, 1927.

Mayer, Martin. *The Met: One Hundred Years of Grand Opera*. New York: Simon & Schuster, 1983.

Metropolitan Opera Milestones. New York: The Metropolitan Opera Guild, 1944.

Mitchell, Donald G. *The Lorgnette, or Studies of the Town by an Opera Goer*. New York: Stringer & Townsend, 1851.

Mitchell, Ronald E. *Opera: Dead or Alive*. Madison: University of Wisconsin Press, 1972.

Mordden, Ethan. *Opera in the Twentieth Century*. New York: Oxford University Press, 1978.

Odell, George C. D. *Annals of the New York Stage*. New York: Columbia University Press, 1927.

Olson, Kenneth E. *Music and Musket*. Westport, Conn.: Greenwood Press, 1981.

Parsons, Charles H., ed. *The Mellen Opera Reference Index*. Lewiston, N.Y.: E. Mellen Press, 1989.

Pollock, Thomas Clark. *The Philadelphia Theatre in the Eighteenth Century*. Philadelphia: University of Pennsylvania Press, 1933.

Ponte, Lorenzo da. *Memoirs of Lorenzo da Ponte*. Translated by Elisabeth Abbott and edited by Arthur Livingston. Philadelphia: Lippincott, 1929.

Ritter, Frederic L. *Music in America*. New York: Johnson, 1970.

Robinson, Paul. *Opera and Ideas*. New York: Harper Row, 1985.

Sadie, Stanley, ed. *The New Grove Dictionary of Music and Musicians*. London: Macmillan, 1980.

Seligman, Vincent. *Puccini among Friends*. New York: Benjamin Blom, 1971.

Smith, Cecil and Glenn Litton. *Musical Comedy in America*. New York: Theatre Arts Press, 1981.

Smith, Patrick J. *The Tenth Muse: A Historical Study of the Opera Libretto*. New York: Knopf, 1970.

Sokol, Martin. *The New York City Opera, An American Adventure*. New York: Macmillan, 1981.

Sonneck, Oscar G. *Early Opera in America*. New York: Benjamin Blom, 1963.

Swain, Joseph P. *The Broadway Musical: A Critical and Musical Survey*. New York: Oxford University Press, 1990.

Timberlake, Craig. *David Belasco, The Bishop of Broadway*. New York: Library Press, 1954.

Traubner, Richard. *Operetta: A Theatrical History*. Garden City, N.Y.: Doubleday, 1983.

Upton, George P. *Musical Memories: My Recollections of Celebrities of the Half Century, 1850–1900*. Chicago: A. C. McClung, 1908.

Weaver, William. *Puccini: The Man and His Music*. London: Hutchinson, 1977.

Wechsberg, Joseph. *The Opera*. New York: Macmillan, 1972.

Winter, William. *The Life of David Belasco*. New York: Moffat, Yard & Co., 1918.

———. *Other Days, Being Chronicles and Memories of the Stage*. New York: Moffat, Yard & Co, 1908

List of Contributors

Monica T. Albala works at the Long Island Studies Institute, a part of Hofstra University, and also writes about opera.

Edith Borroff is a professor in the Department of Music at the State University of New York at Binghampton. In addition to being a composer of operas and other forms of music, she has written *Music in Europe and America: A History*.

Phillipa Burgess teaches in the Music Department of the University of Kentucky–Lexington, where she writes about music and opera history.

Martin Chusid has edited *Rigoletto* and other works by Giuseppe Verdi and other composers. He is also director of the Verdi Institute of New York University.

Shelby J. Davis is a member of the School of Music and Theatre Arts of Washington State University, where she writes about opera.

John Louis DiGaetani is a professor of English at Hofstra University, where he writes about opera and the connections between opera and literature. His books include *Richard Wagner and the Modern British Novel*, *Penetrating Wagner's Ring*, *Puccini the Thinker*, and *An Invitation to the Opera*.

Michael B. Dougan is a professor in the Department of History of Arkansas State University. His specialties include opera and American history.

Gary D. Gibbs is Director of Education at the Houston Grand Opera where he arranges educational programs about opera for the community.

MARIO HAMLET-METZ is a professor in the Department of Foreign Languages and Literatures at James Madison University. His research interests include European literatures and opera.

JOAN KRIEG is a professor of English at Hofstra University. Her books include *Long Island Architecture, Walt Whitman: Here and Now*, and *Epidemics in the Modern World*.

ALICE LEVINE is a professor of English at Hofstra University. She has re-edited *Manuscripts of the Younger Romantics: Byron*.

JULIAN MATES is a professor at the C. W. Post campus of Long Island University. He has written *America's Musical Stage: Two Hundred Years of Musical Theatre*.

CHRISTOPHER NEWTON teaches at Tufts University, where he specializes in modern trends in the arts.

JUNE C. OTTENBERG is a professor in the Department of Music History at Temple University. Her special subject is the history of American opera.

ZOLTAN ROMAN is a professor in the Department of Music at the University of Calgary. His books include *Gustav Mahler and Hungary* and *Gustav Mahler's American Years, 1907–11*.

EMANUEL RUBIN is a professor in the Department of Music and Dance at the Amherst campus of the University of Massachusetts where he specializes in opera history.

SHEILA SABREY-SAPERSTEIN is a professor in the Department of Theatre of Northwestern University, where she specializes and writes about opera and musical theater.

MICHAEL SAFFLE is a professor in the Department of Music of Virginia Tech University, where he writes about American opera history. He has written *Franz Liszt: A Guide to Research*.

MARJORIE MACKAY SHAPIRO is a professor at the Graduate Center of the City University of New York. She does research and writes about the history of American opera.

NADINE SINE is a professor in the Department of Music of Lehigh University. Her specialty is Richard Strauss and other opera composers.

JOSEF P. SIREFMAN is a professor in the School of Business of Hofstra University. His books include *Managing Faculty Disputes* and *Immigration and Ethnicity*.

JON SOLOMON teaches in the Department of Classics of the University of Arizona. He has written *The Ancient World in Cinema*.

ROXANA STUART is a professor in the Department of Performing Arts of Adelphi University. She has written about Giacomo Puccini and other opera composers.

JOSEPH P. SWAIN is a professor in the Department of Music of Colgate University where he writes about opera and other forms of American musical theater.

JEAN-FRANÇOIS THIBAULT is a professor in the Department of Romance Langagues and Literatures at George Washington University. His specialty there is the history of opera, particularly French opera.

THOMAS WARBURTON is a professor in the Department of Music at the University of North Carolina–Chapel Hill. He writes about Puccini and other opera composers and also composes music.

Index